OUTLINE OF
IRISH RAILWAY
HISTORY

OUTLINE OF
IRISH RAILWAY
HISTORY

H. C. CASSERLEY

DAVID & CHARLES

NEWTON ABBOT LONDON

NORTH POMFRET (VT) VANCOUVER

0 7153 6377 8

© H. C. Casserley 1974

Set in 11pt on 13pt Monotype Aldine Bembo
and printed in Great Britain
by Latimer Trend & Company Ltd Plymouth
for David & Charles (Holdings) Limited
South Devon House Newton Abbot Devon

Published in the United States of America
by David & Charles Inc North Pomfret
Vermont 05053 USA

Published in Canada by Douglas David & Charles Limited
3645 McKechnie Drive
West Vancouver BC

CONTENTS

6 CONTENTS

ILLUSTRATIONS

ILLUSTRATIONS IN THE TEXT

ABBREVIATIONS

AER	Athenry & Ennis Junction Railway
BBCPJR	Belfast Ballymena Coleraine & Portrush Junction Railway
BCDR	Belfast & County Down Railway
BCRBR	Belfast Cushendall & Red Bay Railway
BHBR	Belfast Holywood & Bangor Railway
BLR	Ballymena & Larne Railway
BNCR	Belfast & Northern Counties Railway
BR	Ballycastle Railway
BWR	Bagenalstown & Wexford Railway
CBPR	Cork Blackrock & Passage Railway
CBSCR	Cork Bandon & South Coast Railway
CDJR	City of Dublin Junction Railway
CDRJC	County Donegal Railways Joint Committee
CIE	Coras Iompair Eireann
CKAR	Castleblayney Keady & Armagh Railway
CLR	Cavan & Leitrim Railway
CMDR	Cork & Macroom Direct Railway
CMLR	Cork & Muskerry Light Railway
CVBT	Castlederg & Victoria Bridge Tramway
CVR	Clogher Valley Railway
DBJR	Dublin & Belfast Junction Railway

DER	Dublin & Enniskillen Railway
DGR	Dundalk & Greenore Railway
DNGR	Dundalk Newry & Greenore Railway
DSER	Dublin & South Eastern Railway
DWWR	Dublin Wicklow & Wexford Railway
GNR	Great Northern Railway
GSR	Great Southern Railways
GSWR	Great Southern & Western Railway
GWR	Great Western Railway
L & BER	Londonderry & Burtonport Extension Railway
LCR	Londonderry & Coleraine Railway
L & LSR	Londonderry & Lough Swilly Railway
LMS	London Midland & Scottish Railway
LNER	London North Eastern Railway
LNWR	London & North Western Railway
LSWR	London & South Western Railway
MGWR	Midland Great Western Railway
MR	Midland Railway
NCC	Northern Counties Committee
NIR	Northern Ireland Railways
PDOR	Portadown Dungannon & Omagh Railway
SECR	South Eastern & Chatham Railway
SLNCR	Sligo Leitrim & Northern Counties Railway
SSR	Schull & Skibbereen Railway
TCLR	Timoleague & Courtmacsherry Light Railway
UTA	Ulster Transport Authority
WCIR	Waterford & Central Ireland Railway

WDLR   Waterford Dungarvan & Lismore Railway

WKR   Waterford & Kilkenny Railway

WLR   Waterford & Limerick Railway

WLWR   Waterford Limerick & Western Railway

WTR   Waterford & Tramore Railway

WWR   Waterford & Wexford Railway

CHAPTER 1

GENERAL SURVEY

Ireland has a total area of some 32,588 square miles, exclusive of the numerous inland lakes, and consists in broad terms of an extensive central plain bounded by large mountain ranges, of which the most considerable are the well-known Killarney group in the south-west, the Wicklow Mountains of the south-east, and the wild areas of mountain and moorland in Donegal in the north-west. Cutting through this central plain is the River Shannon, 240 miles long and the longest river in the British Isles, which rises in the Cuilcagh Mountains and flows in a roughly north to south-westerly direction through a marshy rain-soaked area, swelling in places into broad and shallow lakes, which are a distinctive feature over much of the country.

Away from the cities the land is sparsely populated, and it is in fact one of the few countries in the world where the population has decreased over the last 125 years, starting with the great potato famine of 1846–8, which forced so many Irishmen to emigrate. The population in 1845 stood at some 8,000,000 but by 1851 had fallen to 6,500,000. Between 1847 and 1851 over 1,200,000 people emigrated, more than a million of them to the United States. Another 4,000,000 left between 1851 and 1905, and by 1926 the total population stood at some 4,229,000, little more than half of what it had been eighty years earlier.

Since then it has risen slightly, but only to about 4,300,000, mainly concentrated in and around Dublin and Belfast, the two principal cities. The general drift from the country areas, not peculiar to Ireland alone, is well exemplified by the fact that of the twenty-six counties in what is now the Irish Republic, all except Dublin, Kildare and Cork have populations of less than a hundred per square mile, and large areas, especially in the west, together with the greater part of Wicklow, have less than fifty. In these circumstances it is easy to understand how such a lot of the railway system away from the main centres has disappeared—quite apart from the universal consequence of road competition. It is indeed surprising how many lines in the Republic still remain, thanks to the sensible policy of the government, which still regards railways as essential to the needs of the community, even if they can no longer be self supporting, a fact which practically all countries of the world have now come to realise.

B

The position in Northern Ireland is not so happy, as a strong anti-rail element was active in the Stormont government in the 1950s and caused the closure of all but the principal main lines linking Belfast with Dublin and Londonderry, and one or two others of vital importance. However there are signs of a welcome change of heart and it seems unlikely that any more closures will occur, but at present only passenger services are operated, all goods being carried by road, which seems an uneconomic policy. Nevertheless the entire north-west of the country is now devoid of rail communication, and indeed the whole western coast, most of which lies in the Republic, is in a like position, the principal reason being of course the general decline of population.

Ireland has never been a wealthy country, having practically no natural resources of any consequence. The only fuel found to any extent is peat, or turf, as it is more commonly known in Ireland, of which there are immense areas, forty-feet thick in some places, and this is recovered on a considerable scale for use as domestic fuel, largely by 3ft gauge railway systems operated by Bord na Mona (Irish Turf Board). Unfortunately it is of little use in a locomotive firebox, and severe recurring shortages of coal, particularly during the world wars and afterwards, resulting from difficulties with shipments from England, was one of the main reasons for the rapid change to diesel working in the 1950s and early 1960s. Apart from turf, the central area consists largely of limestone, now being exploited to a useful extent. Because of this lack of mineral resources there are no major industries outside Belfast, which has engineering and shipbuilding, and consequently the heavy freight trains which are such an essential part of the British railway scene have never been known in Ireland.

The climate is generally more equable than in the rest of the British Isles, without the extremes of winter and summer generally found in England and Scotland. The rainfall is heavier on the west side, exposed to the Atlantic, and less so away from the mountainous areas, but is considerably more than in Great Britain. The Irishman has only two standards of weather, a 'soft day' when it is raining, and a 'grand day' when it is not! Nevertheless it is a most charming and attractive country, with a people who are indeed friendly—despite any impressions to the contrary derived from the old conflict between Catholics and Protestants, the former mainly in the south and the latter in the north, the Catholics being in the great majority.

Such 'troubles', starting with the 1916 rebellion which led in 1921 to the partition of the country, and the secession of what became the Irish Free State, and later the Irish Republic, from the Commonwealth, affected the railways to a considerable extent, particularly those whose systems were partly in one country and partly in the other, the chief sufferer being the Great Northern. Much damage was done by sabotage, signal boxes set on fire, and so on, and many instances occurred of derailment of trains, with consequent destruction of rolling stock. Several engines were so badly damaged that they had to be scrapped.

Most railways were involved, particularly the Dublin & South Eastern, Great Southern & Western, Midland Great Western, and Great Northern, and even the poor little Sligo Leitrim & Northern Counties had more than its fair share. The most serious incident was the blowing up of Mallow viaduct in 1922, which severed rail connection between Cork and the rest of the country. Until a new one was built, passengers were conveyed by road between Mallow and Mourne Abbey, a small wayside station which was closed in 1963.

This period of unrest was not the first time that the railways had suffered through political dissensions; there had been trouble in 1867, the year of the Fenian Rising. On 6 March disruption had been caused on the same stretch of line at nearby Rathduff, when over 1,000 men ripped up rails and shovelled tons of earth and boulders on to the line. This Fenian movement marked the beginning of the later events which were to establish the demand for Home Rule, for which Gladstone introduced several bills in Parliament, designed to give some measure of self government, but they were all rejected by the Commons or Lords. These moves were strongly opposed in the six counties forming the province of Ulster, with its strongly Protestant element, and the same conflict of opinion unfortunately still rages today. The establishment of the Sinn Fein movement in the south and west (the nearest equivalent being the French 'Nous même') and the 1916 rebellion led eventually to the creation of the Irish Free State (Saorstat Eireann, usually abbreviated to Eire) which came into being on 15 January 1922, with the status of a British dominion, the six counties of Northern Ireland remaining part of Great Britain. This involved the setting up of a customs barrier at the ports and also along the political boundaries, which caused many difficulties for railways like the Great Northern whose lines crossed the border. In 1949 Eire left the Commonwealth and adopted the title of Republic of Ireland.

An interesting geographical curiosity arising from the partition was that, in true Irish fashion, the most northerly point of the entire railway network, and indeed in the country itself as a whole, now lay in 'Southern Ireland', on the Carndonagh branch of the Londonderry & Lough Swilly Railway.

Although the Irish Republic is now technically a foreign land, one does not in any way feel that this is so when visiting the country. The language as spoken every day is of course the same, although Erse is the official one and appears on public notices alongside English; the money is the same currency, and traffic drives on the same side of the road. Away from the busy streets of Dublin itself, things proceed at a leisurely pace, a welcome relief in these hectic days. The casual attitude of the southern Irish is well illustrated by the story of the level-crossing keeper who kept one gate over his single line open to the railway and the other to the road, because he was 'half expecting a train'.

The first idea of railway construction in Ireland occurred as early as 1825, the year of the opening of the Stockton & Darlington, and before the Liverpool & Manchester had come into being. This however came to nothing and it was not until 17 December 1834 that the country's first railway, the Dublin & Kingstown, was actually opened. In the 1840s things really got going; the Railway Mania which spread far and wide in Great Britain affected Ireland on a similar scale, numerous schemes being promoted, many of them destined to be stillborn.

In all about 180 one-time separate railway concerns come into the general story of Irish railway history, some of them only very briefly while others never materialised at all; in addition there was a number of other abortive schemes of such little importance as hardly to warrant any reference. There must, therefore, have been something like 200 all told, quite a total for such a comparatively small country.

By 1853 there were 840 route miles of railway open in Ireland (compared with 990 in Scotland), of which 130 had been opened during that year. Seven million passengers were conveyed and the total receipts amounted to £537,000 for passengers and £294,000 for goods. This was partly accounted for by the Dublin International Exhibition in the grounds of Leinster House, which ran from May to October 1853. Thereafter the route mileage rose to 2,091 in 1872, 3,044 in 1894, and a maximum of 3,442 in 1920. When the Tramways of Ireland Act of 1883 was passed, there were already 94 miles of 3ft gauge railway in existence, and under this Act and the Light Railways Acts of 1889 and 1896 a further 332 miles of narrow-gauge line were built.

The 1883 Act provided for the construction of light railways, or tramways (usually under a baronial guarantee, whereby the government either provided part of the capital or guaranteed some of the interest), to serve outlying or sparsely populated areas which would not justify the provision of a railway of main-line standards. The distinction between light railways and tramways lay in the fact that whereas the former usually had its own private right of way, as with a normal railway, a tramway ran alongside the public highway on its own reserved track, although some lines embraced both features. After 1920 the total mileage began to decline; by 1939 it was down to 3,183, but there were few closures during the war, and it had only fallen to 3,153 by 1946. By 1957 however it was only 2,557 and today it stands at about 1,550. These figures include both Northern and Southern Ireland.

The pattern of railway development followed very closely that of the rest of the British Isles; the gradual absorption of small companies by larger ones, sometimes followed in turn by even larger amalgamations, led to the unification of all railways lying wholly within the Free State in 1925, and finally to nationalisation both in the south and in the north. The number of individual railways, large and small, had by the earlier 1920s, before any closures had taken place, reduced to about thirty.

It seems that the railway map of Ireland at the present time has become more or less stabilised; at any rate there are unlikely to be any mass closures, as seemed possible only a few years ago. Indeed, there have been within recent years several new lines built to serve industrial needs. Nevertheless a recent inquiry into the finances of CIE, undertaken in 1971 by a consulting firm, McKinsey, recommended certain further closures, amongst which was the North Kerry line, from Limerick to Tralee, which lost its passenger service in 1963, and one or two others, including practically all of the few remaining country branches. However, it accepted that the network of principal main lines is still essential to the needs of the Republic, both in a commercial and a social sense, and must be supported by government assistance or grants, in one form or another, where necessary. There was a number of other recommendations which largely paralleled what had already been done in Great Britain, such as the conversion of some intermediate main-line stations into unstaffed halts served by pay-trains with conductor-guards. Bulk trains and container services, first introduced in 1969, were found to be profitable and recommended for further development, although the potential is limited in view of the country's lack of heavy industry.

Although the railways of Ireland are largely similar in many respects to those of Great Britain, they differ in one essential respect, namely the gauge. In Great Britain there were the rival claims of Brunel's 7ft on the Great Western, against the rest of the country's adoption of Stephenson's 4ft 8½in, which was already almost universal. Exactly how the use of the latter rather curious dimension came about in the first place no one is quite sure, but it seems that George Stephenson adopted it because it was already to be found on the Wylam wagon way and the Killingworth and Hetton colliery lines, where it had developed naturally from the earlier conversion of road waggons, which were about that width, when they were first adapted to run on primitive rails. It is an interesting point moreover that, whether or not by coincidence, Roman chariots were made to this dimension, as traces of ruts both in this country and at Pompeii show. At an early stage it was realised that the whole railway system would eventually be linked together, and it was essential that a single standard be laid down for future construction; there were already difficulties in transhipment where the GWR made contact with other systems, and Parliament decreed that 4ft 8½in must prevail.

In Ireland it was not quite so simple. So far as Great Britain was concerned, it did not matter if a different gauge was adopted in Ireland, as nothing in the nature of through running by means of ferries, as now operate to the continent, has ever been considered across the Irish Sea. However, by 1843 the position was already complicated by the fact that whereas the gauge of the original Dublin & Kingstown Railway, the first in Ireland, had been laid down to the English specification of 4ft 8½in, the Ulster Railway had adopted a figure of 6ft 2in, and moreover another projected line, the Dublin & Drogheda, was planning on a 5ft 2in basis. At this point the Board of Trade stepped in and appointed Major-General Pasley of the Royal Engineers to make a decision. He sought the advice of the Stephensons, who were already committed to 4ft 8½in in this country, ignoring Brunel, who was still firmly advocating 7ft. The Stephensons suggested as a compromise for Ireland something between 5ft 0in and 5ft 6in, whereupon the major-general came up with the discovery that the average between the two figures was exactly 5ft 3in, and this was the figure which was decided upon. The little extra width in most Irish coaches makes an appreciable difference in comfort to the four-a-side arrangement in main-line coaches, both of the side corridor and centre gangway type.

Apart from the standard 5ft 3in adopted for main lines, there also appeared in later years a considerable number of railways of a light nature in more sparsely populated districts, built to a gauge of 3ft, mostly under the Tramways and Light Railways (Ireland) Act of 1883. This became in effect a second standard which could be usefully applied, with great economy in construction, when the question of through running was not of paramount importance. Not all these lines were small systems by any means. The Londonderry & Lough Swilly, for instance, with its Burtonport extension, had a main line 74 miles long, and the County Donegal with its associated lines had a total route mileage of 111.

The railway companies themselves, whilst developing much in their individual ways, in some cases were very similar in certain respects to British lines. The Great Northern of Ireland, for instance, although it had no connection whatever with its English namesake, managed to achieve a striking resemblance to it with its coaching stock; and indeed some of its engines, the smaller 0–6–0s in particular, with the initials GNR on the tender, might at first glance have been taken for their English counterparts. Similarly, on the Great Southern & Western A. McDonnell, locomotive superintendent from 1864 to 1883, not only built some 0–6–0s, the 101 class, that strongly resembled Ramsbottom's DX goods on the LNWR, but also adopted distinctive oblong numberplates very much like those of that company. These remained standard until World War II when they were replaced by painted numbers. The small Dundalk Newry & Greenore Railway was actually owned by the LNWR, and its six engines, built at Crewe between 1873 and 1898, were as pure North Western as could be imagined, although not exactly like anything on the parent system. They were in fact 0-6-0STs, an unmistakeable cross between the old Ramsbottom DX goods 0-6-0 tender engines and F. W. Webb's 'Special Tanks'. Mr McDonnell later went to the North Eastern, where he built a class of 4-4-0s of striking similarity to some which appeared concurrently from Inchicore during the regime of his two successors, J. A. F. Aspinall and H. A. Ivatt; in view of the similarity between the two classes he must have been largely responsible for the design.

An indication of the relative longevity of engines in the two countries is shown by the fact that whereas the last of the North Eastern engines disappeared in 1923, many of the Irish counterparts survived into the 1950s.

There are numerous instances of Irish locomotive engineers gravitating to England. J. A. F. Aspinall succeeded McDonnell on the GSWR for three years before going over to the Lancashire & Yorkshire. He was replaced by H. A. Ivatt in 1886, who took over from Patrick Stirling on the Great Northern (the English company) in 1896. J. G. Robinson was locomotive superintendent of the Waterford, Limerick & Western Railway from 1888 until 1900, after which he became well known on the Great Central. In more recent years R. E. L. Maunsell, loco superintendent of the South Eastern & Chatham from 1913 to 1922 and of the Southern from 1922 to 1937, came from the GSWR at Inchicore, and finally, in the reverse direction, that very distinctive designer O. V. S. Bulleid, who succeeded Maunsell in charge of Southern Railway locomotive affairs, finished his career at Inchicore.

One striking similarity between railways on both sides of the Irish Sea is not at all surprising, as the old Belfast & Northern Counties Railway was acquired by the enterprising Midland Railway of England in 1903. By the 1920s the most marked and obvious 'Midlandisation' of the Northern Counties Committee (MR) as it had now become—to graduate to NCC-LMS after the grouping—was the adoption of the famous crimson lake livery, both for engines and coaching stock, as on the parent system. It was moreover applied to all engines, both passenger and goods, and all were kept in sparkling condition, pure joy to a lover of the Midland, of which the NCC was by the 1930s a sort of miniature version. Many of the locomotives after the takeover were actually built at Derby, and although not quite like any on the parent system bore very strong Midland characteristics.

As regards actual locomotive design, engines were generally smaller than their contemporaries in Great Britain. Traffic was very much lighter and there was no heavy industry. Consequently the mineral train was practically unknown, and there was no need for the heavy 0–6–0, 0–8–0 or 2–8–0 engine. In fact only six eight-coupled engines ever ran in Ireland, two rather short-lived 4–8–0Ts on the GSWR and two 4–8–0s and two 4–8–4Ts on the Lough Swilly; they were, incidentally, the only engines of these wheel arrangements ever to be seen in the British Isles. These are not the only instances of types to be found more often among the 950 or so locomotives in Ireland, at its peak period in the 1920s, compared with over 20,000 in England, Scotland and Wales. The 2–6–0T is another; it was the principal type on the narrow-gauge Tralee & Dingle, which had seven, and there were also one each on the Castlederg & Victoria Bridge, Timoleague & Courtmacsherry and the Northern Counties Committee. Over the years England has produced only two, and these on such obscure lines as the Garstang & Knott End and the Wrexham Mold & Connah's Quay. The NCC was also responsible for the only 2–4–4T anywhere in Great Britain and Ireland.

In the field of express engines, the 2–4–0 type, and later the 4–4–0, formed the mainstay of the larger companies. The 4–2–2, much favoured by several English railways towards the end of the nineteenth century, was represented by only two examples, on the GNR. Atlantics were entirely unknown, and nothing as large as a Pacific was ever really a likelihood, although one was considered by the GSR in case the 21 ton axleload for the 800 class express engine proved unacceptable to the civil engineer. In fact even the 4–6–0, which became so popular on British lines, numbered only twenty-two in Ireland, all on the GSWR and GSR, and of these only sixteen came into the express category. The GNR might have found a use for a 4–6–0 but was restricted by the length of the traversers in Dundalk works. Consequently it relied entirely on 4–4–0s for its principal expresses, and had in fact the distinction of producing in 1948 the last example of this once numerous type in the British Isles, and probably in the whole world.

The ubiquitous 0–6–0, as might be expected, was found in considerable numbers on the GSR and GNR, but its tank counterpart, the 0–6–0T, so common on British lines, was a comparative rarity. So too was the use of a saddle tank, commonly seen in Great Britain, particularly on the GWR and innumerable industrial railways, but examples in Ireland were possibly less than fifty all told.

Another aspect in which Irish locomotive design followed very closely the earlier English pattern was the almost total preference for inside cylinders, whereas most foreign lines placed them outside. However, a couple of 0–6–2STs on the Cork Bandon & South Coast Railway violated the usual conceptions in several ways. Not only did they have both saddle tanks and outside cylinders, but they also had bar frames instead of the otherwise universal plate frames; all this was because they were of American design, the only Irish steam engines ever built there. Other rare machines on the CBSCR were a few inside-cylinder o–6–oSTs and some 4–6–oTs, a type also used by the West Clare, the Lough Swilly, and the County Donegal, but otherwise almost unknown on both sides of the Irish Sea. The North Eastern built some but later converted them to 4–6–2Ts.

On the 3ft gauge outside cylinders were a necessity owing to the restricted width between the frames, but otherwise were found, with few exceptions, only on the multi-cylinder engines, the GSWR four-cylinder and GSR three-cylinder 4–6–os and the GNR three-cylinder 4–4–os. Notable exceptions were the modern two-cylinder 2–6–os and 2–6–4Ts on the NCC and the Woolwich 2–6–os of the Great Southern.

Compounding was seen on only a limited scale and, except for the GNR 4–4–os, was chiefly on the Worsdell von Borries two-cylinder system. A few of these were built for the Belfast & County Down, but more particularly for the BNCR, principally before its absorption by the Midland in 1903. Some more however appeared during the Midland regime, and one narrow-gauge 2–4–2T was in fact built at Derby as late as 1920, the last new Worsdell von Borries in these islands, though some were built in subsequent years for the Argentine. The GSWR also made two experimental and temporary conversions in the 1890s.

The change to diesel working followed much the same pattern as in Great Britain, with a few experimental engines in the 1930s on the NCC and BCDR, chiefly for shunting. The County Donegal was however the principal innovator and was in fact the first railway in the British Isles to introduce diesel passenger railcars, which it did in 1931, followed by the Great Northern which, like the GWR, introduced some single units for main-line working. It was this company which pioneered the modern multiple-unit diesel railcar, the first of which appeared in 1950 for the main line between Dublin and Belfast. The CIE followed suit in the next year, a considerable number of units being turned out both for main-line and local work, chiefly on the DSER suburban services, but also on the isolated Waterford & Tramore. In due course they also appeared on the UTA lines of the former BCDR and NCC. CIE, after initial experiments with five shunting engines in 1947 and two mixed-traffic in 1951, decided in 1953 on the complete elimination of steam working (three years before British Railways). Sixty main-line engines were ordered from Metro Vickers, together with a number of smaller designs for mixed traffic and secondary services. The large ones, known as class A, were not entirely satisfactory; they were built straight off the drawing board, a mistake which British Railways was also to make to its cost in the following years, being entirely unable to profit by the experience of CIE. In the event the A class had to be re-engined, and meanwhile recourse was made to the later B class for main-line passenger work; these were imported from General Motors of the United States, which of course already had wide experience in the diesel field. With the arrival of a second batch of these engines in 1961 steam working was reduced drastically and came to an end in 1965, anticipating British Railways by three years. Thus the Republic of Ireland became the first country in Europe to be completely dieselised.

During the period between the wars the railways of Ireland were a pure delight to the connoisseur, and this continued to a certain extent into the 1950s, although by this time one too frequently encountered dirty engines no longer cared for and lying in sheds or sidings awaiting their final demise—a depressing sight soon to be repeated on a far larger scale in Great Britain. Nevertheless, it was possible even as late as 1955 to travel along a main line in a vintage Edwardian twelve-wheeled clerestory coach, still gas-lit, on the Limited Mail from Sligo to Dublin, and as far as Mullingar behind a 2–4–0 at that!

Away from the main lines, the Irish railways corresponded by and large to what could have been found a generation earlier in the rest of the British Isles. One could still find, on the long cross-country branches, trains which meandered peacefully through the green and pleasant countryside or perhaps the more mountainous west, with considerable pauses at wayside stations, where the staff and the occasional passenger, or farmer bringing his cattle to be loaded, would exchange the time of day; no one would ever be in a hurry. The train itself would probably consist of some ancient six-wheelers, with probably a 'tail' of vans or cattle wagons, and hauled by a small and aged 4–4–0 or 0–6–0. After the war there were still a few railways of such individuality as the Sligo Leitrim & Northern Counties, although one had if possible to avoid the diesel railcar or railbus which latterly worked the passenger services. Then there were the delights of the dozen or more 3ft gauge lines, but less than half of these survived the war.

All this has now gone for ever, and the present Irish railway system, particularly in the Republic, is completely modernised and can bear comparison with anything to be found in Great Britain, except perhaps for the high speeds and frequency of service within the Inter City complex, and for such developments as the electrified West Coast route and the Advanced Passenger Train.

CHAPTER 2

DUBLIN & SOUTH EASTERN RAILWAY

Important main line based on Dublin serving the south-east, chiefly the counties of Wicklow and Wexford.

Principal constituents:

DUBLIN & KINGSTOWN RAILWAY   Incorporated 1831 (first railway in Ireland). Opened 1834.

WATERFORD WEXFORD WICKLOW & DUBLIN RAILWAY   Incorporated 1846 became DUBLIN WICKLOW & WEXFORD RAILWAY   Incorporated 1859 (opened in stages) renamed DUBLIN & SOUTH EASTERN RAILWAY in January 1907. Became part of GREAT SOUTHERN RAILWAYS 1925.

Route mileage in 1922: 156 miles.

Principal places served:

Dublin, Kingstown (Dun Laoghaire), Bray, Wicklow, Enniscorthy, Wexford, New Ross, Waterford.

The origins of this system lay in the Dublin & Kingstown Railway, the first public railway in Ireland, incorporated in September 1831 and opened on 17 December 1834. With a length of 6 miles, it was built to provide more satisfactory communication between Dublin and Kingstown Harbour. Ships from Holyhead and Liverpool were diverted from the Port of Dublin on the completion of Victoria Wharf at Kingstown (now known as Dun Laoghaire), and although a canal was proposed the idea was abandoned in favour of the railway.

The Dublin & Kingstown Railway was remarkable in that, although it came in later years to be worked successively by the Dublin & Wicklow, Dublin Wicklow & Wexford, and Dublin & South Eastern Railways, it retained its nominal status as an independent company right up to the grouping of 1925, when it became part of the Great Southern.

A fact not generally realised is that the Dublin & Kingstown's independent life of ninety years would constitute a record for any railway in the British Isles but for two exceptions, one of them the Londonderry & Lough Swilly Railway. The other exception is of course the Great Western Railway, which retained its independence from its original incorporation in 1835 right through to the creation of British Railways in 1948.

The line was double from the start, and was originally laid to the 4ft 8½in gauge; it was converted to 5ft 3in when it was leased to the Dublin & Wicklow. It was an expensive line to construct, averaging about £63,000 a mile, a large amount in those days. At the Dublin end it had to be carried on embankments and bridges to clear the city streets, whilst between Merrion and Blackrock it ran along the seashore, which involved the construction of a 6,660ft embankment comprising a sea wall built of heavy blocks of granite. This had to be strengthened and concreted in the course of time, but nevertheless it has withstood the gales and storms of nearly 140 years with comparatively few interruptions to traffic. The present sea wall embodies some of the original Dublin & Kingstown stone sleepers.

Westland Row was a two-platform station and at the other end the line terminated at Victoria Wharf, until the construction of the present Carlisle Pier, opened on 12 December 1859, which could accommodate the larger ships then being put into service by the London & North Western Railway and the City of Dublin Steam Packet Company. Another pier for goods traffic, served by a separate branch, was opened in 1863. This was known as the Mineral Wharf, and at first was largely used for transporting exports of sulphur ore from the Avoca mines.

The first extension southwards from Kingstown was to Dalkey, 1¾ miles; this was at first worked on the atmospheric principle then in vogue on some railways, the best known probably being the London & Croydon and the South Devon, and was the only application of this form of traction in Ireland. The stationary engine was situated at Dalkey, which was at a higher level than Kingstown; the trains being hauled atmospherically only in the upward direction, the descent from Dalkey being made by gravity. It was a single line, and was built over the course of an older mineral tramway used for carrying granite blocks during the construction of Kingstown Harbour. It operated as an atmospheric railway from 29 March 1844 to 12 April 1854, after which it was converted to ordinary locomotive haulage.

Two railways authorised in 1846 for southward extensions through the counties of Wicklow & Wexford were the Waterford, Wexford, Wicklow & Dublin, self-explanatory from its title, and the Dublin Dundrum & Rathfarnham Railway. The latter replaced an abortive proposal for a Dublin Dundrum

& Enniskerry Railway, which was planned to serve the more inland area south of Dublin but was abandoned in favour of diverting the route to Bray, a large watering place 14 miles south of Dublin with a present population of nearly 12,000. This was the more obvious immediate objective, since the line could be worked in conjunction with the Dublin & Kingstown, which had already obtained powers for the extension. The two new companies were in fact amalgamated in 1851 as the Dublin & Wicklow, which assumed the Dublin & Kingstown's powers for the Bray extension and on 1 July 1856 obtained the lease of the original line from Dublin to Dalkey. Bray was reached on 10 July 1854 by the new route from Dublin originally planned by the Dublin Dundrum & Rathfarnham, from a temporary terminus at Harcourt Road, Dublin, and by the extension from Dalkey via the coast line. An inland diversion made in 1915 combined the two routes from Shanganagh Junction, 1¼ miles north of Bray. The atmospheric portion had now been converted and the gauge of the Dublin & Kingstown Railway altered to 5ft 3in. The short extension to Harcourt Street in Dublin was completed in February 1859. This station was situated well above road level and facilities for running round were provided by a turntable bounded by a circular stone wall above the street, a somewhat hazardous arrangement. Indeed, on 14 February 1900, 0-4-2 no 17 got out of control and charged through the retaining wall, only just avoiding plunging into the street below. On 30 October 1855 the railway was extended southwards to Wicklow, another 11 miles, and 28 miles from Dublin.

The City of Dublin Junction was opened on 1 May 1891 and connected Westland Row, which now became a through station, with the Great Northern at Amiens Street, and the Midland Great Western at Newcomen Bridge Junction, from where a loop line skirting the northern boundaries of the city to Liffey Junction gave the Dublin Wicklow & Wexford Railway, as it had by this time become, full interchange facilities with the rest of the Irish railway system. Previously its only physical connection had been at Macmine Junction, over the Bagenalstown & Wexford Railway, completed in 1873. The suburban services thenceforth normally ran from Amiens Street. Nowadays there are some through trains between Bray or Dun Laoghaire and Howth on the former Great Northern Railway.

One of the first constituents of the Dublin & Wicklow Railway was the first-styled Waterford Wexford Wicklow & Dublin. This project had the backing of the Great Western Railway of England, which wished to obtain a share of the cross-channel Irish traffic, then largely a monopoly of its rival the London & North Western. Its aspirations lay in the idea of a sort of back-door access to Ireland via Waterford or Wexford, then an important port. For the same reason it also secured financial interest in the Waterford Limerick & Western Railway.

However, it was not until a good many years later, with the opening of Ross-lare Harbour on 31 July 1906 and the institution of the direct service from Fish-guard, that the Great Western was able to secure a good share of the Irish traffic. This was after Rosslare had been reached by the Great Southern & Western. Fourteen miles south of Wicklow is Avoca, where there were large deposits of sulphur ore. For exporting this product from the mines, which were intensively exploited until the 1880s, a mineral tramway had been constructed to Arklow Harbour, but with the coming of the railway, which purchased the tramway and used a greater part of the site for the construction of its line, this important traffic was diverted to Kingstown. An Act of August 1859 authorised the exten-sion of the railway, henceforth to be known as the Dublin Wicklow & Wexford Railway, as far as Gorey, and another one in 1860 onwards to Enniscorthy. The section as far as Rathdrum was opened on 20 August 1861, onwards to Avoca on 18 July 1863, and the 34¾ miles to Enniscorthy on 16 November 1863. Between Rathdrum and Arklow a 16½ mile branch from Woodenbridge Junction westwards to Shillelagh, a small township in the heart of County Wicklow, was opened in 1865. The terrain on the inland side of the railway between Bray and Arklow comprised the extensive Wicklow mountain range, the wildest, most desolate and inaccessible in the whole of the country, the highest summit being Lugnaquilla, 3,039ft. The stretch of line through the well-known Vale of Avoca down to Arklow is one of the most picturesque on any Irish railway.

Wexford was finally reached on 17 August 1872 with a station at the north end of the town. Although it has to a great extent lost its importance as a harbour, at any rate for cross-channel traffic, it still has a population of about ten thousand and as the capital of the county is one of the largest and most important towns in the southern half of Ireland.

The Dublin Wicklow & Wexford was the first railway to reach Wexford, although a rival scheme had been authorised as early as 1846. The Wexford Carlow & Dublin Junction planned to leave the Great Southern & Western at Carlow and approach Wexford by a more inland route down the valley of the River Slaney. Meanwhile the South Eastern Railway, originally promoted in 1845, and worked by the Great Southern & Western Railway from Carlow to Kilkenny, was opened in 1850. Another scheme now evolved, the Bagenals-town & Wexford Railway, incorporated in July 1854, which was actually a subsidiary of the South Eastern. This followed a still more inland and very difficult course, to the west of the Blackstairs Mountains. It was opened as far as Borris, 8 miles from Bagenalstown, on 11 December 1858, and to Bally-william, another 12¾ miles, on 17 March 1862, but for the time being it got no farther.

The Bagenalstown & Wexford was entirely dependent on the Great Southern & Western, which worked the line; it possessed no rolling stock other than a few wagons of its own, and after the GSWR lost interest and gave notice that it was not prepared to continue its support, there was no alternative to closing the line, which took place on 31 October 1863. In June 1864 the company was declared bankrupt. So matters remained for a year or more until a London barrister, S. H. Motte, approached the GSWR with a view to restoring the BWR. How such a gentleman came to interest himself in an obscure railway in Ireland is problematical. What prospects he saw in such a moribund enterprise, even for those days, it is impossible to say. Anyway he bought the derelict line in 1866 for £25,000. Eventually a new company was formed, the Waterford New Ross & Wexford Junction Railway. This was authorised by an Act of 10 August 1866, which in addition to the construction of 34 miles of new lines also provided for the purchase of the Bagenalstown & Wexford. Mr Motte was named as one of the directors, but after that he seems to have faded from the picture. The old line was reopened as far as Borris on 5 September 1870, and the rest of the disused portion to Ballywilliam, together with the new line as far as Sparrowsland, on 26 October 1870, from where a four-horse coach gave connection to Wexford. The last section to Ballyhoge (Macmine Junction), where it joined the Dublin Wicklow & Wexford, was opened on 1 April 1873. Macmine was purely an interchange station, and had no road approach until 1895. By this time the Dublin Wicklow & Wexford had already completed the last section of its line from Enniscorthy into Wexford, this having been opened on 17 April 1872.

The Bagenalstown & Wexford was worked by the Waterford New Ross & Wexford Junction, partly with its own stock but also with some hired from the Great Southern & Western. It had only one engine, which had come from the MGWR, and it had to borrow others from the GSWR, which would only spare old Bury and Sharp singles, most unsuitable for a route with 1 in 60 gradients. Disputes between the two companies led to the line again being closed on 30 September 1873. Agreement was later reached, another engine and some rolling stock was obtained on hire, and it was reopened on 9 February 1874.

Two years later, in January 1876, the Waterford New Ross & Wexford Junction Railway was sold, being apportioned between the GSWR and the Dublin Wicklow & Wexford. The latter took over the line from Macmine to Ballywilliam, and the section on to Bagenalstown became part of the Great Southern & Western; by agreement the Dublin Wicklow & Wexford Railway worked its own engines and trains through to Bagenalstown until 1885, after which the Great Southern & Western worked its part separately.

As envisaged by the original Act of 1846 authorising the Waterford Wexford

Wicklow & Dublin Junction, the ultimate objective was Waterford. The project was again revived in 1866 by the Waterford New Ross & Wexford Junction. Eventually what was known as the Waterford Extension, which left the Bagenalstown & Wexford Railway at Palace East and proceeded westwards initially to New Ross, 19 miles from Macmine Junction, was opened on 19 September 1887. It was not until 15 February 1904 that the last 14 miles to Waterford were completed. At first the DWWR had to use the Great Southern & Western station there, by reversal over the goods lines, until a new station giving direct access was opened in August 1906.

The opening of this new main line between Macmine Junction and Waterford left an awkward stub between Palace East and Ballywilliam, by then the point of demarcation between Dublin Wicklow & Wexford and Great Southern & Western ownership; this was difficult for the former to operate on its own, and on 1 October 1902 the obvious step was taken of transferring it back to the Great Southern & Western, which could now operate more conveniently between Carlow and Palace East.

Waterford was now served by two routes from the capital city, a situation not often to be found on the railways of Ireland, even in the days of independence. On 1 June 1904 a through dining-car train to Dublin was inaugurated by the DWWR, the first to be seen in Waterford. As the junction at Macmine faced north, this involved reversal there of through trains between Dublin and Waterford.

Because of the completion of the railway the title of the DWWR was changed from 1 January 1907 to the Dublin & South Eastern Railway, and so it remained until its absorption into the Great Southern in 1925.

The DWWR had terminated at Wexford and the final extension southwards was by a separate company, the Waterford & Wexford, which although later incorporated into the Great Southern & Western was at this time closely integrated with the Dublin & South Eastern, to give it its later title. The DWWR terminus at Wexford was at the north end of the town and harbour, and so it remained until 24 June 1882, when the Waterford & Wexford Railway was opened along the quayside and main street to Wexford South and onwards to Rosslare. Although it has the appearance of a double line, it is actually a single main line, this being adjacent to the street, the one next to the quayside being a siding.

The company, the Waterford & Wexford, was incorporated on 25 July 1864, with the object of constructing a railway from the River Suir at Arthurstown in connection, by means of a ferry across Waterford Harbour, with a projected Waterford & Passage Railway, neither of which lines was ever built. Consequently the Waterford & Wexford Railway as such never reached

Page 33 (above) Ireland yesterday: a view in the shed and workshop of the Waterford & Tramore Railway. On the left is one of the original Bury engines, obtained secondhand from the English LNWR, but rebuilt from 2–2–0 to 2–2–2WT, when the line was opened in 1853. The other engine is one of a pair built by Fairbairn in 1855; these lasted for many years, the sister engine no 1 until as late as 1935, when it was scrapped following a derailment. The only other single-wheeler then in service in the British Isles was the celebrated ex-Caledonian 4–2–2 on the LMS; (below) Ireland today: one of CIE's latest air-conditioned inter-city express trains on the Dublin–Cork line. The train is shown in the modified orange and black livery; the coaches were built by British Rail Engineering Ltd at Derby

Page 34 The original Ballygerary Pier at Rosslare, Wexford, opened in 1882, which is the likely date of the photograph. The engine is Dublin Wicklow & Wexford 2-2-2WT no 1, built by Fairbairn in 1853 and withdrawn in 1891. Unfortunately no details are known of the interesting little vertical boiler shunter, which was no doubt a contractors' engine used in the construction of the harbour wall. It is of generally similar design to those built in considerable numbers by the firms of de Winton and Alexander Chaplin for industrial use in Great Britain, particularly in North Wales. It was

Waterford, but what it finally achieved was a continuation of the DWWR lines from Waterford down to Rosslare, at that time a pleasant but insignificant seaside resort on the extreme south-east tip of Ireland, but destined in later years to become an important harbour, and incidentally to usurp Wexford in this capacity almost entirely.

During this period the line was worked by the DWWR, and not unnaturally traffic was very small; after only a few years, on 17 May 1889, it was more or less closed, although some cattle traffic and miscellaneous goods were carried on occasions. It was however the incorporation in 1893 of the Fishguard Bay Railway & Pier Company on the English side, empowered to construct a new harbour at Fishguard, which was to set the pattern for the future of this area. The title of this new organisation very soon became the Fishguard & Rosslare Railways & Harbours, and this company was empowered to take over the Waterford & Wexford Railway. On 1 August 1894 the railway between Rosslare and Wexford was reopened, this time by the Waterford & Wexford itself. The distance to Rosslare Strand is 6¼ miles, with another 3½ miles to the harbour.

The Fishguard & Rosslare Railways & Harbours Company was incorporated jointly between the Great Western Railway of England and the Great Southern & Western. This was the outcome of negotiations which had been taking place since 1898 for the construction of harbours at Fishguard and Rosslare capable of accommodating large passenger ships and for the building of a direct railway between Rosslare and Waterford.

The new direct route between Rosslare Harbour and Waterford, opened in 1906, left the old Wicklow line at Rosslare Strand, 3½ miles from the harbour, and joined the DWWR line from New Ross and Macmine at Abbey Junction, some way east of Waterford station. A short length of about ¼ mile of this from Abbey Junction to New Wharf Junction was then the joint property of the Great Southern & Western and the Dublin & South Eastern Railways, one of the very few cases of joint ownership in Ireland.

The distance between Waterford and Rosslare Harbour is 38½ miles, and the through route from Cork, with steamer connection to Fishguard and by the Great Western Railway to London, was inaugurated on 30 August 1906. This realised the Great Western's long-cherished ambition to secure some Irish traffic, hitherto the preserve of the London & North Western and to a lesser extent the Midland and the Lancashire & Yorkshire. Not only did it now have a more direct route to Cork and southern Ireland, but also an alternative one to Dublin via the Dublin & South Eastern Railway.

The normal all-year-round daily service by the Fishguard to Rosslare route comprised until quite recently a night sailing in each direction, with an ad-

c

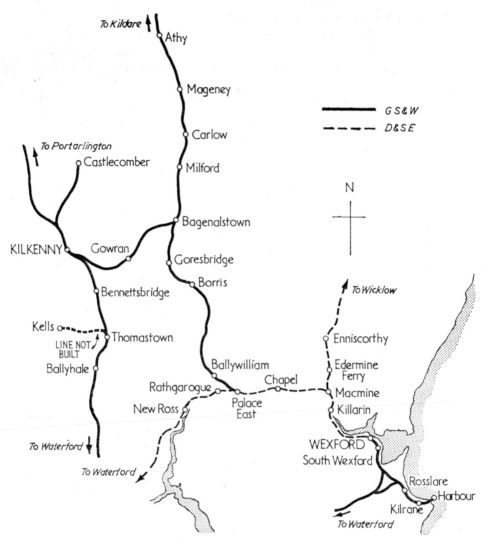

ditional daytime trip during the summer season only. This involved an evening departure from Paddington around 8 pm, the actual times varying over the years, a transfer to the boat in the small hours and arrival at Rosslare about 5 am; the boat expresses to Dublin and Cork left at something between 6 and 7 am. For Waterford passengers there was still sufficient time to enjoy a very welcome breakfast in the hour's run from Rosslare. This is nowadays a popular • route with people taking their cars for a holiday on the uncluttered roads of the Emerald Isle, and British Railways have developed the traffic to a considerable extent. Until quite recently there was no road access to the quayside at Rosslare, and cars had to be offloaded by crane and conveyed by rail over the half mile to the shore. This was provided for by an engine and about half a dozen flat wagons, but there is now a road over which cars may be driven straight off the boats.

When the new railway was opened there was a local service which started on 1 August 1906 between Waterford and Wexford by means of a direct loop line avoiding Rosslare Strand between Killmick and Felthouse Junctions, but this disappeared in 1912. There is now only one train daily in each direction between Waterford and Rosslare serving the intermediate stations.

Original locomotive of the Dublin & Kingstown Railway. *Hibernia*, a 2–2–0, built by Sharp Roberts in 1842, was probably the first engine to run in Ireland

These then were the lines which became part of the Dublin & South Eastern system. Today only the main line between Wexford and Dublin still remains open for passenger traffic, but the old line from Waterford, which lost its passenger service on 31 March 1963, is still used as far as New Ross for freight. The Macmine to New Ross (and Bagenalstown) lines were also closed completely in March 1963. The Harcourt Street line into Dublin from Shanganagh Junction was closed entirely at the end of 1958, and much of the Shillelagh branch in April 1944, although the section from Woodenbridge Junction as far as Aughrim remained open for a daily goods train until 1952.

LOCOMOTIVES AND ROLLING STOCK

The original locomotives of the Dublin & Kingstown Railway, the first in Ireland, were three 2–2–0s built by Sharp Roberts, *Hibernia*, *Britannia* and *Manchester*, and three others by G. Forrester of Liverpool, *Dublin*, *Kingstown* and *Vauxhall*. None of the Sharp engines lasted beyond 1842, when the boiler of *Hibernia* exploded, and the other two were withdrawn in consequence. The stock was of necessity increased during the 1840s, as traffic grew, but details are incomplete. Some of the engines were built at the company's own works at Grand Canal Street, a little south of Westland Row, which remained the locomotive headquarters right into Dublin & South Eastern days very many years later and is still in use as a diesel locomotive shed.

A few of the later Dublin & Kingstown engines survived the conversion to 5ft 3in gauge in 1856 and absorption into the Dublin & Wicklow Railway's stock, and some lasted until the 1880s. Not much is known about the coaches except that three classes were provided, with very great differences between the standards of comfort. At first the service was three trains an hour in each direction, later reduced to two, the sort of frequency which was maintained over the years until the advent of World War I.

The engines of the Dublin & Wicklow and the Dublin Wicklow & Wexford consisted mainly of 0–4–2 and 2–4–0 tender engines, some of the latter having outside frames, for the longer runs, whilst the busy suburban service between Dublin and Bray was largely in the hands of a fleet of 2–2–2WTs, very similar to a couple on the Waterford & Tramore which were in service until the late 1920s and early 1930s. On the Dublin & South Eastern however, all but two, nos 34 and 35, which lasted until 1923 on the Shillelagh branch, had gone by the early part of the century, and had been replaced by 2–4–0Ts. Many of these were later rebuilt as 2–4–2Ts and lasted to the end of steam working in the 1950s. One of them, no 9, *Dalkey*, still a 2–4–0T, around 1912 had three chimneys, two slimmer ones alongside the main one, an experiment which does not seem to have lasted long. The 2–4–2Ts were in turn followed by some 4–4–2Ts, the last two as late as 1924, from Beyer Peacock, being in fact the last new engines built for the DSER before absorption into the Great Southern. There were also six Webb 2–4–2Ts, purchased secondhand in 1902 from the London & North Western, which of course had to be altered to 5ft 3in gauge. Five of them were returned in 1916–17, when they were reconverted and did further work at collieries and for the War Department; the sixth, however, was retained and survived until 1936 as Great Southern no 427. During the 'troubles' it was fitted with armour plating.

The brief history of these engines is tabulated as follows:

Original LNWR *no*	Date built at Crewe	DSER *no*	DSER *name*	Later history
2070	1885	59	*Earl of Fitzwilliam*	Returned to England 1916–17
2502	1883	60	*Earl of Courtown*	,,
2496	1883	61	*Earl of Wicklow*	,,
842	1877	62	*Earl of Meath*	,,
1017	1884	63	*Earl of Carysfort*	,,
2152	1896	64	*Earl of Bessborough*	GSR 427

Nos 59 and 61 were sold to J. F. Wake of Darlington and resold to the Cramlington Collieries, Northumberland, as nos 13 and 14. Nos 60, 62 and 63 were sold to the government, the first two going to the Inland Waterways & Docks at Richborough, Kent, and no 64 to the War Department, Shoeburyness.

For the express trains to Waterford there came in 1895 four handsome 4–4–0s from the Vulcan Foundry, followed by two others from Beyer Peacock in 1905 in anticipation of the inauguration of the Rosslare boat trains. These were no 67 *Rathmore* and no 68 *Rathcoole*, and were the largest express engines owned by the railway. *Rathcoole* came to an untimely end in 1923, being involved in a malicious collision near Palace East. The Dublin & South Eastern was particularly unfortunate during the 'troubles' and suffered several deliberate collisions and derailments; the other engine in the 1923 Palace East derailment also had to be broken up, 0–6–0 no 51 *New Ross*. A similar 'incident' at Palace East in 1922 had caused severe damage to 2–4–0 no 25 *Glenart*, and 0–4–2 no 22 was similarly involved near Macmine. However, one 2–4–0 dating from 1864 survived until 1928, as Great Southern no 422, its last duty being the working of the Shillelagh branch.

For freight there were latterly ten 0–6–0s of varying ages and classes and two inside-cylinder 2–6–0s built by Beyer Peacock in 1922, one of which has been preserved.

As on many English railways during the first few years of the century, small steam railcars, a combined engine and coach, were tried out for short runs and branch-line services. The Dublin Wicklow & Wexford had two, built by Manning Wardle in 1906, nos 69 and 70. They do not appear to have been very satisfactory as such, and they were separated from the coach bodies and worked as independent 0–4–0WTs, later being named *Elf* and *Imp* by the GSWR. No 70 was sold to the Dublin & Blessington but was later returned, and no 69 ran for a time as a 2–4–0WT but was reconverted to 0–4–0WT and finished up in 1931 as Limerick station pilot.

The following is a summary of the Dublin & South Eastern engines which came into Great Southern stock in 1925—

DSER	Name (removed by GSR)	GSR no	Type	Builder	Date	Works no	Withdrawn
24	Glenmore	422	2-4-0	Sharp Stewart	1864		1928
49	Carrickmines	423	2-4-0T	Grand Canal St	1891		1955
9	Dalkey	424	2-4-0T	,,	1890		1953
47	Stillorgan	425	2-4-0T	,,	1889		1953
7	—	(426)	2-4-0T	,,	1895		1926
64	Earl of Bessborough	427	2-4-2T	Crewe	1896	3605	1936
3	St Patrick	428	2-4-2T	Grand Canal St	1898		1953
10	St Senanus	(429)	2-4-2T	,,	1896		1925
11	St Kevin	430	2-4-2T	,,	1896		1953
28	St Lawrence	431	2-4-2T	,,	1887		
45	St Kieran	432	2-4-2T	,,	1886		1957
46	Princess Mary	433	2-4-2T	,,	1888		1957
8	St Brendan	434	2-4-2T	,,	1903		1950
12	St Brigid	435	2-4-2T	,,	1901		1950
27	St Aiden	436	2-4-2T	,,	1907		1953
29	St Mantan	437	2-4-2T	,,	1906		1951
30	St Iberius	438	2-4-2T	,,	1908		1953
40	St Selskar	439	2-4-2T	,,	1902		1953
17	Wicklow	440	0-6-0	,,	1899		1929
36	Wexford	441	0-6-0	,,	1900		1935
13	Waterford	442	0-6-0	,,	1904		1930
14	Limerick	443	0-6-0	,,	1905		1935
18	Enniscorthy	444	0-6-0	,,	1910		1957
65	Cork	445	0-6-0	Beyer Peacock	1905	4647	1957
66	Dublin	446	0-6-0	,,	1905	4648	1957
50	Arklow	447	0-6-0	Vulcan Foundry	1891	1310	1930
4	Lismore	448	*0-6-0	Kitson & Co	1897	3686	1950
5	Clonmel	449	*0-6-0	,,	1897	3687	1940
55	Rathdown	450	4-4-0	Vulcan Foundry	1895		1929
56	Rathmines	451	4-4-0	,,	1895		1934
57	Rathnew	452	4-4-0	,,	1895		1932
58	Rathdrum	453	4-4-0	,,	1895		1940
67	Rathmore	454	4-4-0	Beyer Peacock	1905	4645	1949
20	King George	455	4-4-2T	Grand Canal St	1911		

DSER	Name (removed by GSR)	GSR no	Type	Builder	Date	Works no	With-drawn
34	—	456	4-4-2T	Beyer Peacock	1924	6204	1955
35	—	457	4-4-2T	,,	1924	6205	1960
52	Duke of Connaught	458	4-4-2T	Sharp Stewart	1893	3909	1955
54	Duke of Abercorn	459	4-4-2T	,,	1893	3911	1953
53	Duke of Leinster	460	4-4-2T	,,	1893	3910	1960
15	—	461	2-6-0	Beyer Peacock	1922	6112	pre-served
16	—	462	2-6-0	,,	1922	6113	

Numbers in brackets were never actually carried.
* Formerly 0-6-2T.

Nearly all DSER engines carried names until 1917, after which they were gradually removed. The names were painted in gold lettering with blue shading on the tank sides, or on the splashers of tender engines. The 4-4-0s nos 67 and 68, together with 0-6-0s 65 and 66, however, had brass nameplates, which were retained until removal by the Great Southern in 1925. Rectangular number-plates were carried on the cab or tank sides, and the company's crest was displayed on the upper cabside panel.

The livery was black lined out in red and orange. About the time that the new 4-4-2T King George appeared in 1911, a cigarette card was issued depicting it in a bright red livery, but this was imagination rather than fact. It is known however that the four 4-4-0s built in 1895 ran when new in a reddish-brown livery, but probably not longer than the first repaint. Coaching stock was red-brown lined out in gold.

There were also two survivors of the original Waterford & Wexford Railway, in fact the only engines it ever had. One of these was an 0-6-0ST named Erin, built by Hunslet for the WWR in 1894 (works no 610). It passed to the Great Southern & Western, which allocated it the number 300 but this was never actually carried. The other was an 0-4-0ST named Cambria, built by Hunslet in 1894. This too was acquired by the GSWR, but was never even allocated a number. In 1918 it was sold to the Dublin & Blessington. Erin lasted on miscellaneous duties in the Limerick area until 1930.

After the grouping in 1925 locomotives from other constituents of the Great Southern began to appear on the Dublin & South Eastern section, although it continued to be worked principally by its own engines. Such types as the Great Southern & Western J15 0-6-0s went to Bray along with a few Midland Great Western 2-4-0s, and did many years good work on the suburban services; they were joined also by 4-6-0T no 466 from the Cork Bandon & South Coast.

Great Southern & Western 4–4–0s gradually displaced the DSER engines on the Rosslare trains. Most important of all however was the construction of entirely new types specifically for the section, five 0–6–2Ts nos 670–4, built at Inchicore in 1929 for the Bray suburban service, and solitary 2–6–2T no 850, turned out in 1928 for the Dun Laoghaire boat train; however the latter does not appear to have been very successful.

Electrification of the suburban route to Bray was considered from time to time. It was really the only railway in the country where the traffic, actual or potential, was sufficient, but it never got further than the planning stage and the development of diesel traction finally resolved the matter.

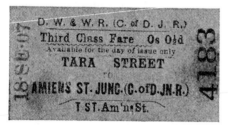

Three specimens of Dublin & South
Eastern Railway tickets

An interesting experiment took place in 1932 with the introduction of two battery-driven articulated railcar sets, which used a design of battery invented by a Dr Drumm. The two cars seated 131 passengers and were equipped with two 200hp motors. Two further sets of an improved design appeared in 1939, seating 140, and this accommodation could be considerably increased by inserting a trailer coach between the two power units. Their range without recharging was about eighty miles, so that theoretically they could make three return trips to Dublin, although in practice they normally did two. Within these limitations they were quite successful, and ran for many years until ultimately displaced by diesel railcars and locomotive-hauled trains.

CHAPTER 3

GREAT SOUTHERN & WESTERN RAILWAY

Ireland's largest railway, comprising the principal route between Dublin and Cork, with many secondary main lines and branches throughout the south and west. Incorporated 1844. Main line Dublin to Cork completed 1849.

Principal later acquisitions:
WATERFORD LIMERICK & WESTERN RAILWAY   Amalgamated 1901.
WATERFORD & CENTRAL IRELAND RAILWAY   Amalgamated 1900.
Many other smaller lines absorbed between 1866 and 1906. Became part o1 GREAT SOUTHERN RAILWAYS 1925.

Route mileage in 1899: 604 miles.

Eventual total route mileage in 1922: 1,150 miles.

Principal places served:
  Dublin, Cork, Queenstown (Cobh), Limerick, Tralee, Sligo, Athlone, Kilkenny, Waterford, Wexford, Rosslare.

The Great Southern & Western was the largest railway in Ireland even in 1900, when it had a route mileage of some 617 miles, slightly exceeding that of the runner-up, the Great Northern, which had about 606. In 1901, however, it absorbed the Waterford Limerick & Western, itself a sizeable railway of some 342 miles, and this placed it well ahead of any other Irish railway system.

It was almost unique in that it was conceived from the start as a through main line between two of the principal cities, Dublin and Cork, and did not grow piecemeal by the fusion of smaller separate concerns. The only other railway which began under similar circumstances was the Waterford Limerick & Western, first promoted to link Waterford with Limerick, a distance of 77 miles.

The 165 miles between Dublin and Cork, however, was not exceeded even in the rest of the British Isles at the time, the nearest rivals being the 118 miles of the original Great Western from London to Bristol and the 113 miles of the London & Birmingham. A good many other lines had been promoted in the 1830s to serve two or more important centres, such as the Grand Junction; Manchester and Birmingham; London and Southampton; North Midland (Leeds and Derby); Great North of England (Newcastle, Leeds and York); Edinburgh and Glasgow; Newcastle and Carlisle and others, but none of these reached the 100 mile mark.

The Great Southern & Western came into being during the Railway Mania of the 1840s, but even in 1844 the planning of a 165 mile main line at one go, as it were, was an ambitious proposal, particularly in a sparsely populated country such as Ireland. The conception was fully justified however in that it would not only provide quick and direct communication between the capital and the third most important city in the country, but also afford a means of opening up the south-west, hitherto difficult of access except by sea.

The original Act of Incorporation was dated 6 August 1844, with a further amending Act of 21 July 1845. It provided for the construction of the main line from Dublin to Cork, to pass through or near Portarlington, Thurles, Tipperary and Mallow, together with a branch to Carlow. As it turned out the latter was the first to be completed, the 55¾ miles from Dublin being opened in August 1846, but construction from Kildare, where the Carlow line diverged, proceeded rapidly. It was not a difficult line to build, there being no great engineering problems to be surmounted except for Mallow viaduct and the approach to Cork itself, with the result that Maryborough (now Portlaoise), 51 miles, was reached in June 1847, Ballybrophy, 66¾ miles, in September 1847, Thurles, 86¾ miles, in March 1848, Limerick Junction, 107¼ miles, in July 1848, Mallow, 144 miles, in March 1849, and a temporary station at Blackpool, on the outskirts of Cork, on 29 October 1849, a remarkable feat of rapid construction with the primitive means then available.

The most famous station on the whole line, at least amongst enthusiasts, is Limerick Junction, which results from the route of the Waterford Limerick & Western Railway, which actually got there about two months before the Great Southern & Western, crossing the latter's line almost at right angles; it was not, and is still not, near any town, although nowadays there is an adjoining racecourse, and is situated largely in the middle of nowhere! It is 22 miles from Limerick itself, and is not even in that county, being in fact in Tipperary. The town of Tipperary itself should have been served by the GSWR main line but is actually three miles to the south of the junction, and it was, and still is, served by the WLWR route.

The purpose of the commodious station, complete with refreshment room, which was built in this out of the way spot, was of course to provide interchange facilities between the trains of both railways, which between them served the four most important cities in the southern part of the country, Dublin, Cork, Waterford and Limerick. In later years alternative routes, rather more direct, were built between Dublin and Limerick and between Limerick and Cork, but although they were somewhat shorter there was not much saving in time, and the direct Cork to Limerick line lost its passenger service many years ago in any case. Limerick Junction, therefore, still sees quite a busy interchange traffic, when three and sometimes four trains are there simultaneously to make connections.

The fame of this unique station derived from the fact that, owing to the peculiar lay-out, a train could only come alongside a platform by reversing (see accompanying diagram). The station consists of a very long platform with a continuous outer face and a bay at either end. However, the track did not run along the main platform continuously but was divided by the centre crossovers into quite independent sections. A train from Dublin to Cork proceeded on the through-running lines past the station until it was clear of the point A, after which it backed over the crossover to take up its position at the east end on the main platform at E. Similarly a train from Cork to Dublin ran past the point B and then backed into the west end of the station at F, so that the two engines were facing each other 'like a couple of Kilkenny cats', as E. L. Ahrons once put it. A train from Waterford to Limerick proceeded northwards past the junction C and then backed into the east bay at G. But the antics of a southbound train were the most extraordinary of all. The train from Limerick left its main line at the point C, proceeded by the loop line, bypassing the station on the north side, to the point D and then backed into the station west bay at H, facing towards Cork. When leaving the station it had to reverse this procedure completely in order to get back to its own direction. Trains to the other three directions, however, had a straight run out without any second reversals.

In pre-war days the station was served by four or five trains daily in each direction over both routes, and as all of these were scheduled in groups of four to call at Limerick Junction for interchange purposes, the station alternated between periods of lively activity, when the four trains were in their respective positions simultaneously, and complete tranquility, save for the passing of the occasional freight train. The two WLWR trains were timed to arrive before and depart after the GSWR ones, and so their passengers had more time to slake their thirst in the refreshment room bar, which would be besieged rather on the lines of a theatre bar during the interval of a play, and moreover in Ireland the situation was not bedevilled by any licensing hour restrictions.

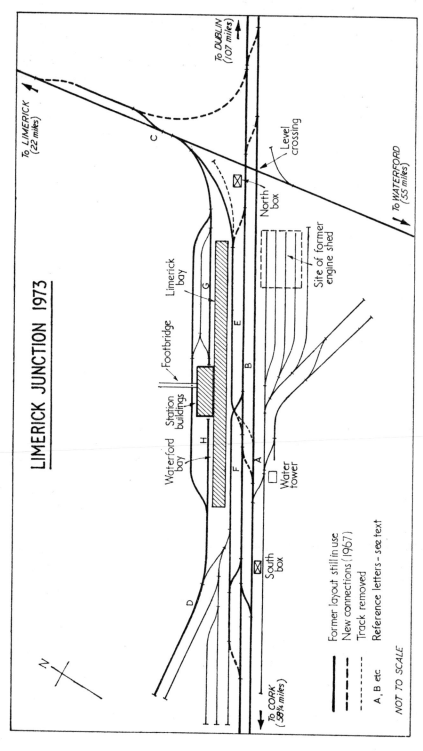

LIMERICK JUNCTION 1973

To LIMERICK
(22 miles)

To DUBLIN
(107 miles)

To WATERFORD
(55 miles)

To CORK
(58¼ miles)

Level
crossing

North
box

Limerick
bay

Site of former
engine shed

Footbridge

Station
buildings

Waterford
bay

Water
tower

South
box

C

A

G

E

B

H

F

D

N

——— Former layout still in use

— — New connections (1967)

- - - - Track removed

A, B etc   Reference letters - see text

NOT TO SCALE

Plan of Limerick Junction

The layout has now been altered so that the Dublin–Cork trains have a straight run-in and exit, and there is also a direct loop from Dublin on to the Limerick line avoiding the station altogether. Despite the apparent absurdity of the arrangement, it had the advantage that as there was only one island platform, passengers could change trains without the necessity of crossing lines by means of overbridges.

At first the GSWR line terminated at a temporary station just outside Cork, and to gain access to the main part of the city it was necessary to build a tunnel, one of the few in Ireland and one of the longest, 1,355 yards. A new station was then opened at Penrose Quay in 1855, but this was in turn replaced in 1893 by the present commodious structure at Glanmire Road, which included an hotel, although it is no longer in use as such. This tunnel approach was on a steep gradient, mostly at 1 in 60–70, necessitating the double-heading of up trains out of Cork. Glanmire Road station has in recent years been renamed Kent. The rest of the main line through to Dublin is easily graded, having nothing worse than 1 in 128 and not much of that, except for the initial rise out of Kingsbridge up to Inchicore, a couple of miles or so at about 1 in 81. The line is double throughout.

From Cork the Great Southern & Western had two branches. The Cork & Youghal Railway started as an independent concern, first presented in 1854 in place of an earlier scheme dating back to 1845 for a railway between Cork and Waterford, which would have taken the course of the Youghal line and reached Waterford by way of Dungarvan. This project was eventually abandoned and the railway constructed only as far as Youghal. The first section to be opened on 10 November 1859, was from Dunkettle, some 3 miles from the centre of Cork, to the small market town of Midleton, 9½ miles, with a present population of about 2,800. This was extended to Killeagh, another 7¾ miles, for some reason bypassing Castlemartyr, through which it might well have passed, but serving it only by a station at the small village of Mogeely, a mile away to the north. Killeagh station was opened on 17 February 1860, and the last 6½ miles to Youghal three months later, on 21 May. It now remained to gain access to Cork itself; it was desired to bring the railway right into the city centre at St Patrick's Hill, but this was found impracticable, and a terminus was built at Summerhill, not far from the present main station at Glanmire Road, but at a somewhat higher level. The complete extension to Summerhill was opened in May 1861 after there had been a temporary terminus for a few months at Tivoli, 1½ miles out.

Meanwhile an important event had taken place in 1859, when Queenstown, situated in Cork Harbour, 11 miles from the city round the shores of Lough Mahon, became a port of call for Atlantic liners. Its original name was Cove, but it had been known as Queenstown since 1849 when Queen Victoria visited Ireland. It was also an important naval base. Obviously a railway was now most desirable, and a branch off the Youghal line at what then became Queenstown Junction, between Littleisland and Carrigtwohill, ran southwards for 5¾ miles to terminate at the harbour. It was opened on 10 March 1862. It was a difficult line to construct, with sea walls and embankments, and it was fortunate that, with commendable foresight, provision was made for conversion from single to double track, as this eventually became necessary. In later years after physical connection with the main GSWR system at Cork had been established, boat trains were run between Dublin, or Kingstown, through to Queenstown. The Cork & Youghal Railway was purchased by the GSWR in 1866, and the line to Queenstown very soon came to be regarded as the main, and that to Youghal the branch. In the 1920s Queenstown reverted to its old name, Cove, but with the Irish spelling, Cobh.

The line is still important with about a dozen trains each way daily (six on Sundays) and with something in the nature of a residential service into Cork in the mornings and outward in the evenings. Incidentally there are no competing buses, as public road transport is controlled by CIE, a very sensible arrangement. Youghal lost its passenger service on 2 February 1963 but the line from the point of divergence, now known as Cobh Junction, is still open for goods.

The railway was joined with the main GSWR system in 1868 by a junction at Grattan Hill, ¾ mile from Summerhill, but the latter station continued to be used by the Youghal and Queenstown trains until 2 February 1893, when Glanmire Road main line station was completed. Tivoli station remained open until 1931. The Queenstown line then came to be regarded as an extension of the through main line from Dublin, and the mileposts in fact show the distances from Kingsbridge, and not, as might be expected, from Cork. The Youghal line however continued with the status of a branch, the mileposts measuring from Queenstown Junction.

The original station at Queenstown was abandoned in early GSWR days. A new one was built in 1888–9 and was enlarged and modernised in the 1950s, now being fully equipped with all facilities, including bar, refreshment rooms, rest rooms and an improved customs examination hall.

Also in Cork was the Cork City Railway, which provided a connection from Glanmire Road through the streets to the Cork Bandon & South Coast and associated lines, hitherto isolated from the rest of Ireland. This ¾ mile link, which included bridges over two branches of the River Lee, was made in 1912, and was the last important addition to the Great Southern & Western system. Although the Bandon lines, connection with which was its original purpose, are now entirely closed, the line still remains open for the conveyance of goods wagons through the city to Albert Quay.

The Cork & Limerick Direct Railway was an independent line incorporated on 3 July 1860 and opened on 1 August 1862. Such a rail link had in fact been mooted as early as 1840 but had come to nothing, and it was to be another nine years before Cork saw its first railway. This line diverged from the Great Southern & Western at Charleville and joined the Limerick to Tralee line at Patrick's Well, 18¼ miles, the trains running for the remaining 6½ miles over the old Waterford Limerick & Western Railway as far as Foynes Junction and then into the Cork & Limerick Direct Railway's own station at Limerick. The Great Southern & Western Railway worked the line and took it over on 1 July 1871. Passenger services ceased in 1934 and the line closed completely in 1967.

Killarney, Ireland's best known beauty spot and holiday centre of world-wide renown, was obviously the next objective once the railway had reached Cork by way of Mallow, some forty miles distant. The famous lakes are bounded by the finest and highest mountain range in the country, Macgillicuddy's Reeks rising precipitately to the west, and on the south the Mangerton Range, rising to 2,756ft; Carrantuohill, 3,414ft, is the highest point in Ireland.

It was not however the Great Southern & Western itself which made the first moves to extend its line in this direction, but the independent Killarney Junction Railway, incorporated in 1846 in anticipation of the Great Southern & Western reaching Mallow under the powers it had already obtained to build its main line to Cork. After the arrival of the GSWR at Mallow in 1849, construction of the 41 miles to Killarney began and the line was opened to Millstreet in April 1853 and to Killarney in May 1854.

Next came the incorporation, on 10 July 1854, of the Tralee & Killarney Railway, striking northwards for a further 22 miles to Tralee, the most important town in that part of the west of Ireland, and with a present population of over 10,000. This line was projected in conjunction with the Killarney Junction, which subscribed part of the capital. It was opened on 18 July 1859. Killarney was, and remains, a terminal station with a single platform and overall roof, and westbound trains have to back out to the junction before proceeding; similarly up trains reverse into the station. In December 1880 Tralee was reached also by the Waterford & Limerick Railway, which made end-on connection with the GSWR, although each company had its own station until the 1901 amalgamation, when the WLWR one was closed. Both of these Killarney lines were worked by the GSWR and were absorbed on 1 May 1860.

There were four branches off the main line from Mallow to Tralee, two of which were of exceptional interest. The first from a geographical point of view, however, was the Banteer & Newmarket Railway, opened in 1889, which left the Mallow to Killarney line at Banteer and ran northwards to Newmarket, 9 miles, with an intermediate station at Kanturk. At first independent, it was purchased by the Great Southern & Western in July 1892. The station at New-market was pleasantly situated in picturesque surroundings, and had the usual one-road shed for the branch engine, together with a turntable. The four daily trains made connection with the main line at Banteer, with sometimes a through working to or from Mallow. First closed in 1947, it was reopened for goods in June 1956, but passenger services were never reinstated, and it was finally closed completely on 2 February 1963.

A little farther on towards Killarney was the Kenmare branch, 19¾ miles, which left the main line at Headford Junction, and ran south-west through very fine mountainous country to the pleasant town of Kenmare, situated on the head of the very long estuary where the Roughty river opens into the River Kenmare, and out of it into the Atlantic.

This branch was constructed under the 1889 Light Railways Act, with a baronial guarantee of £60,000, and was opened on 4 October 1893. In spite of the difficult nature of the terrain it was found possible to limit the severity of the gradients to 1 in 60. The three intermediate stations on the line, at Loo Bridge, Morley's Bridge and Kilgarvan, all in lonely situations, were little more than halts and could have attracted only the minimum of local traffic. The main purpose of the line was to develop the fishing industry, but nevertheless in view of its scenic nature it also attracted much tourist traffic, before the coming of the motor coach and the private car. By its nature it was ill fitted to meet this competition; it was closed on 31 December 1959 and the track was lifted in 1960. The three or four daily trains were usually mixed, with both passenger coaches and freight vehicles. It enjoyed a considerable cattle traffic on fair days at Kenmare, when special cattle trains were run.

Next was one of the most spectacular and interesting railways in the whole of Ireland, the long branch running westwards between Killarney and Tralee, from Farranfore Junction to Valentia Harbour, 39¼ miles, on the extreme west coast overlooking the Atlantic. This outpost had the distinction of being the most westerly railhead not only in the British Isles but in the whole of Europe. It was very closely approached in this respect by the neighbouring narrow-gauge Tralee & Dingle Railway on the other side of Dingle Bay.

The origins of the line lay in the incorporation of the independent Killorglin Railway, which obtained authority in 1871 to build the line from Farranfore as far as Killorglin, a distance of 12½ miles. These powers however were trans-ferred to the Great Southern & Western, which itself undertook the construc-tion and the line was opened on 15 January 1885. Killorglin is but a small town-

Page 51 (above) Rosslare Harbour was rebuilt in preparation for the inauguration of the steamer service to and from Fishguard on 30 August 1906, providing through connections between London and both Dublin and Cork. This view, taken from the evening Cork train in April 1955, shows the steamer *Saint David*, built at Birkenhead in 1947; the engine is Woolwich 2-6-0 no 384. Since this photograph was taken a road has been constructed giving direct access to the quayside, which could previously be reached only by rail or on foot; (below) Although the Fishguard–Rosslare route provides a useful alternative, especially to the south of Ireland, Holyhead–Kingstown has remained the principal artery of communication between the two countries since the opening of the Dublin & Kingstown, Ireland's first railway, in 1834. The pier, as here depicted, was completed in 1859, and this view, taken between the wars, shows the arrival of the mail boat from Holyhead. The connecting train to Dublin is in charge of former DSER 2-4-2T no 434. After the 1925 partition of the country Kingstown was renamed Dun Laoghaire

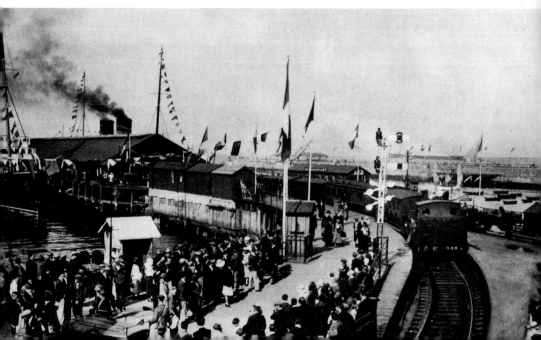

Page 52 (above) A train of the Rosslare & Wexford Railway (later absorbed by the Fishguard & Rosslare Railways & Harbour Co) on Wexford Quay about 1898. The engine, *Erin*, built by the Hunslet Engine Co in 1894, was taken into the stock of the Great Southern & Western, allocated the number 300, but never actually carried it. The only named engines on the GSWR were a few oddments of this sort, as the company did not consider it necessary for an engine to carry both name and number; (below) Cork & Macroom train at the original Cork terminus at Capwell in July 1914. This independent railway originally used the CBSCR terminus at Albert Quay until a dispute caused it to build its own line into the city. This state of affairs lasted until the 1925 grouping, when trains were diverted back to Albert Quay, the more inconvenient Capwell station being closed. Engine no 4 was built in 1881, became GSR no 489 and was scrapped in 1928

ship with a population of about 1,000, but it is the only one of any size on the route to Valentia. Nevertheless the railway took advantage of the Light Railways Act of 1889 to extend the line westwards through this remote and mountainous area. This was completed and opened on 12 September 1893. Even the first section as far as Killorglin had cost £7,000 a mile, but the extension onwards turned out to be more in the region of £8,800. This was made possible only by a grant of £75,000 and a baronial guarantee of £70,000. The Great Southern & Western provided the remaining £65,000.

The railway ran for some of its course along the south shores of Dingle Bay with the Teermoyle mountain range, embracing a summit of 2,542ft, in the background. Intermediate stations were at Caragh Lake, Dooks, Glenbeigh,

DOWN.—Tralee & Farranfore to Killorglin, C'civeen and Valentia Harbour.—WEEK DAYS.

Distance from Farranfore	DOWN TRAINS	1. Sectional Running		2. Empty Train		3. Pas.		4. Goods See Footnote A		5. Empty Train		6. Pas.		7. Pas.		8. Pas.	
		Pas.	Gds.	arr.	dep.	arr.	dep.	arr.	dep.	arr.	dep.	arr.	dep.	arr.	dep.	arr.	dep.
Mls.				a.m.	a.m.	a.m.	a.m.	a.m.	a.m.	p.m.	p.m.	p.m.	p.m.	p.m.	p.m.	p.m.	p.m.
—	TRALEE ... W ● ¶	...	...	...	...	...	...	...	4 30	...	...	...	3 50	...	...	...	...
—	GORTATLEA ● ¶	...	...	...	...	...	...	4 52	5 00	...	...	4 04	4 05	...	...	...	...
—	FARRANFORE ● ¶	...	...	...	...	...	...	5 15	...	...	...	4 13	...	...	...	...	...
—	FARRANFORE W ● ¶	0	0	...	...	...	...	...	6 15	...	...	...	4 30	...	...	...	...
1½	MOLAHIFFE	3	5	...	...	...	...	6 24	6 36	...	...	4 35	4 36	...	...	...	...
6½	CASTLEMAINE ¶	8	12	...	...	...	...	6 52	7 16	...	...	4 46	4 49	...	...	...	...
7¾	MILLTOWN HALT	2	3	...	...	...	...	7 23	7 25 Mxd.	...	...	4 53	4 54	...	...	...	...
12½	KILLORGLIN W ● ¶	10	12	...	...	...	...	7 41	9 07	...	...	5 06	5 10	...	...	...	...
16	CARAGH LAKE HALT	7	9	...	...	...	...	9 18	9 27	...	...	5 19	5 20	...	...	...	...
18	DOOKS HALT	4	5	...	...	...	...	C.	R.	...	...	5 26	5 27	...	...	...	...
20	GLENBEIGH W + ¶	3	6	...	...	...	...	9 42	10 00	...	...	5 32	5 36	...	...	...	...
23½	MOUNTAIN STAGE HALT ¶	12	18	...	...	...	...	10 18	10 23	...	...	5 50	5 51	...	...	...	...
30½	KELLS HALT ¶	24	26	...	...	...	...	10 51	10 53	...	...	6 17	6 18	...	...	...	...
36¾	CAHIRCIVEEN + W ● ¶	11	16	...	7 00	...	...	11 10	...	...	1 35	6 31	6 36	...	...	...	...
39½	VALENTIA HARBOUR ...*	6	7	7 10	...	...	...	...	...	1 45	...	6 45	...	...	...	...	...

*—Train Staff and Single Engine in Steam, Cahirciveen, Valentia.
A—Passenger accommodation provided between Killorglin and Cahirciveen Daily.

UP.—Valentia Harbour, C'civeen & Killorglin to Farranfore & Tralee. WEEK DAYS.

Dist. from Valentia Harbour	UP TRAINS	9 Sectional Running		10 Pas.		11 Pas.		12 Perishable B		13		14		15		16 Empty Train	
		Pas.	Gds.	arr.	dep.	arr.	dep.	arr.	dep.	arr.	dep.	arr.	dep.	arr.	dep.	arr.	dep.
Mls.				a.m.	a.m.	a.m.	a.m.	p.m.	p.m.	p.m.	p.m.	p.m.	p.m.	p.m.	p.m.	p.m.	p.m.
—	VALENTIA HARBOUR ...	0	0	...	7 30	...	...	...	2 10	...	...	...	...	...	...	...	6 55
2¾	CAHIRCIVEEN + W ●	4	7	7 36	7 40	...	...	2 18	2 44	...	...	...	...	...	...	7 05	...
9	KELLS HALT ...	18	32	8 00	8 01	...	...	3 12	3 13	...	...	...	...	...	...	...	...
16	MOUNTAIN STAGE HALT	25	26	8 28	8 29	...	...	3 42	3 43	...	...	...	...	...	...	...	...
19½	GLENBEIGH + W	9	10	8 40	8 44	...	...	3 56	4 04	...	...	...	...	...	...	...	...
21½	DOOKS HALT	3	5	8 49	8 50	...	...	4 11	4 12	...	...	...	...	...	...	...	...
23½	CARAGH LAKE HALT	4	10	8 56	8 57	...	...	4 22	4 24	...	...	...	...	...	...	...	...
27	KILLORGLIN DW ●	6	8	9 05	9 09	...	...	4 34	5 15	...	...	...	...	...	...	...	...
31¾	MILLTOWN HALT	9	12	9 20	9 21	...	...	5 28	5 30	...	...	...	...	...	...	...	...
33	CASTLEMAINE ...	2	3	9 25	9 26	...	...	5 36	5 51	...	...	...	...	...	...	...	...
38	MOLAHIFFE	8	12	9 36	9 38	...	...	6 04	6 09	...	...	...	...	...	...	...	...
39½	FARRANFORE W ●	3	6	9 43	...	...	...	6 15	...	...	...	...	...	...	...	...	...
—	FARRANFORE ●	...	...	...	9 50	...	...	...	6 35	...	...	...	...	...	...	...	...
—	GORTATLEA ●	...	...	9 58	9 59	...	...	6 45	6 46	...	...	...	...	...	...	...	...
—	TRALEE ... ●	...	...	10 11	...	...	...	7 00	...	...	...	...	...	...	...	...	...

C.R.–Stops when required. B–Passenger accommodation provided between Valentia and Tralee Daily.
Bogie Coaches can work between Killorglin and Valentia Harbour provided they be fitted with Elliptical Buffers, or with Round Buffers of not less than 18 inches diameter.

Working timetable of Valentia (often spelt Valencia) Harbour Branch in CIE days. September 1954

D

Mountain Stage and Kells, these last three all being passing places. Glenbeigh possessed watering facilities, as did Killorglin, and engines needed to take water at both these places in view of the arduous nature of the line. Cahirciveen was the principal township in the area, with about 1,800 inhabitants and two hotels, and for practical purposes was really the end of the branch. The engine shed and turntable were situated there, and the first and last workings of the day comprised an outwards and inwards trip over the remaining $2\frac{1}{2}$ miles to Valentia Harbour, which consisted of nothing more than a bare platform and a small corrugated iron shed, in fact a halt, albeit unusually a terminal one. A ferry crossed the $\frac{1}{2}$ mile strait to Valentia Island, 7 miles long, of which the farthest tip, Bray Head, is the ultimate western extremity of Europe.

The scenery of this route was magnificent. Between Mountain Stage and Kells it ran close to the seashore, but at a considerable height above sea level along ledges on the hillside, with several short tunnels through protruding cliffs. At Gleensk, near Kells, was a very fine curved viaduct; it consisted of eleven spans and was built 73ft above river level on a radius of 10 chains, which necessitated check rails.

As on the Kenmare branch, the trains, which ran through to and from Tralee, were usually mixed, at one time three per day in each direction. For a long time only six-wheelers were allowed, but in later years the use of bogie coaches was authorised, with certain restrictions. By 1954 the service had been reduced to only one advertised passenger working each way daily, but with accommodation provided for passengers on the much slower daily goods. With this timetable it was not practicable to do the return trip in one day, and the night had to be spent in Cahirciveen.

In early days the line was worked by 2–4–2Ts and 4–4–2Ts but for the majority of its existence it was entirely in the hands of the ubiquitous 101 class 0–6–0s, and it is doubtful whether any other types were ever seen. For the last two or three years these were supplanted by diesels of the C class but such marginal economies as these might have achieved could give no hope for the future. Never a paying proposition, such a remote railway, expensive to maintain, has no place in the present day, and to the great regret of all who ever knew it, the last train ran on 30 January 1960. It is in fact remarkable, and from the enthusiast's point of view, fortunate, that it lasted as long as it did. Other comparable lines, such as the Midland Great Western's Achill and Clifden branches, succumbed very much earlier, as did such narrow-gauge systems as the Tralee & Dingle and the Letterkenny & Burtonport Extension.

Nearer to Tralee was the short conventional branch to Castleisland, $4\frac{1}{2}$ miles without intermediate stations, leaving the main line at Gortatlea, 7 miles out from Tralee. Castleisland is a market town of about 1,650 inhabitants, with a ruined castle, but its main claim to fame derives from its quarries of red marble, used effectively in ecclesiastical decoration. The unusual colour is due to the infiltration of iron oxide.

The Castleisland Railway was originally a separate company, authorised on 13 May 1872 and opened on 30 August 1875. The Great Southern & Western provided a combined 0–6–4T engine and coach, no 90, built at Inchicore in 1875 to the design of A. McDonnell, to work the line. It could haul either an independent coach or two or three wagons. The railway was acquired by the Great Southern & Western in 1880, and as traffic grew, this early form of steam railmotor was replaced by various types of tank locomotives, and sometimes by the inevitable 101 class 0–6–0s, with ordinary trains, and for a short period by a Sentinel locomotive. Two more of these combined engines and coaches were built at Inchicore, nos 91 and 92. The latter retained this form and was a familiar sight in recent years as the Inchicore 'works cab', conveying staff between the works and Kingsbridge station. The coach portion was however removed from no 90, which became an ordinary 0–6–0T and still survives at Mallow, one of the all too few Great Southern engines preserved.

This branch was closed in February 1947, but thereafter continued to run specials on 'fair days', and a regular daily goods train from Tralee was reinstated on 7 January 1957. The line is still open, along with the Tralee & Fenit.

What eventually became the through direct line between Dublin and Limerick, as an alternative to the earlier route via Limerick Junction, started as it were at both ends with what were originally separate and entirely unrelated branches. The Limerick Castleconnell & Killaloe Railway was opened as far as Castleconnell on 28 April 1858, Birdhill on 10 July 1860, and Killaloe on 12 April 1862. From Birdhill, which now became a junction, the line was extended to Nenagh on 5 October 1863, Killaloe then being relegated to a branch. Passenger services between Birdhill and Killaloe ceased in 1931, and freight in 1944, although the track was not lifted until 1952.

Before all this, however, there had been authorised in 1853 a 22½ mile branch from the Great Southern & Western main line at Ballybrophy to Parsonstown, which is now more usually known as Birr but sometimes by its old Celtic name of Biorra. It is situated in the southern part of the central plain of Ireland, more or less equidistant from the east and west coasts, and is a pleasant town of some 3,250 inhabitants. It has a castle, in the grounds of which Lord Rosse set up some great astronomical telescopes in 1845, at the time some of the largest in the world, but they have long since disappeared.

The line was opened as far as Roscrea, 10¼ miles from Ballybrophy, on 19 October 1857, and reached Parsonstown, another 12 miles, on 8 March

1858. The intervening section between Roscrea, which now became the junction for the Parsonstown branch, and Nenagh, was opened in 1863, at the same time as the extension to Nenagh from the Birdhill end, which completed the through route between Ballybrophy and Limerick. It was not until the amalgamation of the Great Southern & Western and the Waterford Limerick & Western in 1901, however, that through trains were operated. There is nowadays one daily express with buffet car in each direction between Dublin and Limerick by this route, with an additional working (which also runs on Sundays) between Limerick and Ballybrophy, with Dublin connections. The through trains reverse at Ballybrophy as the junction faces the Cork direction. Most services between the two cities however continue to be provided by the old arrangement of changing at Limerick Junction, but in one or two cases trains bypass the junction by means of the recently constructed avoiding line, thus obviating the change. As for the branch from Roscrea to Birr, all services ceased on 31 December 1962 and the line was lifted. Another independent company, the Parsonstown & Portumna Bridge, was authorised on 11 July 1861, to construct a 12½ mile railway to Portumna Bridge, at the head of Lough Derg, into which runs the Shannon. Portumna actually lies in the county of Galway, the boundary with the northern part of Tipperary being the Shannon itself. Parsonstown however was in the neighbouring Offaly county, formerly known as Kings County. This, together with the adjoining Queens County to the south, was renamed when Eire came into being, and they became respectively Offaly and Laoighis, or Laois.

Portumna, although not a large town, with nowadays only about 1,000 inhabitants though probably more then, was considered of sufficient importance to have a railway, and after some delay in acquiring the necessary capital, the line was at last completed and opened on 5 November 1868. Parsonstown remained a terminal station and the new branch left the line from Roscrea by a trailing connection. It was worked by the Great Southern & Western, to which it was leased for ten years. The only engineering work of any note was a girder bridge supported by stone piers over the Little Brosna river at Riverstown. The line terminated on the east bank of the Shannon at Portumna Bridge; there was already a road crossing over the river into Portumna itself. An Act dated 29 July 1864 for the Parsonstown & Portumna Bridge Extension Railway authorised a railway bridge and continuation of the line another 1½ miles into the town, but this was never built.

Traffic was poor from the start, and never came up to expectations. The hoped for exchange with the steamers of the Shannon Navigation did not somehow materialise. A timetable of 1871 shows only two trains per day in each direction, the first of which left Portumna Bridge for Parsonstown at the uncomfortable hour of 6 am, no doubt designed to give early connection with a Dublin train at Ballybrophy, allowing a day in the city and a return late in the evening at 9.28 pm. Such timings would be very inconvenient for local passengers, however, and the only other train was around mid-day.

When its lease expired in 1878, the GSWR refused to continue the operation of the line, saying it was losing £2,000 a year, and it was consequently closed to all traffic in December. Several attempts were made in the ensuing years to reopen it, and it was not until 1907 that such ideas were finally abandoned. Up to that time the railway had been nominally left intact, and until 1880 some attempt was made to keep it in order, but after that it gradually disappeared. It was not long before everything that was movable, from the rails to the station buildings at Portumna Bridge, had been removed by scroungers from far and near, who helped themselves to anything that might be useful. The police did what they could, but no prosecution was practicable as there was no one prepared to take proceedings, probably for fear of being liable for possible claims as a result of presumed ownership. There was even an attempt to remove the girders of the six-span bridge by means of cranes and other apparatus, but it was stopped by the police, and the bridge remains, or did until not so long ago, as the only tangible relic of the line.

A new line was built in this area, albeit only a short one of 1¼ miles, as recently as December 1966. This is the Silvermines branch, between Nenagh and Birdhill, on the south side of the main line, and it serves mining operations of barytes and zinc deposits which are conveyed to Foynes for export, a lucrative traffic developed with commendable enterprise by the CIE.

Farther along the Cork main line is Thurles, an important town with a fine cathedral, and today a centre of considerable sporting activity. A railway with the somewhat grandiose title of Southern of Ireland was incorporated on 5 July 1865, to construct a 22¼ mile line from the Great Southern & Western to Clonmel, on the Waterford Limerick & Western. There had been such a scheme in 1846, the Clonmel & Thurles Railway, but the powers lapsed before construction could begin. Clonmel is an important town of 10,000 inhabitants, the largest in the county of Tipperary. It was the original intention that the new railway should be worked by the GSWR, but by the time it was opened, from Clonmel to Fethard on 23 June 1879 and through to Thurles on 1 July 1880, this arrangement had fallen through and it was in fact operated by the Waterford Limerick & Western until that railway was absorbed by the GSWR in 1901.

The status of the Southern Railway Company of Ireland seems to have become somewhat vague in later years. Although still remaining nominally an independent concern, it was to all intents and purposes a part of the Great Southern & Western system. No one seemed to bother about this, and the matter was more or less forgotten until the creation of the Great Southern in 1925, the amalgamation of all railways in the Free State, when the question of the actual ownership had to be considered. By that time the Southern Railway of Ireland seemed to have no company offices or address, directors, officials or shareholders, and there was no response to advertisements; so on 17 November 1925 the matter was officially forgotten and the Clonmel and Thurles line became part of the new Great Southern Railways.

For many years this became the principal route between Clonmel and Dublin, rather than the slightly longer one via Limerick Junction. In earlier times there were normally no through trains to the capital, but interchange was not always effected at Thurles, as might have been expected, some branch services running through to Ballybrophy, 20 miles farther up the main line, to connect with Limerick–Dublin trains. By 1954 there were only two trains daily over the branch, latterly worked by a railbus obtained from the SLNCR, but this ceased on 7 September 1963, and the line was closed completely in 1967. Clonmel passengers therefore have to travel via Limerick Junction, and with only three trains each way daily, not all of them making main-line connections, this important town is now poorly served with rail facilities.

The last country branch to be built by the GSWR was from Goolds Cross, on the main line between Thurles and Limerick Junction, to Cashel, a short line of 5¾ miles with one intermediate station at Ardmayle. A branch with no particular features of interest, it was opened on 19 December 1904. The 1910 timetable shows an unbalanced service of five trains in one direction and six in the other. Regular passenger services were withdrawn on 25 January 1947, but occasional excursions still ran until 1954, when the line was closed altogether. The chief interest of the town of Cashel, which has some 2,700 inhabitants, is its rock, 300ft high, dominated by its thirteenth-century cathedral.

Portarlington, 41¾ miles out from Dublin is the junction for the Great Southern & Western line to Athlone, a rival route to that of the Midland Great Western, which had reached there in August 1851. The GSWR started in that direction by constructing a line from Portarlington as far as Tullamore, 16¼ miles, which was opened in October 1854, at first to a terminal station, but this was closed and a new one built when the railway was extended in 1859. Tullamore is an agricultural town of over 6,000 inhabitants, with an important malting industry.

In 1856 a bill was presented to Parliament for authority for an extension to Athlone and thence via Roscommon through to Sligo. The MGWR had already reached Longford in 1855, as the first part of its own route to Sligo, and powers were obtained in 1857 for the construction of the remaining 58 miles via Carrick on Shannon. Further complication occurred by the incorporation in 1857 of

the Great Northern & Western Railway for a line from Athlone to Roscommon and Castlerea. This was to become part of the Midland Great Western's
third main line to Claremorris and Westport.

Relations between the two companies, already none too good as a result of
disputes over the ownership of the Grand Canal, which ran through Tullamore,
became very strained and were at their worst in 1858. Various proposals were
made in an endeavour to secure some sort of working arrangement between the
three railways involved, the Midland Great Western, Great Northern &
Western and the Great Southern & Western, but no agreement could be
reached. The Midland tried to get to Tullamore by a branch of its own from

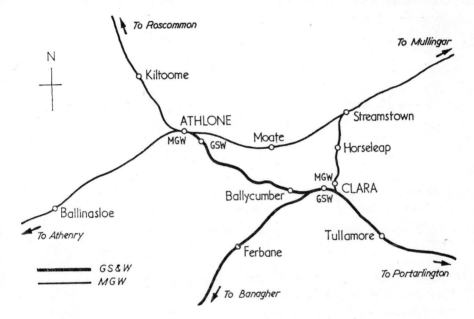

Streamstown, but this only reached Clara (in 1863), whereas the GSWR achieved
its objective by getting as far as Athlone, with its own station at Clara, this line
being opened on 3 October 1859. Here too, and at Athlone, there were separate
stations until 1927, although a connection between the two lines had been put
in during 1860. After the 1925 grouping the Great Southern ran trains from
Portarlington through to the former MGWR station. The construction of this
line however more or less finished the Great Southern & Western's aspirations
as far as Connaught and the north-west was concerned, until its absorption of
the Waterford Limerick & Western in 1901, which railway had already reached
Sligo by its western route from Limerick.

The year 1860 was really the end of the disputes between the GSWR and the

MGWR, which had been going on since 1853, including the contentious ownership of the Grand Canal. The relevant matters were submitted to arbitration,
which duly announced its findings on 8 February 1860. Under these rulings a
line of demarcation between the two companies was declared, outside of which
each should henceforth operate. This ran from Dublin to the mouth of the
Shannon via Edenderry, Athlone, the Shannon, mid Lough Derg, Ennis and
south of the Midland Great Western Galway main line. Athlone itself presented
a little difficulty, but the agreement provided that traffic originating there would
be apportioned 65 per cent of passenger and 55 per cent of goods to the Midland
Great Western; similar percentages, but in favour of the Great Southern &
Western, were to be made in respect of Clara on the opening of the latter's
branch from Streamstown, which did not take place until 1863.

The Midland Counties & Shannon Junction Railway was incorporated on
6 August 1861 to construct a 19 mile branch from the GSWR at Clara to Banagher.
This pleasant town formerly had a very ancient bridge over the Shannon but
this was replaced in 1843 by a more modern structure and was regrettably not
preserved. The line should have continued along the east side of the Shannon
for about 3 miles and then crossed the river into County Galway at Meelick
but this was never built. It was even envisaged as part of a 'Main Trunk Railway'
from the west and north, but this was one of those grandiose schemes destined
never to materialise. The branch, worked by the GSWR from the start, was
vested in that company on 14 May 1895. Passenger services ceased in 1947 and
the line was entirely closed on 31 December 1962. The 1972 timetable shows
two through trains each way between Dublin and Westport, calling at Tullamore, and also two local services between Portarlington and Athlone, some of
these serving Clara in addition.

From Sallins, 17¾ miles out of Dublin, a long 35 mile branch ran southwards
over the western edge of the Wicklow Mountains to terminate at Tullow, on
the River Slaney, in County Carlow, a busy little town of 1,700 inhabitants.
Among the more important intermediate places was Naas, of 4,000 inhabitants,
now much more easily reached by road from Dublin, only about 20 miles
distant, as it lies on the main routes to Cork, Limerick and the west. Another
small intermediate town was Baltinglass, of about 1,000 inhabitants. It was in
fact the original terminus of the line, which was opened as far as Colbinstown
on 22 June 1885; the full 24½ miles to Baltinglass were opened on 1 September
in the same year. The remaining 10½ miles, the Tullow extension, followed on
1 June 1886. The normal service was three trains each way daily, one on Sundays, making connections with the main line at Sallins. However, being so
near to Dublin the area is more suited to bus services, particularly in view of the
inconvenient distance of Kingsbridge (now Heuston) station from the city

centre, and there is now no outer suburban service of any sort out of Dublin on the former Great Southern & Western; in fact of all the intermediate stations in the first 30 miles to Kildare, Clondalkin, Lucan, Hazlehatch, Straffan, Sallins and Newbridge, only the latter, now known as Droichead Nua, remains open, served by three or four trains a day. Formerly all these stations had a service of about ten trains daily. Not surprisingly the Tullow branch lost its passenger service in 1947 and was closed entirely in 1959.

All the four main railways out of Dublin, the Dublin & Kingstown, Dublin & Drogheda, Midland Great Western and Great Southern & Western, the first portions of which were opened between 1834 and 1846, were for many years unconnected with one another, or with the docks. This situation obviously had to be dealt with sooner or later, as it became apparent that railways were destined to serve more than purely local needs, and must inevitably form an embracing network over the whole country. The Midland Great Western was the first to appreciate the need for some sort of communication with the outside world, and its first effort in this direction was the construction in 1864 of the Liffey branch from Liffey Junction, a mile out of its Broadstone terminus, along the course of the Royal Canal to North Wall, which gave it access to the harbour and shipping routes.

In the 1860s several alternative schemes were put forward for a general link-up of the four railways, but it was to be many years before this was finally achieved. Amongst the abortive schemes was one put forward for a line from Ringsend Docks alongside the Grand Canal to join the Great Southern & Western at Inchicore. It would have had a connection with the Dublin & Kingstown Railway and given the GSWR much earlier access to Kingstown Harbour than it eventually gained early in 1892. Another proposal was for a railway passing under the Liffey by means of a tunnel 72ft below the quays. Yet another idea, the Dublin Metropolitan Junction Railway, which was actually authorised on 6 July 1865, was for elevated lines from Westland Row to Amiens Street and Kingsbridge, the first part of which anticipated to a large extent the City of Dublin Junction Railway.

The earlier scheme however had provided for a large central station at Eustace Street, near College Green, which could have been used by both the Dublin Wicklow & Wexford and the Great Southern & Western, and would have provided the latter with a far more convenient station than Kingsbridge. This bill, however, although passed by the House of Commons, was rejected by the Lords.

By this time other schemes had been projected. The Dublin Railway was to have a large bridge over the Liffey, embodying a nine-track station, presumably to be used by the Dublin Wicklow & Wexford and the Dublin & Drogheda.

The Dublin Grand Junction Railway was a proposal for a line from Ringsend along the course of the Grand Canal, similar to the earlier 1860 scheme, but in this case to Kingsbridge, and thence via Phoenix Park to link up with the Midland Great Western. Then there was the Dublin Trunk Connecting Railway authorised on 29 July 1864, which empowered the construction of 8½ miles of line connecting all stations in the city. This was to diverge from the Dublin & Kingstown Railway near Sandymount, tunnel under the Liffey, and running round the east and north of the city connect the main lines together. Work was actually started on shafts preliminary to the construction of the tunnel, but financial difficulties held up further work and notwithstanding an extension of time until 15 August 1870, the project failed and the concern went into liquidation.

Three plans were submitted to Parliament in 1872. The Great Southern & Western suggested a line from a point about half a mile out of Kingsbridge terminus to be known as Islandbridge Junction, through a short tunnel under Phoenix Park to a junction at Glasnevin with the Midland Great Western Liffey branch. This would give the GSWR access to North Wall docks. Alternative proposals were for a central station over the Liffey between Aston's Quay and Batchelor's Walk, with underground connections to the existing terminus, a somewhat impractical scheme for those days at any rate. Yet a third idea was for a Dublin Port & City Railway, in part a revival of earlier schemes of 1864, particularly the abortive Dublin Trunk Connecting Railway, and the Dublin South Suburban Railway, which did not even get parliamentary sanction. However, this new proposal, too, came to nothing.

There was also the Dublin Rathmines Rathgar Roundtown Rathfarnham & Rathcoole Railway (what a mouthful!) which somehow received parliamentary sanction on 29 July 1864. Yet another Act, on 5 July 1865, sanctioned connecting lines in Dublin similar to those which actually materialised. As it was, the DRRRRRR, as it would have been, was stillborn—perhaps just as well.

The Great Southern & Western scheme, on the other hand, which had the backing of the London & North Western, was the only one which was really at all practicable. It became known as the North Wall Extension, and was opened on 2 September 1877. The LNWR had its own independent short length of line to the riverside, with separate passenger, cattle and goods stations, whilst the Great Southern & Western had a branch and goods station. The passenger service was withdrawn about 1922 but North Wall goods station is still in use.

All the railways north of the Liffey were now interconnected, but the Dublin Wicklow & Wexford was still isolated, and perhaps more important, the

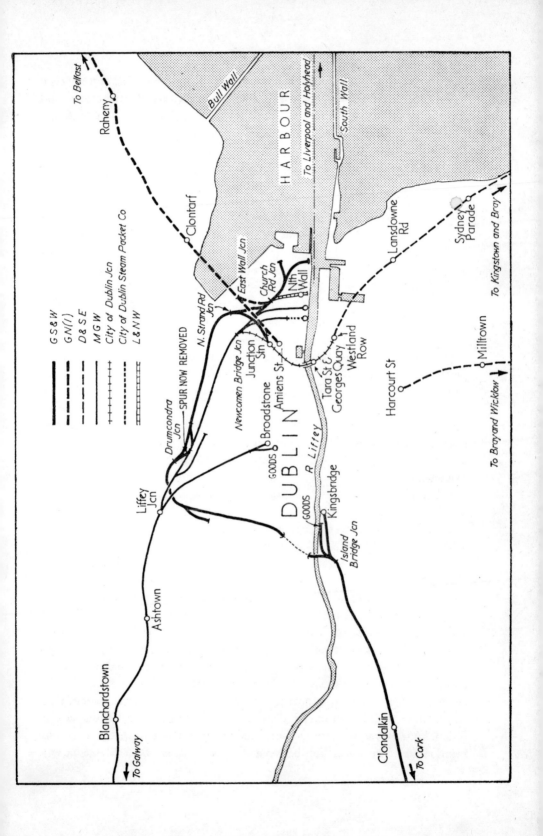

GS&W
GN(I)
D&SE
MGW
City of Dublin Jcn
City of Dublin Steam Packet Co
L&NW

To Belfast
Raheny
Clontarf
Bull Wall
HARBOUR
South Wall
To Liverpool and Holyhead
East Wall Jcn
Church Rd Jcn
N. Strand Rd Jcn
Nth Wall
Landowne Rd
Sydney Parade
To Kingstown and Bray
Newcomen Bridge Jcn
Junction Stn
Amiens St
Westland Row
Tara St & Georges Quay
Harcourt St
Milltown
To Bray and Wicklow
Drumcondra Jcn
SPUR NOW REMOVED
Broadstone
GOODS
DUBLIN
R Liffey
Kingsbridge
Island Bridge Jcn
GOODS
Liffey Jcn
Ashtown
Blanchardstown
To Galway
Clondalkin
To Cork

Great Southern & Western still had no access to Kingstown Harbour, which it badly needed. The obvious route was a connection between Westland Row and Amiens Street, which of course involved bridging the Liffey. An Act of 28 July 1884 eventually authorised construction of the line, known as the City of Dublin Junction Railway, and was sponsored by the DWWR, GNR, GSWR, MGWR and the City of Dublin Steam Packet Co. There were objections by the Port & Docks Board that the bridge would obstruct the view of the Customs House, and it had to be built to the west of this rather than on the seaward side as planned. It had also to be constructed of stone piers instead of iron pillars, to harmonise with the architecture of the Customs House. There is one intermediate station at Tara Street, very handy for the city centre, and much used at busy times. At Amiens Street the new station was alongside the existing Great Northern Railway terminal. The first section of the line was opened in 1891, when Dublin Wicklow & Wexford trains started running through to Amiens Street, and in 1892 the junction with the Midland Great Western Liffey branch was completed at Newcomen Bridge Junction, although not without some trouble arising out of a dispute between the City of Dublin Junction and the Midland Great Western. This was known as the 'Battle of Newcomen Bridge'. The MGWR engineers objected to the fact that the CDJR line, in order to make a junction with their line, had to descend over a sharp curve on a 1 in 51 gradient, which they thought to be dangerous, and they refused to take down their boundary wall. The CDJR however had parliamentary powers to make the connection, and knocked down the wall themselves, whereupon the MGWR promptly rebuilt it. This process was repeated several times, and the matter had to be referred to the Railway Commission, which decided in favour of the CDJR. Thus it was at last possible to run through trains from Kingstown Pier to all parts of the main Irish railway system.

The Great Southern & Western Railway however was still dependent on the Midland Great Western, by having to use the latter's Liffey branch, and wished to have its own line; so the Drumcondra Link Line was built from Drumcondra Junction, off the North Wall Extension from Islandbridge Junction, to Church Road Junction, giving it independent access to North Wall, and was brought into use in April 1901. It was not until December 1906 however that a further short link from North Strand Road Junction to the CDJR at Amiens Street was opened, making the Great Southern & Western Railway entirely independent of the Midland Great Western for access to Amiens Street and Kingstown. A local passenger service was inaugurated between Kingsbridge and Amiens Street, with intermediate stations at Drumcondra, Glasnevin and Cabra, but this was not very successful and was withdrawn in 1910, the stations being closed. The connection between the GSWR and MGWR at Glasnevin was later removed, but after the closure of Broadstone terminus to passengers in 1936, when the MGWR trains were diverted to Westland Row, it was restored, but in the opposite direction, enabling these trains to run over the GSWR loop line and so avoid the awkward 1 in 51 rise at Newcomen Junction, and this is now the normal route for trains between Dublin and the west, Galway, West-port and Sligo.

The South Eastern Railway started as an independent company incorporated in 1845, and was to all intents and purposes an extension of the GSWR Carlow branch. The first 10 miles to Bagenalstown were opened on 24 July 1848, followed by a further 14 miles, striking westwards towards Kilkenny, to Lavis-town on 14 November 1850. From Lavistown it joined the Waterford & Kilkenny Railway, and it used that railway's terminus at Kilkenny, but with its own platform. This arrangement was not satisfactory and there was constant friction, which resulted in the GSWR laying its own single track alongside that of the WKR, though it continued to use the station at Kilkenny for a yearly rental of £1,025. The line, which had been worked by the GSWR from the start, was fully incorporated into that railway on 1 July 1863.

Meanwhile another nominally independent concern, the Bagenalstown & Wexford, had been incorporated in July 1854 to construct a line southwards from Bagenalstown, so as to provide an alternative inland route to Wexford, competitive with the Dublin & Wicklow coast line, which also had Wexford as its ultimate objective, and which it did eventually reach in 1872. The Bagenals-town & Wexford Railway (see Chapter 1) was worked for the most part by the GSWR, and much of it eventually became part of its system. One section of it, between Palace East and Ballywilliam, which at one stage belonged to the DWWR, was transferred back to the GSWR in 1902, to simplify the method of working.

Kilkenny, the capital city of the county, with over 10,000 inhabitants, is the largest centre in a wide area, with its St Canice's Cathedral and the fine Castle of the Butlers, completely restored in the nineteenth century. The Waterford & Kilkenny Railway was authorised on 21 July 1845 to construct a railway between those places, 31 miles apart, together with an additional 6 mile branch to the small township of Kells, but this was never built. The first 11 miles from Kilkenny to Thomastown, which was to have been the junction for Kells, was opened on 11 May 1848, and onwards to a temporary terminus at Jerpoint Hill on 28 May 1850. This station closed on 18 May 1853, when the line was extended farther south for another 16 miles to Dunkitt, just outside Waterford, from which point it had running powers over the Waterford & Limerick Rail-way into what then became a joint terminal station about ¼ mile west of the present one. As at the Kilkenny end the joint operation of a single line proved troublesome, and a second track was laid with the line diverted to a new station at the location of the present Waterford North. The temporary station at Dunkitt was closed in 1855.

The Kilkenny Junction Railway, authorised on 23 July 1860, planned a northward continuation of the WKR to join the GSWR main line at Mountrath. This replaced an earlier scheme of 1846, when the Kilkenny & Great Southern Railway was incorporated to build a direct line between Kilkenny and Bally-brophy, but this too was never carried out. Even the new line only got as far as Abbeyleix, 19 miles, this section being opened on 1 March 1865. Meanwhile a new Act of 6 August 1861 had empowered a diversion to Maryborough in lieu of Mountrath, and this 9½ mile link was duly opened on 1 May 1867. Ballybrophy was again considered by means of a branch from Attanagh, but this again came to nothing.

Another concern, the Central Ireland Railway, was authorised on 23 July 1866 to build a connecting line from Maryborough through to the Midland Great Western at Mullingar. This project was supported by both the Water-ford & Kilkenny and the Kilkenny Junction but it was a long time before any progress was made; even then the line was only built as far as Mountmellick, 7½ miles, opened in 1885, and consequently became a dead-end branch. It diverged a mile out of Maryborough at Conniberry Junction, in such a way that the branch trains had to run round and reverse before proceeding to or from Mountmellick. This branch was closed on 31 December 1962.

Between 1 July 1860 and 1 June 1867 there had been an agreement under which the working of the Waterford & Kilkenny Railway was taken over by the Waterford & Limerick, but on its expiry the WKR resumed its own operation of the line. In the following year, on 13 July 1868, it assumed the title of Water-ford & Central Ireland Railway, and took over control of the Kilkenny Junc-tion and the Central Ireland, although these retained their nominal independence. The last named was duly absorbed by the Waterford & Central Ireland on 12 July 1877, but the Kilkenny Junction was not finally amalgamated until 1 May 1896.

The Waterford & Central Ireland was in turn taken over by the GSWR on 1 September 1900. Between Kilkenny and Waterford it still performs an im-portant function in being part of the direct route between Dublin and Water-ford, via Kildare and Carlow, leaving the main line at Cherryville Junction, the original portion of the Great Southern & Western, and thence via Bagenalstown (now known as Muine Bheag) into Kilkenny over what was originally the South Eastern Railway. Here trains have to reverse before proceeding to Thomastown and Waterford. There are normally three or four trains each way daily, two of them with buffet cars, and two on Sundays. At Carlow there is now a large sugar beet factory, which was built in 1926, and there are extensive CIE sidings.

The old Bagenalstown & Wexford Railway was purchased by the GSWR in 1876, the Ballywilliam to Macmine portion being at the same time repurchased by the DWWR. The section from Palace East to Ballywilliam was closed on 31 March 1963. Kilkenny has become a terminal station, the line northwards to Maryborough (now Portlaoise) having been closed since 1962.

Four miles north of Kilkenny there was a 9¾ mile branch to Castlecomer, a small but important little town in Leinster, and the centre of one of the most important of the few coalfields in Ireland. Very unusually, this field contained high-quality anthracite. Although authorised in 1911, construction was not started until World War I, then it was undertaken by the government under the Defence of the Realm Act, as were Wolfhill and Arigna. It was opened for coal traffic on 15 September 1919, and was the last substantial standard gauge branch to be built in Ireland. It is severely graded, with short lengths of 1 in 41, the steepest on any standard gauge line in the country. The line was worked by the GSWR, and was put in charge of the Board of Works in 1921 when government control of the railways ended. On 1 January 1929 it was vested in the GSR. A passenger service was started in July 1921 between Kilkenny and Castlecomer but it was never extended over the last 2¼ miles to the colliery at Deerpark. An intermediate station at Corbetstown was also provided. The passenger service comprised only two trains daily, and was withdrawn on 1 January 1931, although there were occasional specials afterwards. Coal traffic continued until the end of 1962, when all of these lines, including the Mount-mellick branch, which had lost its passenger service on 27 January 1947, were abandoned.

Another branch was built by the government to serve this coalfield and was opened on 24 September 1918, a consequence of the severe coal shortage which resulted from the limitation of imports from England. It left the Carlow branch at Athy and proceeded westwards to Wolfhill, not far from the Deerpark Colliery terminus of the Castlecomer branch, although the two lines were not connected. Its length, including the branches in the colliery area, was 9½ miles. Rails were in exceedingly short supply at the time, and were obtained by the simple expedient of singling the line between Cherryville Junction and Athy. The Wolfhill line, which never had a passenger service, was also taken over by the GSR on 1 January 1929, and the colliery end of it closed, but 4½ miles as far as Ballylinan continued in use for sugar beet traffic until 23 March 1963; since then only a very short section out of Athy over a viaduct has remained to serve an asbestos factory.

At the beginning of 1900 there were four railways serving Waterford. The

Waterford & Central Ireland, which, as the Waterford & Kilkenny, had been the first to reach the city in May 1853; the Waterford Limerick & Western; the Great Southern & Western; and the small isolated Waterford & Tramore. The Great Southern & Western, which had only recently acquired the previously independent Waterford Dungarvan & Lismore, absorbed the Waterford & Central Ireland on 1 July 1900 and the Waterford Limerick & Western in the following year, thus becoming the largest railway in Ireland, and reducing the number of companies serving Waterford to three, which remained the situation until the 1925 grouping.

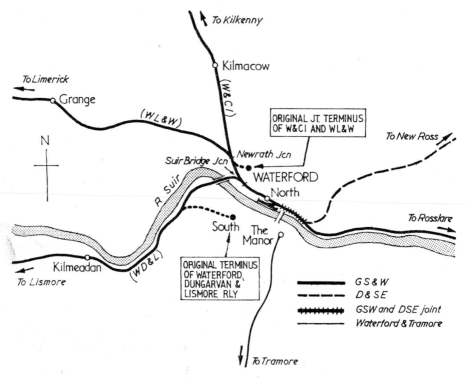

The first terminal in Waterford was shared by the Waterford Limerick & Western and the Waterford & Central Ireland, being opened on 11 September 1854. This joint station, which was about ¼ mile west of the present one, remained in use until September 1864, when the line was extended to a site opposite the north end of the old 832ft long wooden toll bridge dating from 1793. This was freed from toll in 1908 and replaced by the present structure in 1912. The new station has been twice rebuilt, in 1906 and again very recently. It consisted of a long single through platform, 1,210ft in length, the second longest in Ireland, together with four bays (and at one time two others on the

Page 69 (above) Timoleague & Courtmacsherry Light Railway. Train from Ballinas-carthy Junction to Courtmacsherry at Timoleague on 19 July 1939. *Argadeen*, one of the railway's two locomotives, was a 2–6–0T, a wheel arrangement which was rare in Ireland, and of which there were only two examples in the rest of the British Isles; (*centre*) Cork City Railway. Train on the street connection between the main GSWR line at Glanmire Road, and the CBSCR at Albert Quay. Until the construction of this link in 1912 the railways of south-west Cork had no physical connection with the rest of Ireland. The engine is GSWR 0–6–0T no 201, built 1887, the view being taken in 1961; (*bottom*) until World War II, and indeed afterwards in some of the remoter towns of the west, the station 'taxi' was likely to be a jaunting car. This view was taken outside Waterford main station in September 1929

Page 70 Like many railways in Great Britain, several Irish lines experimented with steam railmotors comprising combined engine and coach, during the earlier years of this century, for branch lines and areas of light traffic. The GSWR had built such units as early as 1857, and an 0–6–4T engine and saloon dating from 1880, depicted below, was to be seen up to World War II at Inchicore conveying senior office staff between the works and Kingsbridge station. This view was taken in 1932, when the engine was, uniquely at the time on the GSR, painted green. The Dublin Wicklow & Wexford railmotor, illustrated above, was one of two built in 1906. The coach bodies were later removed and the engines used independently as shunters. Other railways which tried railmotors were the Great Southern & Western, Great Northern, Northern Counties and Belfast & County Down

eastern side). An outstanding feature is a large signal cabin, Waterford Central, which straddles the running lines at the west end of the station. Formerly known as Waterford North to distinguish it from Waterford South and Manor (the Waterford & Tramore station) it is now known as Plunkett, although the distinction is hardly necessary as it is now the only one in the city.

Direct communication between Cork and Waterford was first mooted in 1845 by the incorporation of an Act authorising the construction of a 75 mile railway through Youghal and Dungarvan, but it was reconstituted in 1854 as the Cork & Youghal Railway, which was as far as it got. The next step was the incorporation on 5 July 1865 of two Acts, the Waterford Fermoy & Lismore Railway, and the Clonmel Lismore & Dungarvan Railway. The former was to construct two separated lengths of railway from Waterford to Dungarvan, $28\frac{1}{2}$ miles, and from Lismore to Fermoy, $15\frac{1}{4}$ miles. The intervening $14\frac{1}{2}$ miles between Lismore and Dungarvan was the concern of the other company, a somewhat odd arrangement, although there was a provision that the Waterford company had power to complete this if the Clonmel had not done so by 1868. In the event, neither of the companies carried out any construction, and the Clonmel and Dungarvan link was never built at all.

In their place the Waterford Dungarvan & Lismore Railway was incorporated in 1872 to build the 43 miles of railway between Lismore and Waterford, and this was opened throughout on 12 August 1878. Dungarvan is an important town of 5,000 inhabitants with a fine harbour and castle. Lismore is a charming little town on the south bank of the River Blackwater, with an ancient cathedral. The line was fairly severely graded between Waterford and Dungarvan, with considerable banks of 1 in 66 or so and two summits, as well as one of Ireland's few tunnels, together with a viaduct at Durrow. Between Dungarvan and Fermoy it ran to the south of the Knockmealdown Mountains. The terminus at Waterford was on the south side of the River Suir, known as Waterford South, and for many years there was no connection with the other railways on the north side.

Meanwhile, at the other end, the Great Southern & Western had built a branch from its main line at Mallow to Fermoy, $16\frac{3}{4}$ miles, incorporated on 27 July 1854 and opened on 17 May 1860. This was followed by the independent Fermoy & Lismore Railway, authorised in 1869 to construct a $15\frac{1}{4}$ mile line connecting the two towns, this being opened on 1 October 1872. It was at first worked by the GSWR but was transferred to the Waterford Dungarvan & Lismore on 1 March 1893.

The completion of the WDLR in 1878 made the idea of a through route between Waterford and Cork at last a reality, and was to lead eventually to direct com-

E

munication between Cork and England via Fishguard and Rosslare, with a reduction in the time spent at sea.

On 21 March 1921 the Mitchelstown & Fermoy Railway was opened, a 12 mile branch from Fermoy, on what was by then the through main line between Mallow and Waterford, to Mitchelstown, an important little agricultural centre in County Cork, now with about 2,700 inhabitants in an elevated valley at the southern base of the Galtee Mountains. The line was acquired by the Great Southern & Western in 1900. Once enjoying a service of five trains each way (one on Sundays), making connections at Fermoy, its passenger service was discontinued on 27 January 1947 and the line closed altogether in 1953.

Specimen tickets of the GSWR

The Fishguard and Rosslare Railway and Harbour Act of 12 August 1898 authorised the construction of the new line from Waterford over the River Barrow, which involved the longest bridge in Ireland, 2,131ft, at Campile, to Rosslare, opened August 1906, and the acquisition of the Waterford Dungarvan & Lismore, and the Fermoy & Lismore Railways. The Fishguard Act of 1903 authorised the bridging of the WDLR over the River Suir to connect the railways on both sides of the river, and this was opened in September 1906. The old station at Waterford South was closed on 31 January 1908.

In 1967 it was decided to close the direct route between Waterford and Limerick and reroute the through trains via Limerick Junction; all the intermediate stations were closed on 25 March 1967, most of the track being subsequently lifted. Since then, however, a stretch of 26 miles from Waterford to Ballinrode, between Dungarvan and Durrow, has been restored, and a 1½ mile branch built to a manganese factory at Ballinacourty, which requires large supplies of dolomite ironstone, conveyed on the modern block train principle. This came into operation on 3 April 1970.

Closure of the line between Waterford and Mallow smacked of Beechingisation. Moreover, it bore a strong resemblance to the abandonment, two years earlier, of the direct route between Dumfries and Stranraer, involving a long detour. Curiously, both of these closures resulted in the diversion of boat trains between England and Ireland. To the credit of CIE however, it did not emulate the effrontery of BR in charging an increased fare on the grounds of the additional mileage involved!

LOCOMOTIVES AND ROLLING STOCK

In its independent days the Cork & Youghal had its own engines, seven 2–4–0STs, built by Neilson in 1859–62, and three 2–2–2STs in 1861. There were also two other engines about which details are uncertain.

The first three engines of the Waterford & Central Ireland Railway were somewhat extraordinary 4–2–2Ts built by Tayleur of Newton-le-Willows in 1846 for the original Waterford & Kilkenny Railway (a line drawing appears on page 83 of Ahron's *British Steam Locomotives*). They can make claim to being the first British side tank engines, as distinct from the usual well tanks of those early days. They seem to have been rather poor things, and had disappeared by 1863.

Subsequent engines were of the 2–2–2, 2–4–0 and 0–4–2 wheel arrangement, mostly tender, but one or two tanks. One of them, no 4, built in 1897 by the Vulcan Foundry, was the last 0–4–2 tender engine to be built in the British Isles. It became Great Southern & Western no 252 and lasted until 1909, the last Waterford & Central Ireland locomotive then remaining.

Of the ten engines taken over by the GSWR in 1900, allotted nos 250–9, only two 0–4–2s, nos 10 and 11, dating back to 1872, survived actually to become nos 257 and 258, and these were scrapped in 1906 and 1907. The locomotive livery of the WCIR was dark green with light green lining, black boiler bands and brown frames. The passenger stock at the time of the takeover consisted entirely of four-wheelers of particularly uncomfortable design even for that period, having narrow wooden seats with straight backs not only in the third but also in the second class, and a journey over the 60 miles between Maryborough and Waterford, occupying some three hours, could not have been one of the most pleasant experiences.

At the time of amalgamation the Waterford Dungarvan & Lismore had seven engines, all 0–4–2s except one, which was a 2–4–0ST, originally built for the Cork & Youghal. The six 0–4–2s, nos 1–6, which had come from Sharp Stewart between 1878 and 1892, became GSWR nos 244–9. No 246 was rebuilt as a 0–4–2ST and all were scrapped between 1905 and 1913.

On the GSWR itself the earliest engines were all built by Bury Curtis & Kennedy, and were of their distinctive bar framed design, with haystack fireboxes. Four were ordered in 1844, two for passenger and two for goods, respectively 2–2–2s and 0–4–2s. By the following year, 1845, thirty engines were on order. The passenger engines were numbered 21–40 and the goods 41–50 (later renumbered 100-9). All were taken out of service between 1869 and 1879, but most remarkably no 36 was not broken up, being set aside for preservation, a very rare event for those days. This was indeed fortunate, as it is now the only survivor anywhere of this very early and distinctive design. Its fate was very much in the balance during the period between the wars, when it was turned out to grass in Inchicore yard and began slowly to disintegrate under the ravages of the weather. By 1948 it was in a very poor state, but it was eventually taken in and completely restored. It now stands on a plinth at Cork station. Successors to the Burys were a batch of standard Sharp singles, nos 1–20.

In 1864 Alexander McDonnell assumed the post of chief locomotive superintendent, which he held until 1883. He had previously at the age of 28 held a similar post on the Newport Abergavenny & Hereford Railway, later the West Midland. McDonnell introduced several very efficient designs, at the time much needed, but will be best remembered for his 101 class 0–6–0s, the first of which came out in 1866. These were to be built in considerable numbers over a period of thirty-seven years, being perpetuated with minor modifications by his three successors, J. A. F. Aspinall, H. A. Ivatt and R. Coey. By 1903, when the last one appeared, 111 engines had been built, by far the largest class on any Irish railway, and the only one which can be regarded as standardised. They were true 'maids of all work'; they could, and did, do almost anything from express passenger work to the humblest shunting duties, and could go anywhere on the system except for a few of the lightest branches. They were perhaps most at home on intermediate passenger work on the longer cross-country routes and branches, on which they were inevitably found during the whole of their existence. Naturally they all acquired vacuum brakes, these being fitted to all new engines from 1885 onwards. Most of them were in later years rebuilt with Belpaire fireboxes, together with superheaters and extended smokeboxes, the first of such conversions being in 1930. In appearance they were, before rebuilding, very much like Webb's DX class on the London & North Western, even down to the Crewe style of numberplates, which could often be seen well into Great Southern days. They were among the last engines to be displaced by dieselisation in the 1960s, and two of them have been preserved in working order, no 184, unrebuilt, by CIE, and no 186, rebuilt, by the Railway Preservation Society of Ireland, which frequently uses it on railtours both in Northern Ireland and the Republic.

Among McDonnell's other designs were a set of twelve light 4–4–0s with 5ft 8in wheels for cross-country and branch work, and some interesting 0–4–4 well tanks, the first two of which appeared in 1869 and 1870. These were designed on the single Fairlie system, with a steam bogie in front and an ordinary carrying bogie at the rear. Several similar engines followed, but with coupled wheels carried on the main frames. Mr McDonnell also built the first 0–6–4Ts in the British Isles, the first two coming out in 1876.

A few miscellaneous engines appeared during this period, including two very interesting diminutive 0–4–2Ts, which had 5ft 0in wheels and 9in by 15in cylinders, and which used to haul small four-wheeled saloons known as pay carriages, for distributing the wages in outlying districts. They were based on Limerick Junction, a natural focal point. *Sprite* had been built in 1873, and was originally an 0–4–4T, combined in one frame with a saloon. *Fairy* followed in 1894. They had names only, a distinction allowed only to a few departmental engines. Both ceased these duties in 1927, but in 1929 *Sprite* was still to be found at Inchicore shed supplying hot water for washing out other engines. Then there was *Jumbo*, originally 0–6–4T no 202 of 1876; rebuilt in 1895 as an 0–6–0T, it obtained its name and lost its number, and spent the rest of its working life, until 1957, shunting at Waterford.

In 1883 McDonnell left Inchicore and went to the North Eastern Railway, being succeeded by J. A. F. Aspinall (later to be Sir John Aspinall). His most important contribution to the locomotive stock consisted of two series of 6ft 7in 4–4–0 express engines, the basic design of which must be credited to McDonnell. They worked chiefly on the mail trains and other expresses between Dublin and Cork, which had up to that time been worked by McDonnell 2–4–0s, built between 1869 and 1875. Aspinall's reign at Inchicore was short. By all accounts a difficult man to get on with, he departed in 1886 for the Lancashire & Yorkshire Railway. He was succeeded by H. A. Ivatt, who was in charge until 1896, when he moved to the English Great Northern Railway, his place being taken by R. Coey. So far as tender engines were concerned, Ivatt was content to build more of Aspinall's 4–4–0s, and to turn out another twelve of McDonnell's 101 class. However, he produced a new design of 2–4–2T for branch-line work, which was used amongst other things on the long line to Valentia Harbour. He also carried out some experiments in compounding with Aspinall 4–4–0 no 93 and McDonnell 0–6–0 no 165. These were converted to the two-cylinder Worsdell von Borries system, introduced by T. W. Worsdell on the North Eastern Railway, and adopted extensively by B. Malcolm on the Belfast & Northern Counties Railway. The two Great Southern & Western engines ran as compounds for a few years, but no significant improvement or economies resulted, and they were reconverted to their original form by R. Coey, who was at Inchicore from 1896 to 1911.

During this period Coey built several new classes of express 4–4–0s, and he named the first four of them, nos 301–4, built at Inchicore in 1900. This was an innovation on the GSWR, which, since the early days of the Burys, had only named a few departmental engines. Coey was apparently overruled, as it was not long before *Victoria*, *Lord Roberts*, *St Patrick* and *Princess Ena* lost their appellations and only one more main-line engine was destined to receive a name during the history of the GSWR. Nos 301–4 and Coey's subsequent 4–4–0s, nos 305–14 and 321–40, underwent sundry forms of rebuilding later in their careers, with the result that by the 1930s it was difficult to find two of them exactly alike. All had 6ft 7½in driving wheels except nos 333–40, which had 5ft 8½in. Some were fitted with coned boilers, the first in Ireland, and only used subsequently on the Woolwich 2–6–0s, but these were replaced in later years by parallel boilers with Belpaire fireboxes and superheaters. For goods work Coey introduced new classes of 0–6–0, after construction of the 101 class ceased in 1903, and for express freight duties some inside-cylinder 2–6–0s and 4–6–0s with 5ft 1½in driving wheels. Tank engines constructed during this period consisted mostly of a few 4–4–2Ts, 0–6–2Ts and 0–6–0Ts.

The livery changed early in Coey's regime from olive green, lined out in black and cream with red-brown frames, to black, lined red and white. This was replaced in 1918 by unlined grey.

In 1911 R. E. L. Maunsell succeeded Coey as locomotive superintendent but it stayed for only two years before moving to the South Eastern & Chatham Railway. During his short stay he built a large 4–4–0 for the Cork to Dublin main line, which came out from Inchicore in 1913 as no 341 *Sir William Goulding*. Unfortunately it does not seem to have been such an unqualified success as were his later English engines. One interesting innovation was the use of inside Walschaert's valve gear. In outward appearance it bore a distinct resemblance to his later D1 and E1 rebuilds on the SECR but it was a much heavier engine, 59 tons 7cwt in working order (without tender), and this is believed to be one of the reasons why it was never multiplied. It had a very short life by Irish standards, and in 1929 was on stationary boiler duties at Inchicore works. However, Maunsell's designs were still to play a considerable part in Great Southern locomotive history. The next locomotive superintendent was E. A. Watson, whose principal effort was a large 4–8–0T banking engine no 900, which appeared from Inchicore in 1915. Another one, 901, came out in 1924 after J. R. Bazin had succeeded Watson in 1922. He was the last locomotive superintendent on the GSWR but continued to act in that capacity for the first few years after the formation of the Great Southern Railways in 1925.

It is curious that this second 4–8–0T was built nine years after the first, as by that time the fact that the design was unsatisfactory, as seems to have been the case, must have become apparent. Both engines were scrapped, respectively in 1928 and 1931, again with very short lives for Ireland.

Watson's main achievement however was the introduction of the express 4-6-0, never used on any Irish railway but the Great Southern. It had four cylinders and 6ft 7in driving wheels, and was numbered 400. It came out in 1916, and was followed by nine others, nos 401-9, in 1921, some from Inchicore and others by Armstrong Whitworth. As four-cylinder engines, they were not an unqualified success, and most of them were later rebuilt with two cylinders, some with Caprotti valve gear, and these lasted until the 1950s and 1960s. Nos 400/4/8 however were never rebuilt and were scrapped in 1929 and 1930.

Another two-cylinder 4-6-0, no 500, appeared in 1924 to the design of Mr Bazin and was followed by nos 501-2 in 1926. These had 5ft 8½in driving wheels, and the last two belong strictly to the Great Southern period.

As on other Irish railways, GSWR engines were for the most part very long lived; the great majority even of the earlier McDonnell and Aspinall engines were still active at the formation of the Great Southern in 1925, some of them already forty or more years old, and many survived much longer, well after World War II, to the end of steam in the 1960s. Classified tables of Great Southern engines are given at the end of Chapter 14.

CHAPTER 4

WATERFORD LIMERICK & WESTERN RAILWAY

A long straggling main line from Waterford in the south to Sligo in the north-west, with secondary lines and branches. Incorporated as WATERFORD & LIMERICK RAILWAY *1845. Opened 1848–54. Extended in subsequent years to Tralee, Claremorris and Sligo.*

Became: WATERFORD LIMERICK & WESTERN RAILWAY *in 1896.*

Amalgamated with GREAT SOUTHERN & WESTERN 1901.

Route mileage in 1901: 342 *miles.*

Principal places served:
   Waterford, Clonmel, Limerick, Tralee, Ennis, Athenry, Tuam, Claremorris, Sligo.

The Waterford Limerick & Western had a total route mileage of 342½, only 32 of which was double line, and was exceeded only by the Great Southern & Western itself, with 606 miles in 1900, the Midland Great Western, 538 miles, and the Great Northern, 617 miles. It resulted from the acquisition of a number of other lines which were originally independently promoted. The parent body, the Waterford & Limerick Railway, 77¼ miles long, the first part of which, between Limerick and Tipperary, was opened on 9 May 1848, was completed throughout in 1854, the later section by means of a government loan of £120,000. There had been a much earlier proposal for a rail link between Waterford and Limerick, in 1826, only a year after the successful opening of the Stockton & Darlington, but although parliamentary powers were obtained the scheme was not proceeded with.

   Limerick, which was a terminal station, then became something of a railway centre, from which lines began to radiate, worked by the WLR and later to be absorbed by it. Westwards was the 70½ mile line to Tralee, known as the 'North Kerry' line. It came into being by the formation of three originally independent companies, the Limerick & Foynes, incorporated on 4 August 1853 and opened in 1856; the Rathkeale & Newcastle Junction, incorporated on 22 July 1861 and opened in 1867, which left the Limerick & Foynes at Ballingrane Junction (Foynes then becoming a branch); and the Limerick & North Kerry, incorporated on 5 July 1865 and opened in December 1880. All of them were worked by the Waterford & Limerick. Passenger services were withdrawn between Limerick and Tralee and over the Foynes branch on 1 January 1963.

Railway letter stamps of the WLR and WLWR

Newcastle was another terminal station, where through trains had to reverse, and at Tralee an end-on connection was made with the GSWR line from Killarney, but with independent stations until the WLWR was absorbed by the GSWR in 1907. Out of Tralee a branch to Fenit, 8 miles in length, was opened in 1887, and near to Limerick a new branch to a factory at Castlemungret was opened as recently as October 1957.

This completed the south-western leg of the WLWR. Out of Limerick there was another branch which started as the Limerick, Castle Connell (later spelt as one word) & Killaloe Railway, opened to Castle Connell on 28 August 1858, and to Killaloe on 12 April 1862, with a pier extension in August 1863. This branch lost its passenger service in 1931; it was not used at all after 1944 and closed officially in 1952. Castleconnel station was closed in 1963.

Another branch left the original WLR line from Clonmel to Thurles, where it joined the GSWR main line from Dublin to Cork. This line, 28 miles long, was known by the grandiose title of Southern of Ireland Railway. It was incorporated in 1865 and opened throughout in July 1880.

The first section of what was to become the long straggling line northwards from Limerick to Sligo, 145¾ miles, was the Limerick & Ennis, 24¾ miles, incorporated on 4 August 1853 and opened in 1859. It was worked by the WLR with which it was amalgamated in 1874. Next came the Athenry & Ennis Junction, another 36 miles, incorporated on 20 August 1860 and opened on 15 September 1869, and the Athenry & Tuam Railway, incorporated 23 July 1858 and opened on 27 September 1860. This line was at first leased for a period of ten years to the MGWR, whose main line to Galway made contact with both of the smaller concerns. The AER was leased to the WLR on 1 November 1872, and both lines were taken over by it from 27 July 1893.

From Tuam onwards the line was extended to Claremorris on 30 April 1894 by the Athenry & Tuam Extension Railway (which actually retained its nominal independence until the 1925 grouping) but was naturally worked by the WLR. Here contact was made with the Midland's secondary main line to Westport. From Claremorris the final section to link up with the MGWR's Sligo line at Collooney was opened on 1 October 1895, from which point running powers were obtained over MGWR metals for the last 6 miles into Sligo.

By this time the original title of Waterford & Limerick Railway seemed no longer wholly appropriate in view of its long northwards extensions, and from 1 January 1896 it became known as the Waterford Limerick & Western.

This last section of line was almost unique in Ireland in that it was used by three different railways, the MGWR as owners, the WLWR, which became after 1901 the Great Southern & Western, and also the Sligo Leitrim & Northern Counties. To gain direct access to the latter the WLWR put in a loop at Collooney, which though little more than a village of about 600 inhabitants, was an important centre for livestock traffic. It was remarkable in possessing three separate stations, owned by each of the three railways, and there was no way in which they could be embodied into one, as all were situated before the junctions at which the WLWR and SLNCR separately converged on to the MGWR. But how such an uneconomic arrangement would have horrified Dr Beeching!

The long trek from Claremorris to Sligo came in later years to be nicknamed after the notorious railway constructed by the Japanese, the 'Burma Road'. The leisurely progress of the trains was undoubtedly extremely tedious to the ordinary traveller, as distinct from the railway enthusiast. Nowadays the journey has, even worse, to be made by bus, the passenger service having been discontinued on 15 June 1963. In 1910 the two daily trains each way, stopping at all stations, took the almost incredible time of about 6½ hours for the through 145¾ mile journey. But perhaps it was not quite so difficult to understand in view of the leisurely way of life in the west of Ireland and the fact that station time allowances had to be sufficiently elastic to allow for dealing with general merchandise, not to mention the likelihood of having to attach or detach a van or two, or a cattle wagon or horsebox. By 1955 there was only one daily train throughout, in each direction, and the time had been reduced to 6 hours in the down direction (from Sligo) and 5½ hours in the up.

Nevertheless it was a journey to think about carefully beforehand, particularly as there were no refreshment facilities except for the possibility of popping into the buffet at Claremorris whilst the train was waiting for its connections.

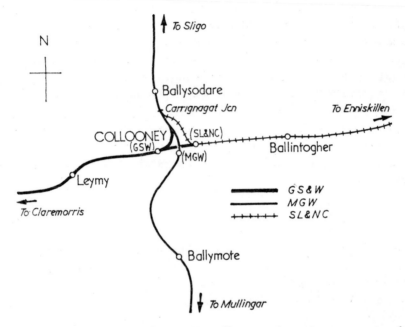

When I did it in 1938, behind a McDonnell 4–4–0, the train was composed of non-corridor six-wheelers, with a lavatory compartment in the first-class accommodation but not in the third. Ticket inspection was very rigorous on the Great Southern (probably it had to be to stop fare evasion and prevent third-class ticket holders from invading the first) and was successfully and sensibly achieved by having the guard also act as travelling ticket inspector. He would make several checks en route and even if tickets had already been seen, make a fresh clip each time, so that at the end of the journey only about half of the ticket might be left.

Essentially a cross-country route, the 145¾ miles between Limerick and Sligo represented about the longest journey of this nature which one could make without change of train. Main line expresses had longer runs of course, such as the 165½ miles of the GSWR between Dublin and Cork, and through trains to

Killarney and Tralee, 206¾ miles. Until 1934, when passenger services ceased, there was a through coach from Achill to Dublin, 187 miles, attached to the main Galway train at Athlone. Again, between 1950 and 1953 the GNR Enterprise express between Belfast and Dublin ran through to Cork over the CIE, a total of 278 miles, and there were through services between Dublin and Londonderry by two different routes of 175¾ and 162¾ miles. There were also holiday expresses between Dublin and Bundoran, 159¾ miles, and Dublin and Portrush, 178¾ miles.

The through length of the main line of the WLWR totalled 222½ miles, and in 1910, for instance, one could leave Sligo at 8.45 am, and with a 20 minute break at Limerick and a halt of anything up to half an hour at Limerick Junction, whilst the two main line connections arrived and departed, reach Waterford at 7.40 pm—an enterprise not to be undertaken without due forethought and preparation. By 1955 it was no longer possible to make this journey in the day, as there was no through connection southwards from Limerick, although it could still be done in the other direction. Surely however this must have been the only instance in British railway history when it was not possible to traverse the whole length of the main line of what had once been one company in a day.

LOCOMOTIVES AND ROLLING STOCK

The head offices were at Waterford and the locomotive and carriage workshops were conveniently situated at Limerick. These workshops were maintained after absorption into the GSWR in 1901, and indeed remained as a supplementary complement to Inchicore right through to CIE days and the end of steam.

For working the whole of the 342½ mile system there were, at amalgamation with the GSWR, only 58 locomotives, of which about half would be found on the original section between Waterford and Limerick, and the rest thinly scattered on the branches and on the long route to Sligo. This was not exactly a lavish provision of motive power, but the service over much of the system comprised only three or four trains a day, sometimes only one. The only comparable railway in the rest of the British Isles was the Highland, which required 150 locomotives to operate its total mileage of about 500, but with the difficulty of making provision for high variations of traffic between the busy summer season and the winter.

In the early 1880s there were still three old Bury 2–2–2s in service together with another engine of the Jenny Lind type. Main line goods traffic was mainly in the hands of 0–4–2s and the passenger services were worked by 2–4–0s, ten

No. 718 Waterford and Limerick Railway.

(LOCOMOTIVE DEPARTMENT.)

Second Class.   Free Ticket.   Not Transferable.

(AVAILABLE FOR ONE JOURNEY ONLY.)

Pass ....

From .... to ....

on the .... 189......

.... Loco. Superintendent.

N.B.—For Conditions upon which this **Pass** is granted see back hereof.

If not used within the time for which it is available, or not collected by the Company's Servants, this Ticket is to be returned.

(714)—Harvey & Co., Printers, Waterford.

Free pass, paper ticket, Waterford & Limerick Railway

of an express type with 5ft 6in wheels and half a dozen older ones with 5ft wheels, which were really mixed traffic engines. Some of these were later reconstructed as tank engines and others as 0–6–0 tender engines, and lasted well into GSWR days, but most of the others had gone by 1901.

In 1888 the then locomotive superintendent, H. Appleby, was succeeded by J. G. Robinson, later of Great Central fame, who proceeded to turn out a number of more modern engines, until the line was taken over by the Great Southern & Western in 1901. For express work there were eight 2–4–0s built by Dübs between 1889 and 1893:

10	Sir James	43	Knockma
20	Galtee More	44	Nephin
22	Era	47	Carrick Castle
23	Slieve-Na-Mon	48	Granston

They were handsome engines with a distinctly Great Western appearance, complete with brass domes, though their smart red livery, very similar to the crimson lake of the Midland could hardly have been less like the GWR. On being taken over by the GSWR they lost their names and became nos 263, 273, 275, 276 and 290–3. Four were scrapped in 1909–10 but the others lasted into CIE days. No 291 was still at work in Limerick in 1959.

Three rather similar 4–4–0s were built by Kitson in 1896–7, no 53 *Jubilee*, 54 *Killemnee* and 55 *Bernard*, which became GSWR 296–8, also losing their names. No 297 was scrapped in 1928 but the other two lasted until 1949.

Tank engines consisted of two 2–4–2Ts, 13 *Derry Castle* and 14 *Lough Derg*, built by the Vulcan Foundry in 1891 for the Limerick to Tralee line, later becoming GSWR 266 and 267. The first of these was sold to the Cork & Macroom Direct Railway in 1914, to appear in the Great Southern list at the 1925 amalgamation as no 491; it was withdrawn in 1935. No 267 had gone in 1931. A couple of 0–4–4Ts for the Tuam service came from Kitson in 1895, no 51 *Castle Hacket* and 52 *Brian Boru*. As GSWR 294, the first disappeared in 1910, but the second, no 295, finished its days in 1954 on the Ballybrophy to Birr branch.

For the opening of the line to Sligo, Robinson built four 4–4–2Ts, nos 16 *Rocklands*, 17 *Faugh a Ballagh*, 18 *Geraldine* and 21 *Castle Blarney*, turned out by Kitson in 1896–7. These became GSWR 269, 270, 271 and 274. The last three were withdrawn in 1949, but no 269 lasted until 1957.

Of the 0–6–0s for main-line goods work, four were built by Dübs in 1895–7:

45	Colleen Bawn	49	Dreadnought
46	Erin Go Bragh	50	Hercules

and four by Kitson in 1897–9:

56	*Thunderer*	58	*Goliath*
57	*Cyclops*	2	*Shannon*

Two more which were under construction by Kitson in 1901, when the GSWR took over, were to have been 4 *Shamrock* and 11 *Samson*; they were purchased by the MGWR, on which they became 141 *Limerick* and 142 *Athenry*, and came into the GSR fold in 1925 as 233 and 234. The eight WLWR engines were renumbered 233–9 and 222 respectively and were scrapped between 1911 and 1951.

The original livery of the Waterford Limerick & Western engines was green. This was changed to red-brown, lined out in blue, and in its later years, before absorption by the Great Southern & Western, to crimson lake, very similar to the Midland Railway of England, lined out with yellow bands. The engines also had copper-capped chimneys, a fair amount of brasswork, such as the beading around the splashers and, in the case of the 2–4–0s and some of the tank engines, brass dome casings as well, although this did not apply to the 4–4–0s.

The carriages, mostly six-wheelers, though some bogie coaches appeared during the last years for the Waterford boat trains, were painted crimson lake lined out in gold.

CHAPTER 5

WATERFORD & TRAMORE
RAILWAY

A small isolated line serving the two places comprising its title without intermediate stations. Incorporated 1851. Opened 1853. Became part of GREAT SOUTHERN RAILWAYS *1925.*

Route mileage: 7¼ miles.
No physical connection with any other railway.

Principal places served:
   Waterford, Tramore.

Closed 1960.

This was a 5ft 3in gauge railway running between the city of Waterford and the popular watering place of Tramore, 7 miles away on the southern shores of County Waterford, with a population of about 3,000.

The earliest attempt to provide Tramore with a railway was an ambitious scheme authorised in 1846 to construct a 78 mile line from Cork to Waterford along the south coast through Youghal and Dungarvan. Tramore would have been reached by a branch, and another was planned to Fermoy. The authorised capital was £1 million, but the venture failed.

The alternative of a short railway directly connecting Waterford with Tramore received very much better support, and the required capital of £77,350 was soon raised. It was authorised on 24 July 1851, and was officially opened on 5 September 1853. It was unusual in that it never had any physical connection with the several other lines which later reached Waterford. Except for the Waterford Dungarvan & Lismore, all these were on the north side of the River Suir.

Another unusual feature was that it consisted of a single main line, 7¼ miles long, with no intermediate stations and no branches. Two such deviations, to

Page 87 (above) An engine which successively acquired four different ownerships. Built in 1891 for the Waterford & Limerick Railway as no 13 *Derry Castle*, it became GSWR 266 on amalgamation in 1901, was sold in 1914 to the Cork & Macroom, becoming no 6, and was reabsorbed into the Great Southern at the 1925 grouping as no 491. It was scrapped in 1935; (below) MGWR 0–6–0 no 82 *Clonbrock*, built at Broadstone in 1892. It later became GSR 583 and was scrapped in 1963. Note the distinctive type of flared cab. With it is 2–2–2ST no 29 *Fairy*, built 1852 and scrapped 1906. In early days this type worked the night mail trains to Galway. The photograph was taken about 1899

Page 88 (above) One of the handsome Cork Bandon & South Coast 4–6–oTs, no 464, on a railtour, 17 March 1961, organised by the Irish Railway Record Society, crossing Innishannon viaduct. This railway is now closed; (below) the famous Limerick Junction in 1932. The 4–4–0 no 312 on an up train for Dublin, and 4–6–0 no 405 in the distance on the down main platform with a train for Cork. The complicated lay-out is best understood by reference to the diagram on page 46

Dunmore and to Passage, were planned but never built, although the last named got as far as an Act of Parliament, dated 7 August 1862, the Waterford & Passage Railway.

The line was single throughout, with easy gradients, nothing steeper than 1 in 134, and had no engineering features of any consequence. The journey time was about sixteen minutes. As the one engine in steam principle was used, no signalling was necessary except for one signal controlling a level crossing at Waterford, and another covering the approach to Tramore station. In steam days the engines were invariably turned at the end of each journey, always working chimney first. Small turntables were used, beyond the ends of the platforms, and they also served as switches for the running-round loops. Both terminals were substantial stations, each with a single platform and overall roof, and the quite ornate exteriors were so incredibly alike as to be almost indistinguishable from photographs, an extraordinary feature for those days of individuality, although common enough in these days of box-like prefabricated buildings. The Waterford terminus was known as Manor station to distinguish it from Waterford North, $1\frac{1}{4}$ miles away on the other side of the river, and used by the other railways serving the city.

The headquarters of the line were at Waterford, along with the engine shed and workshops, which were capable of carrying out major overhauls. Delivery of new engines and rolling stock had to be made by sea in the early years, until the WDLR reached the south bank in 1876; latterly transfers were effected through the streets and over the river bridge by means of laying temporary rails, a slow job usually performed on Sundays.

Unlike many Irish railways, the Waterford & Tramore was a prosperous line in its early years, paying dividends up to $7\frac{1}{2}$ per cent. In the height of the summer season the traffic at weekends was sometimes almost more than the railway could take, but this was only for a few weeks in the year. The line was run on strictly economical grounds and by the time it was absorbed by the Great Southern in 1925, the newest item of equipment was an engine which had been built in 1908. The other three dated back to the 1850s and 1860s, whilst the coaching stock, all four-wheelers, was of ancient origin.

To replace it the Great Southern sent over six bogie vehicles articulated in pairs, which were conversions of the body work of Clayton steam railcars built in 1928 for branch-line work. The last phase in modernisation came in 1954 and 1955, when there arrived three twin diesel railcars, nos 2657-9, together with two trailers. Steam working was thereafter abandoned, and the turntables and running-round loops at the termini were taken out.

By 1930 the inevitable bus competition had begun to make serious inroads into the most profitable traffic, but fortunately the Great Southern obtained

F

Waterford & Tramore Railway.

Week Days, 1st & 3rd Class.

From Waterford.—7.45, 10.45, 12.15, 2.0, 4.15, 5.30, 7.20, 9.0.

From Tramore.— 9.10, 11.15, 1.15, 2.50, 4.45, 6.0, 7.50, 9.30.

NOTE.—On SATURDAYS the departure of the 2 p.m. Train from Waterford will be delayed until 2.15 p.m.

1st Class Single 1/-.   Return 1.6.
3rd Class Single 8d.   Return 1/-.

Sundays, 1st & 3rd Class.

From Waterford.—8.0, 11.15, 12.30, 3.0, 4.30, 6.0 7.20, 9.0,

From Tramore.—9.15, 11.45, 1.30, 4.0, 5.30, 6.30, 7.50, 9.30.

From Waterford.—Return Tickets at Single Fare—1st Class, 1s.; 3rd Class, 8d., will be issued by the 4.15, and 5.30 on Week Days, and on Sundays by all Trains except the last.

Excursion Tickets 1st & 3rd Class, will be issued (until further notice), on Week Days and Sundays by the 7.20 p.m., and every Monday, Tuesday and Thursday, by the 12.15, available for return by any Train same evening. Fares—1st Class, 1s.; 3rd Class, 6d. Children—1st Class, 6d.; 3rd Class, 4d.

Bathing Tickets are issued every Week Day by the 7.45 a.m., and on Sundays by the 8.0 a.m. Trains, available for return only by the 9.10 a.m. and 9.15 a.m. Up Trains respectively. Fares—1st Class, 6d.; 3rd Class, 4d.

Weekly Bathing Tickets are issued every Monday Morning, available for same Trains. Fare—1st Class, 3/6; 3rd Class, 2/4.

From Tramore.—Special Return Tickets, 1st and 3rd Class, will be issued on Week Days by the 2.50 p.m. Train, and on Sundays by all Trains except the last, at Single Fare, available for Return by any Train same evening.

Children under three years of age travel free; over three and under twelve years, half-price. Return Tickets are available only on the day they are issued, and are not transferable. 3rd Class Return Market Tickets are issued on the First Monday in each month (if a Fair Day), and every Wednesday and Saturday morning by the 9.10 a.m. Up Train, available for Return by any Train during the day. Fare 8d.

YEARLY TICKETS £9; Half-yearly ditto, £6 for Summer six months, and £4 for Winter six months. MONTHLY TICKETS—1st Class £1 10s.. available for all Trains as above. £1 4s.. available for one double journey only, each day; 3rd Class ditto, £1, available for all Trains as above, and 17s. 6d. available for one double journey only, each day. WEEKLY TICKETS, available for one double journey only each day, are issued every Monday; Fares—1st Class, 7s. 6d.; 3rd Class, 5s.

ARTHUR PROSSOR,
Secretary and Manager.

Waterford Terminus, May 16th, 1908.

It is requested that any complaints or irregularity may be immediately reported to the Manager.

---

control of the principal competition under a government Act of 1932, which placed severe restrictions on destructive and unnecessary rivalry. In 1953, the year of the railway's centenary, it was busier than at any time during its existence, trains being run for seventeen hours out of twenty-four, and at times the whole of the coaching stock and all three surviving engines were in steam.

WTR ticket and WTR left-luggage ticket

Nevertheless, in spite of the reduction in working expenses upon dieselisation in 1954, it soon became quite obvious that the CIE was intent on closing the line completely and substituting its own buses. The nowadays all too familiar cries of 'uneconomic to maintain', 'the line loses money', 'cannot pay its way' and so on, were heard with increasing frequency, and despite the usual protests the last train ran on 31 December 1960, and the line was completely lifted by the following May. After 106 years of service to the local community, the Waterford & Tramore was no more.

LOCOMOTIVES

Not the least interesting aspect of the Waterford & Tramore was its locomotives, of which three of the earliest were still in service when the line was taken over by the Great Southern in 1925. The first locomotives were three Bury engines, obtained secondhand from the London & North Western Railway. These had originally been London & Birmingham 2-2-0 tender engines built in 1837, which had been rebuilt at Wolverton to 2-2-2WTs. They were however only a stopgap, pending the arrival of two new engines on order from Fairbairn & Sons; in the meantime this firm loaned another engine, of which only scanty details have survived.

The Burys were found to be in poor condition and underpowered, and only one of them, no 4, was retained as a spare engine after the arrival of the new ones, but for some years after it ceased work, which seems to have been around 1906, it was kept in Waterford shed with a view to its preservation. Regrettably it was cut up in 1912.

The two new locomotives from Fairbairn arrived in 1855 and became WTR nos 1 and 2. They were neat little 2-2-2WTs, radically different from the old bar-framed Burys which they replaced. Another somewhat similar engine, but an 0-4-2WT, came from Slaughter Gruning (later the Avonside Engine Co) in 1861, works no 452, and became WTR no 3. These three engines, which underwent sundry rebuilds over the years, assisted occasionally by the aged no 4, worked the entire traffic until 1908, when a new no 4 came from Andrew Barclay, works no 1137. This was another 0-4-2WT, but of much more modern design, and considerably more powerful. Nevertheless it does not seem to have been used to a great extent outside the busy season, and for lighter trains the older engines were still preferred.

On absorption by the Great Southern the four engines were allocated nos 483-6, but no 3 never ran as 485. No 484 was scrapped in 1926 and no 3 in 1930. The larger 0-4-2WT no 486 lasted until 1941, as might well have done the old no 1, which could easily have attained its century. This gallant little 80 year-old engine was still merrily at work until 24 August 1935, when it was unfortunately derailed at speed and fell down an embankment. H. Fayle has suggested sabotage was the cause but this now seems unlikely. Several were injured but there were no fatalities. The engine was severely damaged and was cut up on the spot. This was a great tragedy, as even at that time there were thoughts of possible preservation, and its loss was even greater than that of the old Bury, because whereas a GSWR engine very similar to the latter now stands in retirement at Cork station, no Fairbairn engine now survives, at any rate in the British Isles. With the exception of a couple of NER 2-2-4Ts mainly used on departmental duties, which were still in occasional use until 1937, this was, together with the better-known Caledonian 4-2-2, also withdrawn about the same time, the last single wheeler in regular use in Great Britain and Ireland.

To replace the WTR engines, the GSR sent over three small Midland Great

Western 0–6–0Ts, which were found very satisfactory. The first one, no 560, a Kitson engine of 1893, arrived in 1930 to replace no 3 and two others duly followed in substitution for nos 483 and 486. These were Great Southern 553 and 555, and the three engines then worked all traffic on the line until the end of steam operation in 1954. No 560 was then returned for further service on the main CIE system, but the other two were scrapped at Waterford.

CHAPTER 6

MIDLAND GREAT WESTERN RAILWAY

Ireland's third largest railway before the 1925 grouping, with a principal main line extending from Dublin in the east to Galway in the west and numerous subsidiary lines and branches covering the great central plain and the west coast. Incorporated 1845. First section Dublin to Mullingar completed 1848. Extended to Galway 1851 and to Sligo 1862 with subsequent additions and absorptions of independent railways.

Eventual route mileage in 1922: 538 miles.

Principal places served:
   Dublin, Mullingar, Athlone, Galway, Clifden, Westport, Achill, Longford, Sligo.

The Midland Great Western was Ireland's third largest railway, its route mileage of 538 being exceeded only by the Great Southern & Western and the Great Northern. Unlike the Great Northern, however, which grew up out of several constituent companies and did not actually become the Great Northern as such until amalgamation in 1876, the Midland Great Western, as did the Great Southern & Western, retained its original identity and independence for a period of eighty years, until absorbed by the Great Southern in 1925. Although it acquired certain other subsidiary undertakings, these were nothing like as numerous as in the case of the Great Southern & Western, and much of the Midland Great Western system was added on its own account right from the start.

The original incorporation was by an Act of 21 July 1845, for a main line from Dublin to Mullingar, 50 miles, the ultimate objective being Galway, with a 26 mile branch to Longford. Another Act of 1846 authorised extension from Mullingar as far as Athlone, another 26 miles, and a further one on 19 July 1847 for completion to Galway, on the west coast, 126 miles from Dublin. This provided for a main trunk route right across the heart of Ireland from east to west, traversing the central plain, bounded both to north and south by various mountain ranges, and within which area almost the whole of the ultimate system of the railway eventually lay. A noticeable feature of the Midland Great Western Railway map was the fact that, apart from three small branches, the whole of the railway lay to the north of its basic main line, radiating from two important junctions, Mullingar and Athlone, and a third of rather less importance, nearer to Dublin. Thus the Midland Great Western was aptly named; it was just what it described itself to be. In Ireland itself it was more often just known as the Midland, being unlikely to be confused with the English railway of that name or with its offshoot in Northern Ireland.

Of the towns served by the Midland, outside Dublin itself there are only four with present populations in excess of five thousand: Galway, with 22,000; Sligo, 13,000; Athlone, 9,600; and Mullingar, 5,900. These figures have increased considerably during the present century because of the usual immigration to the towns from the countryside, where the population is much less than it was a century ago, when the railway was young. Galway, situated on the large inlet known as Galway Bay, is one of the principal fishing ports on the west coast of Ireland, and has considerable industries manufacturing woollens and agricultural implements. Sligo is another prosperous and busy port, from which there were once regular steamer services to Liverpool and Glasgow, and also to Belmullet, a small isolated community on the remote north-west tip of County Mayo, which never had a railway although one was once proposed. Mullingar, which has an extensive cattle and horse trade, is an ancient town dating back to the thirteenth century, when the Anglo-Norman invaders built a formidable stronghold. It is now dominated by a Roman Catholic cathedral with twin towers 140ft high. Athlone, which from very earliest times has been one of the most important strategic points in the country, lies in what may be roughly regarded as the centre of Ireland.

The first 35 miles of the route to Mullingar follow very closely that of the Royal Canal; in fact the first thing the new company did was buy out the canal company, which it was able to do for a fifth of the original cost. By following the course of the canal, it obtained the necessary land cheaply and construction was easy. No major earthworks were required and the steepest gradients, except for some short sections at 1 in 100, were 1 in 150, many stretches of the line being indeed level. The first sod was cut on 8 June 1846, and the first 26 miles as far as Enfield completed for a trial trip in the remarkably short time of ten months. The opening of this section of the line took place on 28 June 1847, followed by another 9 miles to Kinnegad (later known as Hill of Down), on 6 December 1847, and the last 15 miles to Mullingar on 2 October 1848. The last part of the line into Mullingar deviates from the course of the canal and cuts across the northern part of the marshy area known as the Bog of Allen, where there are large quantities of turf. The 26 mile branch to Longford, although part of the original Act, was not actually finished and opened until 8 November 1855 for passenger traffic, and 14 December for goods, some years after the completion of the main line to Galway. The Acts of 1846 and 1847, which provided for the building of the rest of the main line, were implemented by opening throughout to Galway on 1 August 1851. The only engineering work of importance was a bridge over the river at Athlone.

At Athenry the Midland's monopoly of the county of Galway was being encroached upon by the gradual extension northwards from Limerick of the Waterford & Limerick. Two subsidiary companies, the Athenry & Ennis Junction and the Athenry & Tuam, both of which were worked and eventually taken over by what became the Waterford Limerick & Western, made contact with the Midland at Athenry. The Athenry & Ennis, opened on 15 September 1869, was at first worked independently but was leased on 1 November 1872 to the Waterford & Limerick and amalgamated with it on 27 July 1893. The Athenry & Tuam, opened on 27 September 1860, was leased by the Midland for the first ten years and then worked independently until November 1872, when the Waterford & Limerick obtained a lease, absorbing the line completely on 27 July 1893. From 1 October 1895 the WLR obtained running powers over the Midland between Collooney and Sligo.

The Midland resented the intrusion into its territory, and in 1901, when the Waterford Limerick & Western was taken over by the Great Southern & Western, it attempted to regain possession of the disputed lines, but without success. However, it obtained running powers from Athenry as far as Limerick, a distance of 60½ miles, which it exercised for a good many years both for passenger and goods traffic. Athenry Junction, used by both railways, remained Midland property, with running powers granted to the Waterford Limerick & Western.

Already owning the Royal Canal, which ran from Dublin to Mullingar and beyond for another 30 miles north-west to Tarmonbarry, on the River Shannon, the Midland in 1852 extended its operations in a southerly direction into what was definitely Great Southern & Western territory, by leasing the somewhat parallel Grand Canal, running from Dublin to a point farther downstream on the Shannon. These two canals had been in direct competition with each other, and the reason for the existence of the Royal, sometimes known as the Shoemaker's Canal, was that a shoemaker, ousted from the Grand Canal board, built the new one in opposition.

Be that as it may, the Midland now found itself in possession of more mileage of canal, something over 200, than of railway, which at that time only covered the 126 miles to Galway! This last move was naturally looked upon with disfavour by the GSWR, but an agreement was reached between the two railways, and the Midland retired into its own territory. Under the original terms of agreement for the purchase of the Royal Canal, the Midland was obliged to keep it open for traffic. The passenger service ceased after the opening of the railway, but it was maintained in navigable condition until about 1956. It was officially closed on 6 April 1961.

From Mullingar the second most important line of the Midland was the long branch—if such is the right term—to Sligo, 134 miles from Dublin. The Midland itself called it its 'Principal Line' as distinct from its 'Main Line', Dublin to Galway, 8 miles shorter.

In view of the expansion of the railway system which took place in Ireland in the 1840s and 1850s, it is surprising that it took so long for railways to reach Sligo, then the fifteenth largest town in the country. There had been numerous abortive schemes, particularly during the Railway Mania of 1844–6, amongst which were the Sligo & Shannon Junction (the only one to obtain an Act), the Athlone & Sligo Junction, Sligo Ballina & Westport, Enniskillen & Sligo (later successfully revived as the Sligo Leitrim & Northern Counties Railway), Irish West Coast, Dundalk & Sligo, Londonderry Ballyshannon & Sligo and the Great Waterford Kilkenny Longford & Sligo. These were some of the more ambitious of the projects, none of which came to anything.

The first section of what later became the first main line into Sligo was the branch from Mullingar to Longford, authorised under the original MGWR Act of 1845 but not opened until 1855. On 27 July 1857, however, powers were obtained for the building of the remaining 58 miles. This was eventually opened on 3 September 1862, when Sligo at last got its first railway. The 51 mile section between Longford & Collooney was never more than a single line, and it had only one branch (although in later years Dromod became the junction for the narrow-gauge Cavan & Leitrim). Opened on 1 November 1874 by the nominally independent Sligo & Ballaghaderreen Junction Railway, this 9 mile branch left the Midland main line at Kilfree Junction and ran to Ballaghaderreen, an important market town of some 1,400 inhabitants. It was worked by the Midland, in which it was vested in 1877.

From Inny Junction, 10 miles out of Mullingar, another 25 mile branch ran to Cavan, opened on 8 July 1856. In March 1863 it was joined by the Great Northern with its own branch from Clones, which used the Midland station by virtue of running powers. This was one of the only two points of contact between the two railways. Off the Midland's Cavan line at Crossdooney a 7 mile branch ran to Killeshandra, opened on 1 June 1886. To facilitate the working of through trains to Cavan, the line was doubled in 1858 between

Mullingar and Inny Junction, and the doubling of the main line was continued to Longford in 1878. It was always double between Dublin and Ballinasloe.

The third important main line was to Westport, another coastal town situated on Clew Bay, in the county of Mayo, on the large Connaught promontory between Galway and Sligo. This diverged from the Galway main line at Athlone. It was promoted by an independent company, the Great Northern & Western, and was backed by the Midland, if only to keep out the GSWR. The original Act dated 27 July 1857 authorised the construction of the railway as far as Castlerea, a distance of 34 miles, the principal intermediate place being Roscommon, to which point the line was opened on 13 February 1860. Castlerea was reached on 15 November. Extensions were duly authorised, and the railway reached Ballyhaunis on 9 September 1861, Claremorris on 19 May 1862, and Castlebar on 17 December 1862. Financial difficulties appear to have arisen at this stage, and Westport was not reached until 24 January 1866, with an extension to the quay on 16 June 1874.

There was also a branch northwards to Ballina, opened as far as Foxford on 1 May 1868 and throughout on 19 May 1873. A later extension to Killala was opened on 2 January 1893. There had been an earlier scheme promoted in 1856 by the imposing title of Grand Junction Railway of Ireland, later amended to North Western Railway of Ireland, for a continuation of the Longford branch to Ballina via Ballaghaderreen and Castlebar. It was to be worked by the Midland but was abandoned in favour of the direct extension to Sligo.

Claremorris, on the Westport main line, which was reached in 1894 by the Waterford Limerick & Western, now became a junction with running powers for a short distance granted by the Midland to the WLWR. Meanwhile another branch had been built by an independent company, the Ballinrobe & Claremorris Light Railway. This was promoted in December 1884 under the Tramways Act (Ireland) of 1883, which encouraged the construction of light railways in rural areas. They were usually of 3ft gauge, but the Ballinrobe was one of two built to standard gauge; both were worked by the Midland, the other being the Loughrea branch.

The 13 mile Claremorris & Ballinrobe line was opened on 1 November 1892 and though worked by the Midland, retained its nominally independent status until taken over by the Great Southern at the 1925 grouping.

With the main lines of the Midland and the Great Southern & Western (as the WLWR became after 1901) intersecting, and the Ballinrobe branch as well, Claremorris became an important and busy junction, sufficiently so to justify a refreshment room. Nowadays trains from Limerick are diverted to Ballina and no longer proceed to Sligo over the 'Burma Road'; this line is still open for goods traffic, however, for which Claremorris remains the junction. It is also the station for Knock, a small village 7 miles away, famous for its shrine, which has come to be regarded as the Lourdes of Ireland. Many thousands of passengers have been carried on Sundays between May and October by pilgrimage excursions run from all parts of Ireland.

Next to be built were two westerly extensions to the Atlantic coast, easily the most spectacular and scenic of all the MGWR system. Both were opened about the same time, in the mid 1890s, and were destined to have comparatively short lives, being closed in the mid 1930s, even before the holocaust which, except for three or four main lines such as those to Sligo, Westport, Galway and Tralee, has now entirely denuded the west coast of rail communication. From Westport the main line was extended by a 27 mile branch which skirted Clew Bay through county Mayo, and struck out westwards to terminate at the small village of Achill, separated by a narrow channel from Achill Island, the largest off the Irish coast, with a population of some 5,000. There were only two intermediate stations, at Newport and at Mallaranny, where the railway built a large hotel. The scenery of mountain, moor and lough is very fine indeed, and the line, which was built with some government assistance, was severely graded, much of it at 1 in 60 and 70, and had two major summits, two short tunnels and several viaducts. It opened as far as Newport on 1 February 1894, Mallaranny on 1 August 1894, and Achill on 13 May 1895.

In the early part of the century there was a proposal to construct a branch from Mallaranny to Bellmullet, one of the remotest townships in Ireland, situated at the most north-westerly tip of the country on a narrow neck of land between Blacksod Bay and Broad Haven, connecting the Mullet peninsula with the mainland. Until the motor age it was extremely inaccessible, and a railway at that time would have been a great boon, although hardly a paying proposition even in those days.

The Achill branch was served by three trains each way daily. One conveyed a through coach to Dublin, attached to the main train at Westport, which was itself attached to a Galway express at Athlone; there was a similar through service in the reverse direction. The 187 mile journey was the second longest in the country, exceeded only by Kingsbridge–Tralee until the 1950s, when for a time the Great Northern Enterprise ran between Belfast and Cork.

To the south of the Achill branch was the somewhat similar line from Galway to Clifden, a 49 mile stretch through Connemara, again very fine scenery. Access to it was by means of a trailing branch out of Galway; trains leaving the terminus had to back out to a point beyond the junction before proceeding over a large viaduct, now demolished, spanning the inlet between Galway Bay and Lough Corrib. The line was opened as far as Oughterard, about a third of the way, on 1 January 1895, and reached Clifden on 1 July in the same year. Other stations were at Moycullen, Ross, Maam Cross, Recess, where the railway also had an hotel, and Ballynahinch. Like the Achill branch, the normal service was three trains daily with none on Sundays. Clifden, known as the capital of Connemara, is a holiday resort on Ardbear Bay, with splendid mountain scenery.

In Dublin, in order to gain access to the docks, the Midland obtained sanction in 1859 for the construction of the Liffey branch, 3 miles to the docks at North Wall, opened on 1 April 1864. This left the main line at Liffey Junction, 1¼ miles short of Broadstone terminus. Like the Mullingar main line, it followed the course of the Royal Canal around the northern edge of the city. All the Dublin freight traffic of the Midland was then handled at North Wall goods station, although cattle traffic continued to use the special depot at Broadstone. Other loop lines and connecting links followed eventually, built by the GSWR and DWWR, and so through running became possible between all four railways.

Although the greater part of the Midland system was constructed by the company on its own account, some sections started as independently owned railways and were later absorbed. Another of these was the Dublin & Meath, incorporated on 23 July 1858 to build a line from Dublin to Navan and Athboy. It was originally intended to be a branch from the GSWR near Lucan, but this was very naturally objected to by the Midland, and agreement was reached under which it became a branch off the Midland main line at Clonsilla, with running powers over the 7 miles into Broadstone terminus; through trains from Navan started running on 29 August 1862. The 12 mile long Athboy line was on a separate branch from Kilmessan, 6 miles short of Navan, and this was opened on 26 February 1864.

From a railway enthusiast's point of view, Athboy has some small claim to be remembered, in that it was the last branch in the whole of the British Isles to be traversed by the late T. R. Perkins, who long ago attempted, and finally achieved, the task of travelling on the whole of the railway network in these islands over which a passenger service operated.

The distance from Clonsilla to Navan was 23 miles. At Navan contact was made with the Great Northern branch from Drogheda, but each line had its own station. A connection was however put in, incidentally without parliamentary sanction, a fact which did not come to light for several years when it was too late to do anything about it. Moreover the Dublin & Meath actually had running powers over part of the Great Northern line as far as Kells. In later years a new four-platform station was built at Navan to accommodate both companies' trains.

Another independent concern, the Navan & Kingscourt, was authorised on 5 July 1865, to extend the line for a further 11 miles to Kingscourt, this being opened on 1 November 1875. It had been planned to extend the railway still further to Carrickmacross, but the Great Northern got there first and this idea was dropped. Some years later the Midland sought powers to extend the line to Armagh, definitely now in Great Northern territory. Naturally the GNR vigorously opposed the idea, and it was dropped. The Midland took on the working of the Dublin & Meath on 1 June 1869, and bought it out completely, together with the Navan & Kingscourt, in 1888.

Of the three Midland lines south of the main line from Dublin to Galway, two were dead-end branches and the third joined the GSWR. The only other point of physical contact between the two railways outside Dublin, despite the fact that they were neighbours, was at Athlone.

The Midland line left the Galway main line at a small place called Streamstown and ran south to Clara, 7 miles. There it had its own station (closed by the GSR in 1925) but there was a junction with the GSWR, whose line continued to Athlone where it had running powers into the Midland station. The Clara branch was authorised in 1856 and opened on 1 April 1863; there was an intermediate station at Horseleap.

Of the two dead-end branches one was the 10 mile Edenderry branch, which left the main line at Enfield, 26 miles out from Dublin. It was authorised in June 1874 and opened on 9 April 1877. Passenger services ceased in 1931 and complete closure took place on 25 March 1963.

The other was the branch from Attymon Junction to Loughrea. Like the Claremorris and Ballinrobe, the Loughrea & Attymon Light Railway, authorised in 1889, was an independent company constructed under the Light Railways Act of 1883, and also built to main-line dimensions instead of the more usual 3ft gauge. Twelve miles long, with an intermediate station at Dunsandle, it was opened on 1 December 1890 and worked by the Midland from the start.

It is one of the few branches which is still open, although it narrowly escaped closure in 1962, and is again in danger in 1972 at the time of writing, but there are hopes that it will be reprieved for a second time. It is of special interest in that it is one of the last purely rural branches still in being in the whole of the British Isles. Moreover it must be absolutely unique for such a line, in that its three daily trains, all making main-line connections with Dublin at the junction, are still locomotive-hauled (diesel of course) despite the almost universal employment of railcars for such duties. This is no doubt because the trains are 'mixed', conveying passengers along with goods and cattle traffic, again a great rarity these days. Until the end of steam working it was almost the final haunt of a Midland Great Western 2-4-0, the final survivors of this type anywhere in the British Isles. Another could be found on the Ballaghaderreen branch. The

2–4–0 had already been extinct in Great Britain since 1954 with the disappearance of the last Midland & South Western Junction engine. The branch train was then usually composed somewhat incongruously of a modern side-corridor coach and an ancient six-wheeler, with such goods vans as necessary.

In Dublin the Midland terminus was at Broadstone, built in 1850, where were also to be found the principal sheds, workshops and the headquarters of the line. Although a fine building in itself, it was awkwardly situated some distance from the city centre, in a rather poor neighbourhood, and not on the tramway system. It was the scene in 1856 of one of the earliest of railway murders, when the booking clerk was attacked and killed one evening for the sake of the day's takings, amounting to about £1,800. The culprit was never identified; there was a strong suspect, but his guilt could not be proved. In 1937 passenger services were diverted from Liffey Junction around the North Wall line to Amiens Street and Westland Row (now known as Connolly and Pearse), where they used the former Dublin & South Eastern stations, and in fact still do. Broadstone station still stands, although now used as a bus and parcels depot.

For the rest, the Killala extension of the Ballina branch was closed in July 1934, followed in April 1935 by the Galway and Clifden lines, and the Westport and Achill in September 1937. Edenderry had lost its passenger service as early as 1931, but remained open for goods traffic until February 1963. No further closures took place until after World War II, when the Killeshandra and the Streamstown to Clara lines lost their passenger service; the former was closed entirely in 1955 and the latter in 1963. The Athboy branch also discontinued passenger trains in March 1947, although it was not lifted until 1963 and saw the occasional goods train. Ballinrobe was closed entirely on 31 December 1959, and Ballaghaderreen on 2 February 1963. From Navan to Kingscourt the line is still open for goods (access being by way of the former Great Northern from Drogheda), although passenger services have been discontinued since 1947. The Clonsilla to Navan section lost its passenger service in 1947 and was closed entirely on 30 March 1963.

In general, the railways of Ireland were self-contained within their own areas of operation, far more so than in the rest of the British Isles, where there was much more intermingling and consequent competition. This isolation was largely the case with the MGWR, notwithstanding its central situation. Away from Dublin it had only two points of contact with the Great Northern, at Cavan and Navan, and as for its early southern neighbour, the Great Southern & Western (before that railway absorbed the Waterford Limerick & Western), the two railways kept almost completely to their own territories. Very few lines in England had such complete monopoly, the most notable being the

North Eastern, which held almost undisputed sway in Northumberland, Durham and a large part of Yorkshire, until challenged by a rival railway which penetrated its preserves to the important port of Hull. The gradual incursion of the Waterford Limerick & Western northwards towards Sligo might be likened to a sort of Hull & Barnsley operation into the domain of the Midland Great Western. The latter, of course, tried much the same thing against the Great Northern with its Meath lines, but again these ended in a sort of no man's land at Kingscourt and got no farther.

Specimen MGWR tickets

Today a fair proportion of the MGWR still survives. The main lines to Galway, Westport and Sligo still form an integral part of the principal Irish main-line railway system. The general pattern of the expresses and mails has not changed greatly over the years, with normally three or four trains each way daily, fully equipped with restaurant cars and, since dieselisation, considerably speeded up. Of the branches however only two have survived, to Loughrea and to Ballina, the latter now having a through coach to Dublin. Loughrea is thus the only station on the Midland that does not now enjoy through services with the capital.

LOCOMOTIVES AND ROLLING STOCK

During the years of its independence the Dublin & Meath had seven engines. Details of them are scanty but there were two single-wheelers, three 0-4-2 tender engines and one 2-4-0, and another four-coupled tender passenger engine which might have been either. The small workshops, with probably an engine shed, were situated at the junction of the Athboy branch at Kilmessan. When the Midland took over the working of the line some of these engines went to the Athenry & Tuam and Athenry & Ennis, which were still independently worked. They passed into the hands of the Waterford & Limerick and lasted until the 1890s.

As for the MGWR engines proper, particularly those which survived to be taken over by the GSR in 1925, one very noticeable feature is the almost complete lack of passenger tank engines. Indeed after the demise of an ancient fleet of 2–2–2WTs the only such locomotives the Midland had were a dozen small 0–6–0Ts, mainly employed on shunting and light duties, and on some of the shorter branches. This was largely because the Midland main line out of Dublin never had any sort of suburban service, as existed from very early days on the Bray line and on the Great Northern. For some reason the country to the west of Dublin has never been developed in this manner even to this day. Moreover the longer branches were almost entirely worked by tender engines, and were provided with turntables accordingly. Most of them were long enough to necessitate the use of tender engines in any case. The locomotive stock from very early days therefore consisted of four very simple, typically British basic types: 2–4–0, 4–4–0, 0–6–0 and 0–6–0T.

The MGWR locomotive stock was unique in that practically every engine was named, a state of affairs unknown on any other large railway in Great Britain and Ireland. Some, particularly the London & North Western and the Great Western, had adopted a consistent policy of naming express passenger locomotives, but this was rarely extended to tank engines (the Brighton was an exception) and hardly ever to the humble goods. Even these however were so honoured on the MGWR and also on the Great Northern. The two railways also had a common feature in that the names were usually carried on brass plates fixed to the boiler barrel instead of the more usual position on the driving-wheel splasher, which was in fact used on new engines after 1902, and on many rebuilt ones. A distinctive feature of earlier Midland tender engines was the peculiar design of the cabs, the roof of which was flared upwards in graceful curves, suggestive of a primitive form of streamlining. The principal locomotive superintendents of the Midland were M. Atock, from 1872 to 1901, E. Cusack, until 1915, and W. H. Morton, until 1925.

The oldest passenger engines at the time of the amalgamation were a series of 2–4–0s built between 1893 and 1898.

GSR no	Former Midland no and name		GSR no	Former Midland no and name	
650	14	Racer	659	13	Rapid
651	16	Rob Roy	660	15	Rover
652	18	Ranger	661	17	Reindeer
653	19	Spencer	662	21	Swift
	20	Speedy	663	22	Samson
654	28	Clara	664	23	Sylph
655	29	Clonsilla	665	24	Sprite
656	30	Active	666	27	Clifden
657	33	Arrow	667	31	Alert
658	34	Aurora	668	32	Ariel

Page 105 (*above*) Irish branch scene in 1934. McDonnell 0–4–4WT no 47 at Castleisland with typical six-wheeled stock; (*below*) branch train at Athboy about 1910. MGWR 0–6–0T no 110 *Bat* (later GSR 555). This quiet backwater was the 'end of the road' for T. R. Perkins in his widespread travels (see page 100)

Page 106 (*above*) MGWR 2–4–0 no 665 in 1955 on the turntable used for running round at the now closed Harcourt Street terminus in Dublin. This was situated at a high level overlooking a busy street, but although on at least one occasion an engine overran and partly demolished the wall, there was never a very serious accident; (*below*) McDonnell (Aspinall) 4–4–0 no 57 at Achill in July 1934, in original condition. Note the distinctive double folding smokebox door. Many of these engines lasted into the 1950s, mostly rebuilt with superheaters, extended smokeboxes and Belpaire fireboxes

No 20 *Speedy* was destroyed during the 'troubles' of 1923 and so never received a GSR number.

All were in service until 1954. They were gradually withdrawn from that year onwards, and the ultimate survivors, no 654, scrapped in 1962, and 653, in 1963, were the last 2-4-0s to remain at work anywhere in the British Isles. It is the greatest pity that one of them was not preserved, and indeed that no Midland Great Western engine now survives.

There was also an earlier series of 2-4-0s built in 1883-7 and withdrawn in 1915-23.

1	Orion	41	Regal
4	Venus	42	Ouzel
5	Mars	43	Leinster
6	Vesta	44	Ulster
35	Airedale	45	Queen
36	Eagle	46	Munster
39	Hawk	47	Viceroy
40	Lily	48	Connaught

Some of the 4-4-0s were rebuilt from 2-4-0s. The oldest of these were nos 530-5, originally built by Beyer Peacock in 1880-1 and rebuilt in 1900-1. In later years they came to be known as the 'Achill bogies', being largely employed on that line. They were small engines, with 5ft 8in driving wheels, and were scrapped between 1949 and 1953. The remaining 4-4-0s were larger machines for express work, with 6ft 3in drivers. Nos 536-44, also nominally rebuilds but better regarded as completely new engines, were turned out between 1910 and 1915. The remaining six, 545-50, were built as 4-4-0s by Broadstone works between 1902 and 1905. All these later engines except 549, which was scrapped prematurely in 1931, survived until the 1950s, the last being withdrawn in 1959.

GSR no	MGWR no	Name
530	36/1	Empress of Austria
531	25/4	Cyclops
532	26/5	Britannia
533	37/6	Wolfdog
534	2	Jupiter
535	3	Juno
536	12	Shamrock
537	9/20	Emerald Isle
538	4/25	Ballynahinch
539	11/26	Croagh Patrick
540	7	Connemara

541	8	*St Patrick*
542	6/9	*Kylemore*
543	10	*Faugh-a-Ballagh*
544	11	*Erin-go-Bragh*
545	127	*Titanic*
546	129	*Celtic*
547	125	*Britannic*
548	126	*Atlantic*
549	128	*Majestic*
550	124	*Mercuric*

There was a variety of classes of 0-6-0, built at various times between 1876 and 1924. Nos 623-45, built in 1921-4, were never named. Named engines were as follows (numbers in brackets were allocated but never actually carried):

233*	141	*Limerick*	596	57	*Lough Corrib*
234*	142	*Athenry*	597	58	*Lough Gill*
(563)	49	*Marquis*	598	59	*Shannon*
(564)	50	*Viscount*	599	60	*Lough Owel*
(565)	51	*Baron*	600	61	*Lynx*
(566)	52	*Regent*	601	62	*Tiger*
567	53	*Duke*	602	63	*Lion*
(568)	54	*Earl*	—†	64	*Leopard*
(569)	76	*Lightning*	603	65	*Wolf*
(570)	78	*Planet*	604	66	*Elephant*
(571)	83	*Lucan*	605	67	*Dublin*
(572)	84	*Dunkellen*	606	68	*Mullingar*
(573)	95/85	*Bulldog*	607	69	*Athlone*
574	80	*Dunsandle*	608	70	*Ballinasloe*
575	92/135	*Bittern*	609	71	*Galway*
576	74	*Luna*	610	72	*Sligo*
577	86	*Bullfinch*	(611)	140	*Wren*
(578)	79	*Mayo*	612	75	*Hector*
(579)	91/64	*Bear*	613	81	*Clancarty*
582	73	*Comet*	—†	85	*Meath*
583	82	*Clonbrock*	—†	87	*Buzzard*
584	130	*Ajax*	—†	88	*Buffalo*
585	131	*Atlas*	—†	89	*Bison*
586	132	*Pluto*	—†	90	*Beaver*
587	133	*Titan*	—†	93	*Butterfly*
588	134	*Vulcan*	—†	94	*Badger*
—†	135	*Arran Isles*	619	96	*Avonside*
589	77	*Star*	620	97	*Hibernia*
590	136	*Cavan*	621	98	*Caledonia*
591	137	*Maynooth*	622	99	*Cambria*
592	138	*Nephin*	646	143	*Canada*

593	139	*Tara*	647	144	*Australia*
594	55	*Inny*	648	145	*India*
595	56	*Liffey*	649	146	*Africa*

* Were to have become 580 and 581; they were originally Waterford Limerick & Western engines.

† Scrapped by 1925 and not included in renumbering.

No 64 was destroyed at Streamstown in January 1923 during the 'troubles'.

No 74 *Luna* was the last engine to remain in Midland colours, and did not become Great Southern 576 until 1931. Nos 619–22 were built by Avonside in 1878 for the Waterford Dungarvan & Lismore Railway, and transferred to the Midland in 1880. Scrapping took place gradually over the years, but a number lasted until the end of steam in the 1960s, the final withdrawals taking place in 1965.

There were two classes of 0–6–0Ts; the smaller ones, which were actually of later construction, were built between 1891 and 1894.

GSR	MGWR		GSR	MGWR	
no	*no*	*Name*	*no*	*no*	*Name*
551	106	*Lark*	557	112	*Hornet*
552	107	*Robin*	558	113	*Gnat*
553	108	*Swallow*	559	114	*Stork*
554	109	*Fly*	560	115	*Achill*
555	110	*Bat*	561	116	*Cong*
556	111	*Wasp*	562	117	*Moy*

These were used on passenger services on the shorter branches; no 560, which had been on the Waterford & Tramore, finished up on the Tralee & Fenit line until withdrawn in 1963, the last of the class. The others had been scrapped from 1955 onwards.

The larger 0–6–0Ts, dating from 1881 to 1890, were purely goods shunting engines:

614	100	*Giantess*
615	101	*Giant*
616	102	*Pilot*
617	103	*Pioneer*
618	105	*Hercules*

These were withdrawn between 1949 and 1959.

From before the turn of the century the livery of Midland engines was emerald green. Various styles of lining out were used, and the brass name and numberplates had vermilion backgrounds. The 2–4–0s had individual brass numerals on the splashers, and the 0–6–0s and 0–6–0Ts had them on the sand-boxes on the frames at the front. From 1903 until about 1906 an experiment was made with a royal blue livery, but this was abandoned owing to its poor weather resistance, and green was reverted to. From 1914 all engines were painted black, the superheated passenger and mixed traffic types being lined out in red.

Coaching stock also adopted a livery of blue with white upper panels con-currently with the blue engines, but this in turn gave way to the former brown, later changed to crimson lake.

Although the Midland was not slow in providing comfortable corridor coaches for its main expresses it also retained an unusually large number of old six-wheelers for secondary and branch services until quite recent years. Many were drafted to other sections of the Great Southern system, and some even lasted until well into the 1960s, almost certainly the last of the type in the British Isles.

Although three classes of passenger travel were offered on many Irish rail-ways until World War II, the MGWR provided only two, as early as 1914. Until 1865 a fourth class had been tried as an experiment, mainly for the benefit of harvestmen. Some railways in England also had fourth class for a time, nor-mally known as 'Parliamentary'.

For such a large railway the MGWR has fared particularly badly in the field of preservation. The only specimen of MGWR rolling stock still in existence is a six-wheeled coach known as Dargan's saloon, now to be found in Belfast Museum. This vehicle dates back to 1844; it was used as a state carriage until renovated in 1904, and later became a first-class vehicle in ordinary service.

CHAPTER 7

CORK BANDON & SOUTH COAST RAILWAY, TIMOLEAGUE & COURTMACSHERRY RAILWAY and CORK & MACROOM RAILWAY

A group of railways serving the area of county Cork west of the city itself.

CORK BANDON & SOUTH COAST RAILWAY

Principal constituents:

CORK & BANDON RAILWAY   Incorporated 1845. Opened 1851.

CORK & KINSALE JUNCTION RAILWAY   Incorporated 1859. Opened 1863.

WEST CORK RAILWAY   Incorporated 1860. Opened 1866.

Later extensions by independent companies:

All amalgamated in 1888 as CORK BANDON & SOUTH COAST RAILWAY. Became part of GREAT SOUTHERN RAILWAYS in 1925.

Route mileage: 94 miles.

Principal places served:

Cork, Bandon, Bantry, Skibbereen, Baltimore.

Completely closed by 1961.

TIMOLEAGUE & COURTMACSHERRY LIGHT RAILWAY

Mainly a roadside tramway serving small fishing villages and resorts on the south coast.

Incorporated 1888 under Tramways (Ireland) Act of 1883. Opened 1891.

Route mileage: 9 miles.

Principal places served:

Timoleague, Courtmacsherry.

Closed 1960.

CORK & MACROOM DIRECT RAILWAY
Incorporated 1861. Opened 1866.

No branches or extensions.

Became part of GREAT SOUTHERN RAILWAYS in 1925.

Route mileage: 24½ miles.

Principal places served:

Cork, Macroom.

Closed 1953.

Cork, the most southerly county in Ireland, is also one of the biggest. The area to the south and west of the county town, third largest city in the whole country, and second only to Dublin in Eire, was until World War II well served by railways, but is nowadays entirely denuded of them.

The outskirts of Cork were reached by the GSWR from Dublin in 1849 but the line was not carried into the city itself until 1855, when there were already two local lines established. The first was the Cork Blackrock & Passage (Chapter 9), which was opened in June 1850. The other, the Cork & Bandon, was incorporated in July 1845 to build 20 miles of line between the two places. Construction started at the Bandon end, and the first 6¾ miles as far as Ballinhassig, were opened on 1 August 1849 and the remaining 13¼ miles into Cork on 1 December 1851. This was a picturesque stretch of line, and between Ballinhassig and Waterfall was a 900yd tunnel known as Goggins Hill, the fourth or fifth longest tunnel in Ireland. Bandon is a pleasantly situated town on the river of the same name, dating from 1608, and was once surrounded by a wall, portions of which still remain.

The Cork & Kinsale Junction Railway, incorporated on 19 April 1859, provided for a branch off the Cork & Bandon to Kinsale, a small fishing town on the south coast; this was opened on 27 June 1863. It was worked by the Cork & Bandon until 1879, when it was purchased outright. Its length was 11 miles. It was off the Head of Kinsale that the *Lusitania* was torpedoed by a German submarine in 1915, with the loss of over 1,000 lives. This branch had the shortest life of any in the south-west Cork area, being closed as early as 1931.

Next came the West Cork Railway, incorporated on 28 August 1860 to extend westwards from Bandon to Dunmanway, 17¾ miles, and opened in June 1866. It was worked independently until 1880. Another separate company, the Ilen Valley Railway, continued the line to Skibbereen, a further 16 miles, and was opened on 21 July 1877. It was worked by the Cork & Bandon but remained nominally independent until 1909; the Cork & Kinsale and the West Cork were taken over on 1 January 1880.

A further extension was from Drimoleague to Bantry, 11 miles, opened on 1 July 1881. Yet another concern, the Bantry Bay Extension Railway, nominally a separate company but worked by the CBSCR, opened on 22 October 1892,

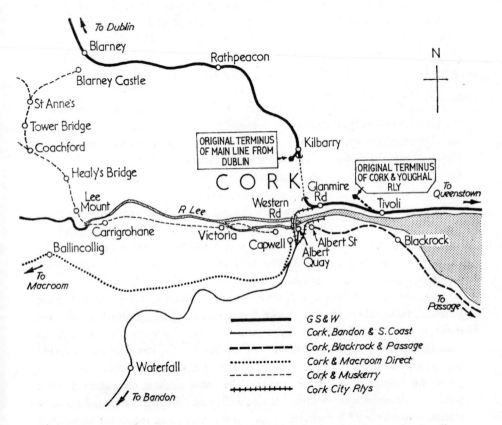

took the line right into the centre of Bantry and continued 1¼ miles in all to the pier at Bantry Bay. At that time only goods traffic was carried by the Bantry Bay Steamship Company, but from 1906 a passenger service was also operated to Glengarriff by the steamer *Lady Elsie*. Finally came the southwards extension from Skibbereen to Baltimore, 8 miles, opened in 1893. This was also a separate company, the Baltimore Extension Railway, but like the others was worked by what had been known since 1888 as the Cork Bandon & South Coast Railway. The CBSCR now had a continuous main line of 61¼ miles. Baltimore was the most southerly outpost on any Irish railway, and is situated at the southernmost extremity of the whole country.

One other branch was from Clonakilty Junction to Clonakilty. The Clonakilty Extension, as it was known, 9 miles long, was opened in August 1886, and was worked by the Bandon.

Associated with the Clonakilty branch was a railway which retained its independence right up to the 1925 grouping, the Timoleague & Courtmacsherry Light Railway, which was built under the Tramways (Ireland) Act of 1883 to standard Irish gauge, though originally intended to be 3ft gauge. There were actually two companies, the Timoleague & Courtmacsherry Light Railway and the Ballinascarthy & Timoleague Junction Light Railway, which were both worked by the Timoleague & Courtmacsherry Extension Light Railway.

The TCLR, which was in fact a branch off a branch, left the Clonakilty line at Ballinascarthy Junction, and ran in an easterly direction to Timoleague, 6 miles, and Courtmacsherry, a further 3 miles, small fishing townships and holiday resorts on the west shore of Courtmacsherry Bay. Part of the line ran alongside the road, so that it was a cross between a light railway and a tramway, as were a number of other systems built under the 1883 Act.

Another railway which remained independent until the 1925 grouping was the Cork & Macroom Direct Railway. Macroom is situated to the north of CBSCR territory, on the river Sullane, and has about 2,000 inhabitants. The CMDR was incorporated on 1 August 1861 and opened on 12 May 1866, there being five intermediate stations in the 24½ miles of line. At first it used the Bandon station at Albert Quay, with running powers as far as Ballyphehane Junction, from where its own tracks diverged. Eventually, however, disagreement arose over toll charges, and because the Bandon gave preference to its own trains. With services hardly on an intensive scale, less than half a dozen trains each way daily on each line, this should not have produced any great problems. However, the result was that the CMDR decided to acquire its own terminus. Premises were obtained at Capwell, some distance away, and the new station opened on 27 September 1879. Now it was more than ever an isolated system, though in 1914 a siding connection was put into the CMDR by order of the British government to enable transfer traffic to be effected. After the 1925 grouping the connecting link to Ballyphehane Junction was restored and trains again ran into Albert Quay, Capwell being closed.

The railways of south-west Cork were reasonably profitable in their earlier years but followed the general pattern of declining fortunes after World War I owing to road competition. The Kinsale branch was closed as early as 1931, and the last regular passenger trains on the Courtmacsherry came to an end in

1947, although there was an occasional excursion up to the late 1950s and a daily goods ran if required until 1960. The last train on the Cork & Macroom ran on 10 November 1953, but the other lines, to Clonakilty, Bantry and Baltimore, remained open until 31 March 1961, since when the whole area has been bereft of rail communication.

A diesel railcar was introduced in 1954 to work the service between Bantry and Cork, which by that time had come down to two trains a day in each direction, with connections to Clonakilty and Skibbereen. In these later years Cork to Bantry had become in effect the main line, whereas earlier it had been the practice to run through trains to Skibbereen with branch connections. There was a Clayton steam railcar at Cork in 1929, mainly for use on the Macroom line, and to Bandon, but apart from the later dieselisation all the services were worked throughout by conventional steam trains.

LOCOMOTIVES

The workshops of the CBSCR were situated at Cork Rocksavage, adjacent to the terminus. The railway never aspired to a covered running shed there, though a couple of favoured engines might be stabled beneath a road over-bridge as shelter. However, there were small one-engine sheds at the branch terminals, and also at Drimoleague and Skibbereen; the train service required at least five engines to be outstationed overnight.

The history of the earliest engines on the Cork & Bandon is obscure; most were obtained secondhand, and some were tender engines, including old Burys from the GSWR. From the 1880s onwards however only tank engines were used on the west Cork lines, not only on the CBSCR but also on the CMDR and TCLR, and this policy continued right to the end of the railways' existence. Of outstanding interest were two engines obtained from Baldwin in 1900, the only American-built engines ever to run in Ireland. They were 0-6-2STs, of typical USA design, with outside cylinders and bar frames, completely unlike anything to be found elsewhere. Numbered 19 and 20, they had comparatively short lives and were scrapped in 1912 and 1914.

The oldest engine taken into Great Southern stock was a 2-4-0T, CBSCR no 1, built by Dübs in 1874; it became no 482 and was scrapped in August 1934. Two 4-4-0Ts, CBSCR nos 2 and 7, became 477 and 478, the latter not being scrapped until 1934, and there were also three 4-4-2Ts, originally 4-4-0Ts, which became Great Southern 479-81, 480 lasting until 1936. Another 4-4-0T, no 10, built by Dübs in 1893, was rebuilt in 1906 as a 4-6-0T. Clearly the conversion was a success, as it was followed by the construction of several engines to a considerably enlarged design.

The rest of the older engines which survived into Great Southern days were five of a class of six 0–6–0STs built by Beyer Peacock between 1881 and 1894. They were very similar to some of Joseph Beattie's engines for the LSWR, built by the same maker. They became 472–6 in the Great Southern list, but two of them, CBSCR 12 and 16, were withdrawn almost immediately and never received their new numbers 474 and 476. Nos 472 and 475 however survived until 1938–9 and 475 was not broken up until 1945.

In 1906 there appeared the first of what became the standard main-line class, if such a term can be applied to a total of eight engines, the enlarged versions of the prototype rebuild 4–6–0T. They came from Beyer Peacock at intervals up to 1920, as CBSCR nos 4, 8, 11, 13, 14, 15, 19 and 20. The Great Southern renumbered them 463–70. They were good sturdy engines and ideal for the needs of the line. Five of them lasted until final closure in 1961. The original small boilered engine became Great Southern 471 and was scrapped in 1933.

The livery of the Bandon engines was olive green and was changed to unlined grey in Great Southern days.

On the Cork & Macroom five of the six engines owned by the company were still running at the 1925 amalgamation. These comprised three of the original four 2–4–0Ts, which became Great Southern 487–9; one 2–4–2T, originally Waterford Limerick & Western no 13 *Derry Castle*, which had been GSWR 266, was sold to the CMDR in 1914 and became Great Southern no 491R (R was the suffix letter applied to CMDR rolling stock, and this was the only instance of it being applied to an absorbed broad-gauge engine); and no 5, an 0–6–2T built by Andrew Barclay in 1905, which became 490. A commercially produced postcard issued about 1916 showed the engine in a red livery; this was incorrect and the card was quickly withdrawn, so that copies are now very scarce and most sought after by collectors. The actual livery was light green, later changed to black with red lining. All of the CMDR engines had gone by 1935.

There was a little interchange of locomotives between the West Cork line and the rest of the system after the Great Southern took over, but not very much. The importations included a few GSWR McDonnell 2–4–2Ts and 4–4–2Ts, one or two similar WLWR engines and a Dublin & South Eastern 2–4–2T; in return, CBSCR 4–6–0T no 466 spent several years in Dublin, doing good work on the Bray suburban service.

The Timoleague & Courtmacsherry had altogether three locomotives, all built by Hunslet: 0–6–0ST *Slaney* (Hunslet no 382 of 1885) was scrapped in 1920, 0–4–2T *St Molaga* (520 of 1890) in 1949, and *Argadeen* (611 of 1894), which was an inside-cylinder 2–6–0T, a very rare type, in 1957. The last two, although taken over by the Great Southern in 1925, were never numbered and continued to be known by their names only. In later years the Courtmacsherry line was worked mainly by two small GSWR 0–6–0Ts nos 90 and 100, former Tralee & Fenit 0–6–0ST no 299, and two former MGWR 0–6–0Ts nos 552 and 557.

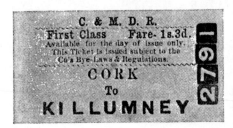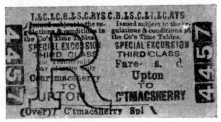

Specimen tickets of West Cork railways

CHAPTER 8

SCHULL & SKIBBEREEN TRAMWAY

A 3ft gauge steam tramway, mainly alongside the public road, serving the village of Schull, remote outpost on the south-west coast.

Incorporated 1883 under Tramways Act 1883 as WEST CARBERY TRAMWAY & LIGHT RAILWAY. Name changed to SCHULL & SKIBBEREEN TRAMWAYS & LIGHT RAILWAY COMPANY and opened in 1886.
Became part of GREAT SOUTHERN RAILWAYS in 1925.

Route mileage: 15 miles

Principal places served:
  Skibbereen, Schull.

Closed 1947.

Originally known as the West Carbery Tramway & Light Railway (Schull & Skibbereen branch), this was one of six 3ft gauge lines which eventually became part of the Great Southern system. Most were incorporated within a short time of one another after the passing of the Tramways Act of 1883. The bill for the West Carbery was actually the first, being incorporated on 7 December in that year; the same month also saw the birth of the Cork & Muskerry, the West Clare and the Cavan & Leitrim.

The small market town of Skibbereen, with a population of something over 2,000, lies in the south-west corner of Ireland, a few miles from the most southerly point of the country. To the west lies one of the mountain promontories, separated from each other by deep arms of the sea, where the forces of wind and wave from the Atlantic have gradually eroded the land over thousands of years.

Skibbereen itself had already been reached in 1877 from Cork and Bandon by the standard-gauge West Cork Railway, and the new narrow-gauge line was to open up the peninsular lying to the west, at the extreme end of which is Mizen Head, 765ft high, the most southerly tip of Ireland. The railway, 15½ miles long, extended only about half this distance, around the shores of the romantic sounding Roaring Water Bay to Ballydehob, the principal intermediate station, and terminated at Schull, a small watering place; both these townships had a population of less than 500. Traffic prospects were anything but rosy, and in fact the railway, supported by a baronial guarantee of £57,000, was never able to pay its way. It was opened for traffic on 6 September 1886, and in 1892 its name was changed to the Schull & Skibbereen Tramways & Light Railway.

The line ran partly alongside the public road, but owing to the undulating nature of the country, it was necessary to provide deviations in places, particularly around Ballydehob, in spite of which it was not possible to avoid gradients of 1 in 30 and even steeper in places. At Ballydehob there was a considerable viaduct of twelve arches, spanning one inlet of Roaring Water Bay. The only intermediate stations with buildings were Hollyhill and Ballydehob; there were small platforms with no shelter at Newcourt, Church Cross, Kilcoe and Woodlands.

Schull had normal station buildings and offices, together with a carriage and engine shed, and a turntable; engines always ran chimney first. One engine and train was housed there overnight. The normal service, weekdays only, was usually only two trains a day, with an extra on fair days. Trains were mixed, passenger and freight, and two classes, first and third, were provided. Most of the passenger coaches were small antique box-like four-wheelers, although there were a couple of bogie vehicles for use on fair days or other times of exceptional traffic. The first class could hardly be described as the acme of comfort, and for third-class passengers the accommodation comprised only wooden seats, in which the journey time of one hour twenty minutes was indeed quite long enough! However, the waits at the stations for shunting of vans and wagons, particularly at Ballydehob, where the engine also took water, gave passengers the opportunity to stretch their legs.

At Skibbereen, the headquarters of the line, where the spare engines and stock were kept, the station was adjacent to that of the broad-gauge line and was a terminal bay, from which trains had to reverse into a siding before setting out for Schull. There was also a small workshop capable of effecting light repairs, but for major overhauls the engines had to be sent to Cork, or in Great Southern days more probably to Limerick. This of course involved transhipment over the broad gauge.

The severe coal shortage which occurred in Ireland during the war years, owing to the restriction of imports from England, caused train services to be drastically pruned or withdrawn entirely; the service on the Schull & Skib-bereen was suspended on 15 April 1944. Attempts had been made in 1942 to run the engines on peat, but with only partial success. Services were resumed on 11 December 1945, but an even worse fuel crisis occurred in 1946, and the trains were again withdrawn on 27 January 1947, this time never to be resumed. An official order of abandonment was obtained by CIE in 1952. It is unlikely that the railway would have survived much longer in any case, as competing buses were already running through to Schull, operated by CIE, which obviously intended to close the railway.

LOCOMOTIVES AND ROLLING STOCK

The first three engines were of the 0–4–0 enclosed tramway type, built by Dick Kerr of Kilmarnock in 1886, nos 1 *Marion*, 2 *Ida* and 3 *Ilen*. They proved insufficiently powerful for the steep gradients and had to be modified; no 2

Specimen ticket of Schull & Skibbereen Tramway

was eventually rebuilt with a larger boiler in 1905. In 1888 a 4–4–0T with inside frames, no 4 *Erin*, was obtained from Nasmyth Wilson. It was notable in being the first engine in Ireland to be fitted with a Belpaire firebox. Another 4–4–0T appeared in 1906, from Peckett of Bristol, no 1 *Gabriel* (the original no 1 being scrapped in that year). This differed from no 4 in having outside frames, much favoured on some narrow-gauge lines, and another similar engine no 3 *Kent*, came from the same maker in 1914, when the original no 3 was scrapped. The rebuilt no 2 lasted until 1925.

These were all the engines which ran on the railway in its independent days. The survivors became GSR nos 1S, 3S and 4S. No 4 had lost its name by 1929, but no 1, scrapped in 1936, and no 3 retained theirs.

In 1938 the Great Southern transferred an engine from the closed Cork & Muskerry Railway, an 0–4–4T built by T. Green of Leeds in 1893. It had been Cork & Muskerry no 6, and became 6S on the Schull & Skibbereen, which never had a no 5. Unfortunately when it first got there it could not be used as it was discovered that the couplings were at different heights from rail level on

SCHULL & SKIBBEREEN TRAMWAY 121

the two railways! The engine was sent to Inchicore for this to be put right, but it was then found to be too large for some platforms. When this matter had also been attended to, it did some useful work.

The last surviving engines, nos 3, 4 and 6, were conveyed to Inchicore on the closure of the railway, but were not officially withdrawn until April 1954.

CHAPTER 9

CORK BLACKROCK & PASSAGE RAILWAY

Originally built to 5ft 3in gauge, later converted to 3ft. Urban railway out of Cork mainly along the western shores of Cork Harbour.

Incorporated 1846. Opened 1850. Extended to Crosshaven under authorisation of 1896 under title of CORK BLACKROCK & PASSAGE EXTENSION ACT. Opened to Monkstown in 1902 and completed to Crosshaven in 1904 with gauge of 3ft, together with the conversion of the original line from Cork to Passage. Became part of GREAT SOUTHERN RAILWAYS in 1925.

Route mileage: 16 miles.

Principal places served:
 South eastern suburbs of Cork, Passage, Monkstown, Crosshaven.

Closed 1932.

The Cork Blackrock & Passage Railway was unusual among 3ft gauge lines in that its origins went back before the Tramways (Ireland) Act of 1883. It was in fact one of the earliest of Irish railways and moreover was the first railway in the city of Cork itself, having started operating a year earlier than the Cork & Bandon and five years before the GSWR finally reached the centre of the city.

 The first proposals for a railway between Cork and Passage were put forward as far back as 1836, at which time there was a good service of paddle steamers to this popular watering place on the western shores of Lough Mahon, which is part of the large sheltered stretch of water known as Cork Harbour. Passage was also at that time an important dockyard town, and it was from there that the *Sirius*, the first steamer to cross the Atlantic, sailed in 1838.

 The 1836 plans were abortive, but in 1845 no less than three companies

Page 123 (*above*) Ireland's most numerous class, the 'maids of all work' of the GS & WR, of which 111 examples were built between 1866 and 1903 and which became class J15 on the GSR. No 255, in final rebuilt condition, as running during one of the periodic coal shortages which were to some extent responsible for dieselisation is seen here at Bray on a Dublin suburban train on 15 April 1948. The white circles on the tender and smokebox door were to indicate that the engine was an oil-burner, if this were not obvious enough from the large oil tank on the tender; (*below*) one of four handsome 4–4–0s built by the Vulcan Foundry in 1895 for the main line of the Dublin Wicklow & Wexford Railway (later Dublin & South Eastern). No 56 *Rathmines* became GSR 451, having already lost its name, and was scrapped in 1934

Page 124 (above) The up Dublin Mail at Sligo on 18 May 1950, with ex-MGWR 4–4–0 no 539 (formerly 26 *Croagh Patrick*, built in 1910, withdrawn 1952). Note the bilingual public notices; (*below*) Valencia Harbour, most westerly station in Europe, July 1934. There never seems to have been any consistency in the spelling of the name. Maps, guidebooks and timetables issued over the years show no marked preference for either Valencia or Valentia and even the GSR seems to have been unable to make up its mind. The extract from the CIE working timetable (page 53) shows Valentia

applied almost simultaneously to Parliament for powers, the Cork Passage & Kinsale Railway, Cork & Passage Railway, and Cork Blackrock Passage & Monkstown Railway. It was the last named that was successful, and it was authorised on 16 July 1846, under the title of Cork Blackrock & Passage Railway.

It was built to the normal gauge of 5ft 3in, and the first 6½ miles to Passage were opened on 8 June 1850. Traffic at the start was exceedingly heavy, several thousand passengers being conveyed during the first weekend alone. The original terminus, known as City Park, was closed in 1873, and its place taken by a new commodious structure with three platforms and overall roof, Albert Street. These buildings still stand and are now used as the offices of Irish Metal Products Limited. The locomotive repair shop was at Passage.

Not until the turn of the century did the company think of extending its line southwards to the southern end of Cork Harbour at Crosshaven. It was suffering much competition from the GSWR, whose branch to Queenstown (now Cobh) on the eastern side had been built in 1862. On 7 August 1896 the Cork Blackrock & Passage Extension Act was passed, authorising the construction of the 9½ miles to Crosshaven. For reasons of economy the important decision was taken to build the extension to 3ft gauge, saving some £26,500. This meant that it was necessary to convert the original line from Cork to Passage accordingly, and also to obtain new rolling stock and locomotives. It was scheduled to open by 1900, but owing to financial difficulties work had to be suspended. It was however completed and opened as far as Monkstown on 1 August 1902, to Carrigaline on 15 July 1903, and Crosshaven on 1 June 1904.

Shipping services were an important part of the CBPR's operations. At the start it had been in competition with them, but over the years, by acquiring interests in shipping concerns, it was able to run its trains in connection and eventually came to own much of the shipping fleet operating in and around Cork Harbour. In all the company possessed over the years sixteen steamships, of which three survived to be acquired by the Great Southern in 1925. One of its principal services operated between Monkstown and Queenstown (on the other side of Cork Harbour) and Aghada, and the times of these steamers were actually incorporated in the railway timetable; in 1910 there were six through trains on weekdays (four on Sundays) between Cork and Crosshaven, with additional workings to Monkstown, where steamer connections were made. Weekend traffic during the summer season was much heavier, requiring all four locomotives to be in use, with no spare available in case of breakdowns.

The CBPR was one of the few narrow-gauge lines to pay its way, in earlier years at any rate. In 1902, for instance, it made a profit of £3,807, taking into account steamship operations. It was however exceptional for a 3ft gauge Irish

H

railway in that it was a busy urban railway out of a large city. Unlike any other narrow-gauge line, its traffic warranted double track, between Cork and Blackrock; this was made possible by the conversion to narrow gauge. The rest remained single track, with passing places at Rochestown, Passage, Monkstown, and Carrigaline. The line was exceptionally well laid and maintained, and much of it was level, skirting the shores of Lough Mahon, with nothing very fearsome in the way of gradients. Consequently speeds over 50mph were commonplace, again unusual for 3ft gauge. There was a tunnel near Passage, about 500 yards long, a substantial viaduct at Crosshaven, and two or three other bridges, one of which was blown up during the 'troubles' of 1922, halting services for several months.

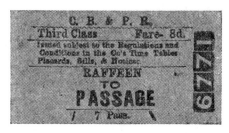

Specimen ticket of the Cork Blackrock & Passage Railway

Traffic was at its peak during the years immediately following World War I, and in fact became more than the railway could handle with its existing resources. Some coaches were borrowed from the Lough Swilly and a small 2–4–0T from the County Donegal, which enabled an extra workman's train to be run from Monkstown to Cork. However, road competition, long present in the shape of the Cork City electric trams, began to be really felt in later years from the inevitable omnibus. In 1932 continued losses caused the Great Southern to close the line, the Monkstown–Crosshaven section on 31 May and the rest of the line at the end of the summer season on 10 September.

LOCOMOTIVES AND ROLLING STOCK

In broad-gauge days the line was worked by three 2–2–2WTs, nos 1–3, built by Sharp Brothers in 1850, makers nos 655/6/62. No 2 later received a saddle tank, but otherwise they were practically unaltered during the whole of their half century's existence, apart from the fitting of vacuum brakes. The livery was light green, lined out in black and yellow.

For the narrow gauge four 2–4–2Ts were built by Neilson Reid in 1899, works nos 5564–7. They were painted black with vermilion and white lines. In spite of their rather clumsy appearance they were very fast engines, and their 4ft 6in diameter wheels were the largest on any Irish narrow-gauge railway.

They were numbered 4 to 7 and the Great Southern duly renumbered them 4P to 7P. On the closing of the line in 1932 they were transferred to the Cavan & Leitrim and renumbered 10L to 13L in that railway's stock, by the casting of new small numberplates of the same pattern as the old CBPR ones. No 7 (13L) was renovated at Inchicore and the other three at Cork, Glanmire Road, workshops, whence they went direct to the CLR. No 11L was scrapped in 1939 and 13L in 1954. The other two lasted until the closure of the Cavan & Leitrim in 1959.

The narrow-gauge coaching stock consisted entirely of bogie vehicles, mostly of the compartment type, but with a few saloons, and provided first- and third-class accommodation.

CHAPTER 10

CORK & MUSKERRY LIGHT
RAILWAY

Began as an urban railway in the streets of the city of Cork, serving outlying villages to the west, mostly a roadside line. 3ft gauge.

Incorporated 1883 under Tramways Act of that year. Opened to Blarney Castle 1887 and to Coachford 1888. DONOUGHMORE EXTENSION RAILWAY (worked by CMLR) authorised 1890 and opened 1893. Became part of GREAT SOUTHERN RAILWAYS 1925.

Route mileage: 18 miles

Principal places served:
   Western suburbs of Cork, Coachford, Blarney, Donoughmore.

Closed 1934.

The other 3ft gauge line out of Cork was quite different from the Cork Blackrock & Passage. The CMLR ran for the first 3½ miles out of Cork along the public highway. It was a little unusual in so far as it actually penetrated the boundaries of a large city. Other narrow-gauge lines were almost all of an entirely rural nature.

   The original Act of incorporation dated 12 December 1883 provided for the construction of 18 miles of line to Blarney and Coachford. The capital of £75,000 was supported by the usual baronial guarantee.

   The line to Blarney, 8¾ miles from the Cork terminus, was opened first, on 8 August 1887, and the branch to Coachford on 18 March 1888. This left the Blarney line at Coachford Junction, 2½ miles short of the terminus, and ran to Coachford, a distance of 9¼ miles. Blarney is a pleasant village of some thousand inhabitants, well known for its fifteenth-century castle, of which only the 85ft high square keep now remains.

The other leg of the CMLR was a separate company, the Donoughmore Extension Railway, authorised on 6 June 1890 and opened on 6 May 1893, 6½ miles from St Anns where it left the Blarney main line. It was worked by the Cork & Muskerry from the start.

When the Cork City Tramways system was opened in December 1898 the route ran for about three-quarters of a mile alongside the CMLR—a unique situation, so far as the British Isles is concerned, of electric and steam tramways running side by side along the public highway, each on its own track without physical connection.

The main shed and workshops were at Cork, where the railway had a considerable area of enclosed space, bounded by the River Lee. Here too was the station with a single platform and an overall roof. There were small locomotive sheds at the three termini, and Coachford also had a carriage shed. There were turntables at Blarney and Donoughmore, but not at Coachford, whence engines had to work back to Cork bunker first; the engines from the other two places were usually turned.

Specimen ticket of the Cork & Muskerry Light Railway

Of all the narrow-gauge systems in Ireland, the Cork & Muskerry was one of the most unsuited to withstand the impact of road competition, and the Great Southern inevitably closed it on 29 December 1934. However, it managed to outlast its first rivals, the Cork City Electric Tramways, which had already ceased operation on 30 September 1931.

LOCOMOTIVES AND ROLLING STOCK

The first three engines were 2–4–0Ts built by the Falcon Engine Company in 1887, works nos 137, 136 and 138, no 1 *City of Cork*, no 2 *Coachford* and no 3 *St Anns*. They had cowcatchers and bells, as they had to work along the public highway, and the wheels and motion were also at first enclosed. They were later rebuilt as 4–4–0Ts.

No 4 *Blarney* was an 0–4–2WT, built by Kitson in 1888. It was rather small, was not popular, and was scrapped in 1911.

Then came two 0–4–4Ts, an unusual wheel arrangement for the narrow gauge, and the inevitable outside cylinders made them almost a unique type (the Caledonian once had some, and there was one on the Swindon Marlborough & Andover Junction Railway). No 5 *Donoughmore* and no 6 *The Muskerry* were from T. Green & Sons, of Leeds, in 1892 and 1893.

Then followed two 4–4–0Ts very similar to the rebuilt nos 1–3, no 7 *Peake* by Falcon in 1898 and no 8 *Dripsey* from the Brush Electrical Co, as Falcon had then become, in 1904.

The last engine was another 4–4–0T from Hunslet in 1919. It became no 4 *Blarney*, in place of the earlier 0–4–2WT, but was even less fortunate than its predecessor, being broken up in 1927 after an even shorter life.

No 3 was scrapped in 1924, but the others all survived to become Great Southern engines in 1925, retaining their numbers with the addition of the suffix K, but losing their names, and of course receiving the inevitable grey unlined livery. After the closure of the line the surviving engines, four 4–4–0Ts and the two 0–4–4Ts, were dismantled, but their frames and boilers were kept at Inchicore for a few years with a view to possible future use; 0–4–4T no 6 was resuscitated in 1938 and sent to the Schull & Skibbereen as no 6S, where it lasted until the line closed in 1944.

At one time it was intended to restore no 5 for use on the Tralee & Dingle as no 9T but most probably it never received this number, as the scheme was dropped. It would have been quite unsuitable for the severe gradients on the Tralee & Dingle, for which six-coupled engines were used exclusively.

The coaching stock, comprising the usual first and third classes, were mostly bogie vehicles of the saloon type with entrances at either end. The slatted wooden seats in the third class were not the acme of comfort, even for the comparatively short journey time to Blarney of 37 minutes, and had to be endured for over an hour on the other branches. At the railway's most prosperous period Blarney usually had some six trains a day, weekdays and Sundays, the other lines rather less, but these services gradually diminished from 1925 onwards. Trains normally conveyed any available freight traffic and so were mixed.

CHAPTER 11

TRALEE & DINGLE RAILWAY

Picturesque 3ft gauge railway running through fine mountainous scenery, with severe gradients.

Incorporated 1888 under Tramways Act of 1883. Opened 1891. Became part of GREAT SOUTHERN RAILWAYS in 1925.

Route mileage: 37½ miles.

Principal places served:
  Tralee and Dingle peninsula, part of Kerry, the most westerly county in Ireland.

Closed 1953.

The Tralee & Dingle was not only the most spectacular of the several 3ft gauge railways which came into the hands of the Great Southern at the 1925 grouping but was among the most attractive lines in the whole of Ireland, a good many of which were the long branches reaching out to the Atlantic coast.

Kerry is the most westerly of all the counties of Ireland and the Dingle peninsula one of its most remote areas. The county town of Tralee is still served by rail from the picturesque Killarney area, probably one of the best-known parts of the country from a tourist point of view. Dingle, with a small harbour and a population of some 1,500, is the most westerly town in Europe. It is one of the few remote outposts where the Irish language is still in everyday use, although it is the official language throughout the Republic.

Under the Tramways (Ireland) Act of 1883 approval was obtained on 17 September 1888 for the building of the railway, and it was opened on 31 March 1891. It consisted of a main line, 31½ miles in length, from Tralee to Dingle, together with a 6 mile branch to Castlegregory, a small watering place on the southern shores of Tralee Bay. The only other place of importance was Annas-caul, some 10 miles from Dingle. The line was dependent on a baronial guaran-tee.

For several miles at either end the railway ran, tramway fashion, by the side of the pulic road, and the first 10 miles from Tralee to Castlegregory Junction, where the branch diverged, were largely level or slightly undulating following the contours of the road. The central portion, however, was of a very different nature. To reach Dingle, the line had to cross the Slieve Mish range of moun-tains, which includes Mount Brandon, 3,127ft, Ireland's second highest summit, and the altitude of 680ft attained at Glenagalt was the third highest point re-corded on any Irish railway. The climb began after leaving Castlegregory Junction at 1 in 35, from which section a fine view of Castlegregory Bay below was obtained, and the gradient, then steepening to 1 in 30, was unbroken for 4 miles through Glenmore Pass until the summit was reached. A long descent followed, much of it at 1 in 29, with another small peak, to Annascaul, 20 miles from Tralee. Then followed another 5 mile ascent, not quite so severe, but continuous and tough enough, to a second peak, Garrynadur. Next came a 2 mile descent, largely at 1 in 29, which had to be surmounted by up trains, and finally an undulating 5 miles into Dingle. Here there was a passenger terminus with one platform and an overall roof, but the line continued for another half mile to the harbour. Dingle was almost, but not quite, the most westerly railhead in Europe, this distinction belonging to Valentia. The upper reaches of the Tralee & Dingle Railway comprised a horseshoe curve and two large viaducts, and was undoubtedly the most gruelling line in the country; there was nothing quite like it anywhere else in Ireland. The nearest approach was per-haps the Ballymena and Cushendall line of the NCC. This section of the Tralee & Dingle was the scene of two major accidents, a runaway train on 29 May 1893, which resulted in the loss of three lives, and another on 1 March 1907, with not quite such serious consequences.

In 1907–8 a grant from the Ireland Development Fund enabled the company, never in a prosperous state, to have two deviations made with a view to safer working; one of these enabled the abandonment of the curved viaduct which had been the scene of the 1893 accident.

The headquarters and workshops of the system were at Tralee, where the station was about a quarter of a mile from the GSWR, but exchange facilities were provided by a connecting line through the streets.

The trains normally comprised two per weekday, with extras on Saturdays and at other times, and one on Sundays; the latter was discontinued in 1925. They were usually mixed and consequently spent a considerable time at inter-mediate stations; the overall journey time was some $2\frac{1}{4}$ hours.

Page 133 (above) The narrow-gauge Tralee & Dingle Railway on the other side of Dingle Bay came a close second to Valencia for the title of most westerly station. This view, taken in 1934, shows TDR 2–6–2T no 5 outside what was at any rate the most westerly European running shed, with the station in the background; (below) Cork & Muskerry Railway. Together with the CBPR, these two were the first of the GSR narrow-gauge lines to succumb, which they did in the 1930s. This view, taken at Blarney Castle in 1934, shows 4–4–0T no 8. Similar engines were used on the Cavan & Leitrim

Page 134 (*above*) First train on the Crosshaven extension, Cork Blackrock & Passage Railway, June 1904; (*below*) the West Clare was the last of the GSR narrow-gauge lines to remain in operation, but even dieselisation could not prevent its closure in 1961. A 1934 view at Kilkee, with 4–6–0T no 11

Page 135 (*above*) A Schull & Skibbereen train pausing at Hollyhill, a roadside stopping place, July 1938. Note the four-wheeled coaches comprising two classes. The engine is 4–4–0 no 4. Services finally ceased in January 1947; (*below*) The Cavan & Leitrim survived until 1959. Steam-worked to the end, it became a Mecca for railway enthusiasts in its final years. This view, taken shortly before closure, shows 2–6–0T no 3 transferred from the Tralee & Dingle Railway

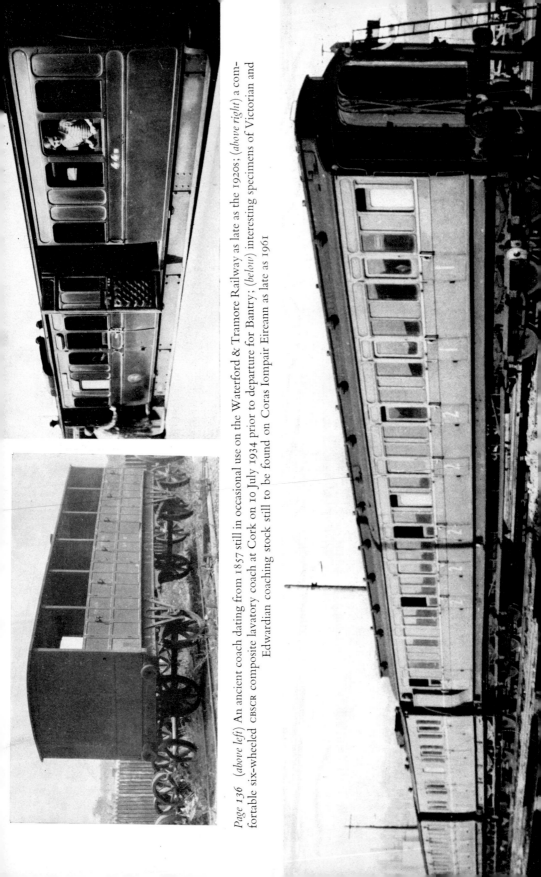

Page 136 (*above left*) An ancient coach dating from 1857 still in occasional use on the Waterford & Tramore Railway as late as the 1920s; (*above right*) a comfortable six-wheeled CBSCR composite lavatory coach at Cork on 10 July 1934 prior to departure for Bantry; (*below*) interesting specimens of Victorian and Edwardian coaching stock still to be found on Coras Iompair Eireann as late as 1961

By 1939 the deterioration of the track was so serious that the alternatives were either extensive improvements or discontinuation of the passenger service, and as the road between Tralee and Dingle had by then been improved, it was decided to substitute a bus service.

In its earlier years before being taken over by the Great Southern the line was not exactly a ramshackle concern but it had been constructed and was run 'on the cheap'. Discipline was undoubtedly lax, and the staff were often to be found somewhat the worse for wear, owing to overindulgence in their favourite beverage. Even the small isolated Castlegregory Junction had a bar, to which it was normal procedure for the crews to adjourn whilst the main and branch trains duly made their connections. Money was always tight and upkeep of rolling stock and track maintenance were kept to a minimum.

All passenger services ceased on 17 April 1939, and the Castlegregory branch was closed entirely. From then on there was but one freight train daily between Tralee and Dingle, and this continued until 1947. Thereafter operation was confined to once a month in connection with Dingle fair day, which occurred on the fourth Saturday, when there was enough cattle traffic to warrant the running of one or more special trains to Dingle. The length of these, which were necessarily double-headed over the severe central section, caused some operating problems, when there were only three serviceable engines.

However, the expense of maintaining a costly line of railway for the running of the occasional train on such a basis could obviously not continue indefinitely and CIE came to the inevitable decision that the line must close completely.

In the final years these monthly cattle specials became famous in the railway enthusiasts' world. Permits to travel were readily granted by CIE, and many were the pilgrimages made from far and wide, especially from England, by devotees taking the last opportunity of travelling over one of Ireland's most interesting and spectacular railways.

The last of these memorable specials ran on 26 and 27 June 1953, the rails were lifted soon after and traces of the trackbed are now almost the only visible evidence of what was an outstandingly fascinating railway.

Specimen ticket of the TDLR

LOCOMOTIVES AND ROLLING STOCK

For working such a line obviously some powerful locomotives were required
and for the opening three 2–6–0Ts were obtained from the Hunslet Engine
Company. The fourth engine, for working the Castlegregory branch, was a
much smaller 0–4–2T, but distinctive in having cabs at both ends and duplicate
controls to obviate the need to turn the engine. On the main line all engines
worked chimney first. Later there were four more 2–6–0Ts, and one 2–6–2T.
The 2–6–0T wheel arrangement has always been extremely rare in the British
Isles, and these seven engines on the Tralee & Dingle outnumbered all the rest
put together.

No	Type	Maker	Date built	Maker's no	Disposal
1	2–6–0T	Hunslet	1889	477	Scrapped 1953
2	2–6–0T	Hunslet	1889	478	Scrapped 1953
3	2–6–0T	Hunslet	1889	479	Transferred to Cavan & Leitrim 1941. Scrapped 1959
4	0–4–2T	Kerr Stuart	1903	836	Scrapped 1908
5	2–6–2T	Hunslet	1892	555	To Cavan & Leitrim 1949. Now preserved in the USA
6	2–6–0T	Hunslet	1898	677	To West Clare 1953, Cavan & Leitrim 1957. Scrapped 1960
7	2–6–0T	Kerr Stuart	1902	800	Scrapped 1928
8*	2–6–0T	Kerr Stuart	1903	836	To Cavan & Leitrim 1941. Scrapped 1959
8	2–6–0T	Hunslet	1910	1051	To West Clare 1953. Scrapped 1955

* Renumbered 4 in 1908.

The engines were never named, and on being taken over by the Great
Southern in 1925 retained their numbers with the addition of the suffix T,
new plates of GSWR design being cast.

The livery was dark green, lined out in red and cream, but the Great Southern
repainted them, at first in plain grey, and later in black.

The coaching stock rather surprisingly consisted of bogie vehicles right from
the start. In all, twenty vehicles were obtained, mostly from the Bristol Carriage & Wagon Company between 1890 and 1907, consisting variously of
thirds, brake thirds, and first and third composites. When passenger services
ceased, most of the coaches were retained for a while, but eventually some of

them were transferred to the West Clare and at least one to the Cavan & Leitrim. The livery of the coaching stock was purple-brown.

The Tralee & Dingle never experimented with railcars or diesel propulsion; in 1922 it built at Tralee workshops a small four-wheeled inspection car with a Ford petrol engine. The Great Southern transferred it to the West Clare, and it was still to be seen at Ennis when that line closed in 1961.

The goods stock consisted of some eighty vehicles of all kinds, and by the very nature of its traffic about thirty were for the conveyance of cattle.

CHAPTER 12

WEST and SOUTH CLARE RAILWAYS

A 3ft gauge railway.

WEST CLARE RAILWAY   Incorporated 1884 under 1883 Tramways Act. Opened 1887 from Ennis to Miltown Malbay.
SOUTH CLARE RAILWAY   Incorporated 1884 as extension of WEST CLARE RAILWAY from Miltown Malbay to Kilrush and Kilkee. Opened 1892.

Both concerns worked as one system.
Became part of GREAT SOUTHERN RAILWAYS in 1925.

Route mileage: WEST CLARE RAILWAY 27 miles
SOUTH CLARE RAILWAY 26 miles.

Principal places served:
Ennis, Ennistymon, Miltown Malbay, Kilrush, Kilkee.

Closed 1961.

County Clare on the west coast of Ireland is largely a barren expanse of country with its coastline exposed to the Atlantic gales. Its first railway was from Limerick to Ennis, the county town, opened in 1859, followed ten years later by an extension northward to Athenry; both lines were worked by and later became part of the Waterford & Limerick Railway.

There was a proposal in 1860 to construct a 5ft 3in gauge line between Kilrush, a busy little port and important market town on the estuary of the Shannon, and Kilkee, 8 miles distant on the coast, an attractive resort well protected from the boisterous Atlantic by the Duggerna ledge of rocks. This project did not however materialise, and the west coast remained without rail communication until 1883. In that year the West Clare Railway was formed, and an order dated 26 May 1884 authorised the construction of the 27 miles of 3ft gauge railway from Ennis to Miltown Malbay, another small resort with a good sandy beach and picturesque surroundings. Interest on the capital was provided in part by a baronial guarantee. Construction was slow, but the line was duly opened on 2 July 1887. Meanwhile a separate company, the South Clare Railway, was authorised on 6 July 1884 to form an extension from the West Clare at Miltown Malbay southwards to Kilkee and Kilrush, again supported by a baronial guarantee. Kilkee was the terminus of the main line, 48 miles in all throughout from Ennis, Kilrush being served by a 4 mile branch from Moyasta Junction. There was a direct spur at Moyasta, by which trains could run direct between Kilrush and Kilkee. There was no platform face to this avoiding loop, which was mainly used by boat trains run in connection with the steamer services from Limerick to Cappa Pier at Kilrush. The South Clare Railway was opened throughout to passenger traffic on 23 December 1892, but freight had meanwhile been conveyed since the previous August. Although the companies were nominally separate, they were worked as one by the West Clare throughout their existence and in 1925 became part of the Great Southern. There were normally four trains each weekday and one on Sundays, throughout between Ennis and Kilkee, with branch connections to Kilrush. The 48 mile journey took about three hours.

Despite the sparsely populated nature of the area, traffic was always reasonably good, both passenger and freight, and the monthly fairs at Miltown Malbay and Ennistymon provided a good revenue from cattle. Dieselisation enabled the overall journey time for passenger trains to be brought down to 2hr 20min, and with a more frequent service the prospects seemed reasonably good. It was hoped that this modernisation would ensure the line's future but it was closed completely in 1961, the last of the once numerous 3ft gauge systems in Ireland.

Specimen ticket of the West
Clare Railway

LOCOMOTIVES AND ROLLING STOCK

The locomotives, which totalled sixteen over the years, were all six-coupled, consisting of 0–6–0T, 0–6–2T, 2–6–2T and 4–6–0T wheel arrangements. The four original 0–6–0Ts were not powerful enough, and until the coming of their larger successors the railway had a bad reputation for timekeeping. The first of the new ones were three 0–6–2Ts, obtained in 1892 by G. Hopkins, then newly appointed as locomotive superintendent, having come from the MGWR. He was succeeded in 1902 by W. J. Carter. These engines were nominally intended for the South Clare Railway, opened in that year, and actually bore the initials SCR on their number plates, but in practice like all the other engines they were used over the whole line. These 0–6–2Ts were unusual in that the trailing wheels were of the same diameter as the six-coupled drivers, namely 4ft. The complete locomotive history is summarised as follows:

Number	Name	Type	Builders	Date	Works no	With- drawn	Scrapped
1	—	0–6–0T	Bagnall	1887	730	1913	
2	—	0–6–0T	Bagnall	1887	738	1900	
3	Clifden	0–6–0T	Bagnall	1887	793	1916	
4	Bessborough	0–6–0T	Bagnall	1887	794	1901	
5	Slieve Callan	0–6–2T	Dübs & Co	1892	2890	1959	*
6	Saint Senan	0–6–2T	Dübs & Co	1892	2891	1956	
7	Lady Inchiquin	0–6–2T	Dübs & Co	1892	2892	1922	
8	Lisdoonvarna	2–6–2T	Dübs & Co	1894	3169	1925	
9	Fergus	2–6–2T	T. Green	1898	229	1954	1955
2	Ennis	2–6–2T	T. Green	1900	234	1955	
4	Liscannor	2–6–2T	T. Green	1901	236	1928	
10	Lahinch	4–6–0T	Kerr Stuart	1903	818	1953	
11	Kilkee	4–6–0T	Bagnall	1909	1881	1953	1955
1	Kilrush	4–6–0T	Hunslet	1912	1098	1953	
3	Ennistymon	4–6–0T	Hunslet	1922	1432	1953	1953
7	Malbay	4–6–0T	Hunslet	1922	1433	1955	

* Restored 1962 to green livery and now stands on a plinth surmounted by a substantial awning at Ennis.

In replacement of the four engines withdrawn in 1953 the Great Southern transferred two 2–6–0Ts from the closed Tralee & Dingle Railway, nos 6T and 8T; 6T later went on to the Cavan & Leitrim. They were found to be less powerful and popular than the 4–6–0Ts which they replaced.

In 1925 the Great Southern removed all the names, which had been displayed by cast plates on the tank sides; the numbers were retained with the addition of the suffix C, new plates of GSWR pattern being cast. The engines were repainted in plain grey. The workshops and headquarters of the line were at Ennis, and there were small one-engine sub-sheds at Kilkee and Kilrush.

The coaching stock was nearly all six-wheelers, mainly of the compartment type, first and third class being provided until diesel days, but some bogie coaches were transferred from the Tralee & Dingle after that line had ceased passenger operation in 1939.

In 1928 two Drewry railcars appeared, nos 395 and 396, but they were unable to cope with the gradients on the main line and were used for a few years between Kilrush and Kilkee.

In 1951 it was decided to change over to diesel traction for passenger working, and four railcars, nos 286–9 (later 3386–9) were obtained from Walker Bros of Wigan. They were unidirectional, with the power bogie articulated from the passenger coach, not unlike those of the County Donegal, and were supplemented by a few trailers converted from locomotive-hauled passenger rolling stock. Finally, to dispense with steam working altogether three diesel locomotives were built in 1955, also by Walker Bros of Wigan; these were of the 0–4–4–0 variety with central cab. As first numbered D31–3, they later became F501–3. All these engines have now been scrapped.

CHAPTER 13

CAVAN & LEITRIM RAILWAY

A 3ft gauge railway in the northern part of the central plain of Ireland.

Incorporated 1883 under Tramways Act of that year under title of CAVAN LEITRIM & ROSCOMMON LIGHT RAILWAY & TRAMWAY COMPANY LIMITED. Opened: main line 1887, branch to Arigna 1888, and $3\frac{1}{2}$ mile extension to coal mines in 1920 under title of ARIGNA VALLEY RAILWAY.

Route mileage (excluding Arigna extension): $48\frac{1}{2}$ miles.

Principal places served:
 Ballinamore, Belturbet, Arigna, Mohill, Dromod.

Closed 1961.

The Cavan & Leitrim was one of the first light railways to be promoted under the Tramways Act of 1883. As its title implied it ran through the two counties named, situated around the edge of the central plain of Ireland, bounded to the north by the Iron Mountain range, with a highest peak, Cuilcagh, rising to 2,188ft. This area was so called because ironstone was once mined there and in later years it was also found to have deposits of coal, almost the only ones in the whole country. The coal was of indifferent quality, but usable, and was one of the reasons for the planning of the railway in the first place, and in its last years for its continued existence, especially during the several periods of severe coal shortage. More recently a 15,000kW coal-burning electric generating station has been built. The area abounds in small lakes, from which the River Shannon rises. Through such pleasant but poor agricultural land, thinly populated, ran the Cavan & Leitrim Railway, serving no townships of any size; only Belturbet, a prosperous little market town could boast more than a thousand inhabitants.

 The line was first incorporated on 3 December 1883 under the title of Cavan

Leitrim & Roscommon Light Railway & Tramway, and was unusual for a railway in being a limited company and not a statutory one. Not all of the originally planned lines materialised, and the railway as finally built consisted of a main line from Belturbet, also served by a branch of the Great Northern, to Dromod, where it made contact with the MGWR main line to Sligo. The Midland incidentally had opposed the building of the CLR, and was unco-operative both during its construction and in providing transfer facilities between the two systems, although the two stations adjoined each other. At Belturbet the one station was shared by the two railways, with adequate inter-change facilities.

The length of the main line was 33¾ miles, and it was opened on 17 October 1887. Gradients on the whole were fairly easy, the steepest being 1 in 50. The principal townships en route were Ballyconnell, Ballinamore and Mohill.

Specimen ticket of the Cavan
& Leitrim Light Railway

Ballinamore was the hub of the system, where the shed and workshops were situated, and was the junction for the branch to Arigna, 14¾ miles, opened on 2 May 1888. Eventually, as late as 1920, the further 3½ miles to the coal mines was constructed, under the title of Arigna Valley Railway. The railways were at that time under government control, and the extension was built by order of the Board of Trade under the Defence of the Realm Act. In 1925, of course, the Cavan & Leitrim became part of the Great Southern system.

Before World War I there were three trains each way daily over the main line, all mixed, with connections to Arigna; the journey between Belturbet and Dromod took a little over two hours. Between the wars there were only two trains on the Belturbet and Arigna sections, and there were never any regular Sunday services. The timetable required an engine to be stationed overnight at both Dromod and Belturbet, where there were small sheds, but otherwise all the locomotives would be found at Ballinamore.

Never a prosperous line, the railway nevertheless managed to secure a reasonable amount of traffic of all sorts, cattle, and in later years, coal, being of predominant importance, and it was not quite so susceptible to road com-petition as some comparable lines.

In the end it was almost the last survivor of the once numerous 3ft gauge

I

railways and was only beaten by the West Clare, which lasted two years longer. Whereas the latter had been modernised by dieselisation, the Cavan & Leitrim remained completely steam worked to the end and never experimented with any other form of power. For this reason it became during the 1950s a mecca for many railway enthusiasts, and to the great regret not only of these devotees but of all regular local users too, the last train ran on 31 March 1959.

LOCOMOTIVES AND ROLLING STOCK

All but one of the locomotives were of the 4–4–0T type, eight of which were built by Robert Stephenson in 1884, works nos 2612–19, no 1 *Isabel*, 2 *Kathleen*, 3 *Lady Edith*, 4 *Violet*, 5 *Gertrude*, 6 *May*, 7 *Olive* and 8 *Queen Victoria*. The names, except no 8, were after daughters of the directors of the company. On absorption by the Great Southern in 1925 they nominally became nos 1L to 8L and officially lost their names, in accordance with Great Southern practice; however some of them retained their brass numerals and nameplates for several years. Nos 5 and 6 were scrapped early, in 1925 and 1927 respectively. No 7 went in 1945, but the others lasted until closure in 1959. No 2 is now in Belfast Museum, and no 3 is preserved in the United States.

One more engine was built for the Cavan & Leitrim; this was a large 0–6–4T, no 9 *King Edward*, by Robert Stephenson in 1904 (works no 3136). It was however much too heavy for the line and was little used, being cut up in 1934. The livery was basically dark green with red and white lining, though there were variations over the years, and this was changed inevitably to grey and then black by the Great Southern.

After the grouping several other engines came to the section. First were the four Cork Blackrock & Passage 2–4–2Ts, which became nos 10L to 13L. Later, four engines came from the Tralee & Dingle, three 2–6–0Ts and one 2–6–2T. These retained their TDR numbers, 3T, 4T, 5T and 6T, so that for a time there were two engines numbered 3 and 4.

Two other strangers which appeared earlier on were a couple of NCC 0–4–2STs, nos 101A and 102A (originally Ballymena Cushendall & Red Bay Railway) which were on loan in 1920–1, when they worked on the newly opened Arigna Valley Railway branch to the coalmines.

The coaching stock, first and third class, consisted of handsome clerestory bogie vehicles, saloon type with end verandahs, American style, and painted red-brown.

CHAPTER 14

GREAT SOUTHERN RAILWAYS
and CORAS IOMPAIR EIREANN

GREAT SOUTHERN RAILWAYS   Compulsory amalgamation as from 1 January 1925 of all railways lying wholly within the Irish Free State. Cross border lines not affected and remained as independent concerns.

CORAS IOMPAIR EIREANN   New company formed under Government control as from 1 January 1945. Fully nationalised on 1 June 1950.

Arising out of the Railways (Directorate) Act of 1924, which had been approved by both the Senate and the Dáil, the Railway Tribunal of the Irish Free State pronounced on 1 January 1925 that the amalgamation scheme was complete and had only to be signed and sealed. This provided for the compulsory amalgamation of the four principal railways lying wholly within the Free State into one company, the Great Southern Railways (Ireland)—to give it its full title—and absorption of the remainder. The GSWR, MGWR and CBSCR had already agreed between themselves for amalgamation from 12 November 1924, under the title of Great Southern Railway, but the DSER had wished to continue its independence.

The new board consisted of fifteen representatives of the four amalgamated railways, the Great Southern & Western, Midland Great Western, Dublin & South Eastern and Cork Bandon & South Coast, and one director nominated by the London Midland & Scottish Railway. The companies to be absorbed were:

Athenry & Tuam Extension
Ballinascarthy & Timoleague Junction
Ballinrobe & Claremorris
Baltimore Extension
Cavan & Leitrim
Clonakilty Extension
Cork Blackrock & Passage

Cork & Muskerry
Cork City
Donoughmore Extension
Dublin & Kingstown
Loughrea & Attymon Junction
Schull & Skibbereen (West Carbery Tramway)
South Clare
Timoleague & Courtmacsherry
Tralee & Dingle
Tralee & Fenit
Waterford & Tramore
West Clare

In addition, the following leased and worked railways were henceforth to be operated by the Great Southern:

City of Dublin Junction (hitherto worked by the DSER)
New Ross & Waterford Extension (hitherto worked by the DSER)
Waterford Joint Lines (worked jointly by the DSER and the Fishguard & Rosslare Railways & Harbour Company)
Fishguard & Rosslare Railways & Harbour (leased to and worked jointly by the GSWR and GWR)

The newly constituted Great Southern Railways, which had its headquarters at Kingsbridge, had now around 2,187 route miles, which comprised 2,924 miles of track. It found itself with 623 locomotives, of which 42 were narrow gauge. The principal railway left outside the amalgamation, because it was partly in the six counties of Northern Ireland, was the Great Northern, and it was to be another 27 years before any attempt at separation was to be made.

From 1931 onwards increasing road competition began to be felt, although the position was helped to some extent by the Road Transport and Railways Act of 1932, which set up a licensing system placing many restrictions on road operators, and again on 1 January 1934 when the GSR took over the Irish Omnibus Company and so gained control of practically all road services outside Dublin. Nevertheless the closure of some of the uneconomic branch lines became inevitable; some were shut entirely, while others lost their passenger services but were kept open for goods traffic. The first casualties in the former category were the spectacular Clifden and Achill lines of the Midland Great Western. The 3ft gauge lines were also amongst the first to succumb, the two local Cork lines going as early as 1932 and 1934. The others survived until World War II, the Schull & Skibbereen only just, and the Tralee & Dingle for freight only, while the Cavan & Leitrim and West Clare lasted until 1959 and 1961 respectively.

World War II did not of course affect the Great Southern Railways directly, as Ireland remained neutral throughout the conflict. There were however various side-effects, chiefly as a result of restriction in the supplies of fuel, both petrol and oil, which affected the road concerns and drove more traffic on to the railways, which were in turn greatly hampered by the shortage of coal, practically all of which had to be imported from Great Britain. During 1942 the position got so bad that some branch lines had to be closed for indefinite periods, in some cases for three years, and services on the main lines had to be restricted to a bare minimum; for a time things almost came to a complete standstill. Various substitutes were tried, of which the most obvious was peat, but it was found to be of little use in locomotive fireboxes. Another fuel crisis occurred during the severe winter of 1946-7, when shipments from England ceased for a time owing to transport difficulties there, and once again services had to be cut practically to nothing. Many Great Southern engines were converted to oil burning, and it was even suggested that this might be permanent in view of the continued uncertainty of obtaining coal, although some was now being imported from America. However by that time the possibilities of dieselisation were being actively explored, and in spite of an inquiry conducted in 1948 by Sir James Milne of the GWR, which recommended the continued use of steam locomotives, the railway was to go over entirely to diesels during the next fifteen years.

Following a general election in the Free State in 1944 the nationalisation of the railway system was considered by the government, and on 29 November of that year a Transport Bill was passed by the Senate and Dáil providing for the creation of a new company, effective from 1 January 1945, to be known as Coras Iompair Eireann (Irish Transport Company). This would be responsible not only for the existing rail and road services of the GSR and the Dublin United Transport Company but also for water and air communication throughout the twenty-six counties. Thus all competition was eliminated as being wasteful and unnecessary—a very sensible arrangement in such a thinly populated country such as Ireland, which can only provide a limited amount of traffic. This has worked out reasonably well in practice, with perhaps a little bias in favour of road operation, but at the same time with a realisation of the importance of the continuation of rail transport under conditions to which it is most suited. Practically every country in the world has come to appreciate that under modern conditions railways can no longer be profit-making concerns (many of them indeed never were) but must receive state subsidy in one form or another to keep them going as a social necessity. Other services, such as postal communication, medical services, hospitals and so on, are experiencing similar problems.

This was still not nationalisation in the full sense, as the newly formed CIE was still a private company, although receiving financial assistance from the government, and it was not until 1 June 1950 that it became completely nationalised under the Transport Act 1950, which gave full government control, with a full-time chairman and six part-time directors, responsible for all transport interests, including inland waterways (the Grand Canal being taken over at the same time).

Tickets of CIE and GSR

Under CIE there have been further closures, indeed the west coast of the country is now almost denuded of rail transport, but the position is not nearly so bad as it would have been under continued private enterprise, or in Northern Ireland, where a vigorous anti-rail policy over the last twenty years—now fortunately showing some signs of abatement—has left only a pitiful vestige of the former system.

Nevertheless even in the south there were rumours of further possible economies and closures, following the McKinsey Report of 1971, by which time the government was subsidising the railways by some five or six million pounds a year. However, there are at least some grounds for hope that this report will not result in wholesale closures.

LOCOMOTIVES AND ROLLING STOCK

The Great Southern Railways drew up a comprehensive scheme to classify all the 623 locomotives inherited from its constituents. The new classification was based on an initial letter denoting the wheel arrangement, tender and tank engines being included in the same group, followed by a number to distinguish the different classes falling within this category. The similarity of the scheme to that adopted by the London & North Eastern Railway two years earlier is so great that it is unlikely to have occurred purely by chance. The letters B, C, D, F, J and K, denoting respectively the 4–6–0, 4–4–2, 4–4–0, 2–4–2, 0–6–0 and 2–6–0 types are in fact identical. The letter A was used by the GSR for its 4–8–0Ts whereas the LNER used it for the 4–6–2 type; and there were some other differences, the LNER using practically the whole of the alphabet, while the GSR did not get beyond P. Narrow-gauge engines were included in the same classification with the addition of the letter N after the initial classification letter.

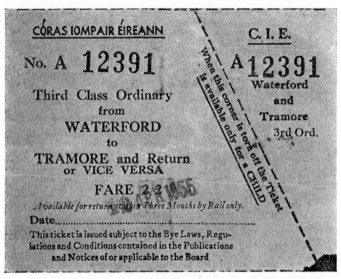

CIE ticket

The scheme was never used in practice amongst the running staff, except perhaps in the case of the ubiquitous J15 0–6–0s. There was an interesting coincidence here, for whilst the J15s of the Great Southern could well be described as 'maids of all work', so did the LNER's J15s occupy much the same position on the old Great Eastern Railway. As for the other classes, they were more often referred to as the '400s' or whatever. Nevertheless it remained the official classification to the end of the steam era.

In spite of the high average age of the locomotives inherited by the GSR, lack of finance prevented replacement on any considerable scale, and after the outbreak of World War II no more conventional steam engines were built. The first and by no means least important, acquisitions were a batch of Maunsell

Woolwich 2–6–0s. After R. E. L. Maunsell had left the GSWR for the South Eastern & Chatham, his initial design was for a 2–6–0 mixed-traffic engine. The first of these appeared from Ashford in 1917, but production was then halted owing to the war. After the war, however, the government authorised the construction of a hundred of these engines at Woolwich Arsenal, mainly as a means of relieving unemployment. Not all were actually erected and the unassembled parts of the remainder were offered for sale as 'do it yourself' kits to any railway interested. Twelve sets were ordered by the MGWR in 1923, and another fifteen by the Great Southern Railways in 1925.

The first engine was actually turned out from Broadstone as MGWR no 49 in April 1925 but before it was even steamed it had been altered to Great Southern Railways 410, the original intention being that the twelve engines would become 410–21. However, when it was decided to purchase another fifteen sets of parts, in order to keep the numbers in one series, no 410 became 372, and the first twenty locomotives 372–91. They were standard with the South Eastern & Chatham N class, with 5ft 6in wheels. Six later ones, nos 393–8, had 6ft driving wheels and corresponded to what eventually became the Southern Railway U class. For some reason there was never a 392, only 26 out of the 27 being completed; possibly the remaining set of parts was used for spares.

This was quite a revolutionary design at the time of its introduction in 1917, Maunsell being one of the first locomotive engineers to appreciate the benefit of long valve travel, and in this respect the engines possessed distinctive features common with Churchward's Great Western Railway engines, particularly the 4300 class 2–6–0s of 1911.

The Great Southern engines were almost identical with their Southern Railway counterparts, except that it was never found necessary to fit them with smoke deflectors. They did yeoman service on the main lines of the Great Southern, principally on the Midland Great Western to Galway, and on the boat trains between Rosslare and Cork.

The first locomotive superintendent of the GSR was J. R. Bazin, who had held the post on the GSWR. In 1929 he was succeeded by W. H. Morton, who was replaced by A. W. Harty in 1932. E. C. Bredin took over in 1937 but became general manager in 1941 and was succeeded by M. J. Ginnetty. C. F. Tyndall took over in 1944 and O. V. S. Bulleid, as 'consulting mechanical engineer', in 1949; he retired on 30 May 1958.

New engines built by the GSR were in fact very few: two mixed-traffic 4–6–0s, nos 501–2, in 1926 to a GSWR design; a 2–6–2T, no 850, in 1928 for the Dublin & South Eastern section, not a very successful machine; a supposedly improved version of the famous 101 class; five 0–6–2Ts, nos 670–4, in 1933 for the DSER section suburban services, which proved to be very good engines indeed;

five 5ft 8½in 4-4-0s in 1936 to Coey's 333 class design of 1907; and three very fine 4-6-0s in 1939.

The first five of the 101 class came out in 1929, nos 700-4, and the second batch, nos 710-19, which had minor differences, in 1934-5. Neither batch was identical to the 101 class, the first having a larger boiler, and these engines never in fact attained the success or popularity of the earlier design.

The final GSR design was an express passenger 4-6-0 for the Dublin–Cork main line. They were the largest express engines to run in Ireland, having a boiler pressure of 225lb psi and three 18½in by 28in cylinders, and were very impressive machines. They were numbered 800-2 and were named after Irish queens, *Maeve*, *Macha* and *Tailte*, in Irish-style lettering on nameplates over the centre driving wheels. Their first livery was a light green, which was later changed to a darker, more bluish shade. *Maeve* is preserved in Belfast Museum.

Two Sentinel four-wheeled shunting engines were obtained in 1927, for work in the Limerick area, and also four Sentinel steam railcars together with six Claytons, for branch-line work. The latter were all dismantled in 1933 and the coach bodies converted for use on the Waterford & Tramore. The Sentinel railcars remained in use until 1941-2, and the engines until 1948.

In the 1930s Drumm battery trains were tried out on the Dublin & South Eastern suburban lines. They consisted of two-coach sets, very similar to a modern diesel railcar, but powered by a 15 ton battery placed between the bogies below floor level. The first train appeared in 1932, followed by another in 1933, and two more in 1939. They did much useful work on the suburban services between Dublin and Bray, and were particularly useful during the coal shortage. They survived until about 1950. Their chief disadvantage was their range, which was restricted by the need to recharge the batteries.

O. V. S. Bulleid was responsible for the only steam engine to be built for CIE. This was not a conventional machine but was designed to make use of indigenous Irish fuel and so was generally known as the 'Turfburner'. Preliminary trials were made with Coey 2-6-0, no 356, suitably converted, but the Turfburner, which was based on Bulleid's unsuccessful Leader class for British Railways and was highly unconventional in many respects, only ran trials and worked a few local goods trains; it never hauled a revenue-earning passenger train.

The Milne report of 1948 did not recommend dieselisation since sufficient utilisation of locomotives could not be achieved in Irish conditions of sparse services to justify the considerable capital expenditure. However, in 1953 this advice was ignored, largely because of the continued difficulties in obtaining suitable supplies of coal, and complete dieselisation was decided upon. As on British Railways subsequently, which might well have benefitted from CIE's experience, no effort was made to build up knowledge of the new form of power slowly, with the result that eventually costly programmes of re-engining and obtaining new locomotives had to be undertaken. Before this only a few diesels had been acquired, five shunters in 1947, nos 1000-4 (later D301-5), and two mixed-traffic engines in 1950, nos 1100-1 (later B113-14). Now sixty main-line engines were ordered from Metro Vickers, twelve for secondary duties from Birmingham Carriage & Wagon, and thirty-four for branch-line work, again from Metro Vickers; these became the A, B and C classes respectively and all were ordered straight off the drawing-board. Such were the difficulties with these locomotives that in 1961 an order was placed with General Motors of the USA, a firm with great experience in the field. The new engines, which were allotted class B, proved extremely reliable, and classes A and C were eventually re-engined on similar lines, class C being redesignated class B. Details of CIE diesel locomotives are given in the following summary:

Numbers	Type	Date	Builders	Notes
A1–A60	Co–Co	1955	Metrovick	Re-engined and numbered A1R–A60R
B101–B112	A1A–A1A	1956	Birmingham Carriage & Wagon	
B113–B114	Bo–Bo	1951	Inchicore	Formerly CIE 1100–1
B121–B135	Bo–Bo	1961	⎰ General Motors, USA	Single cab
B141–B177	Bo–Bo	1962	,,	Dual cabs
B181–B192	Bo–Bo	1966	,,	,,
B201–B234 ⎱ C201–C234 ⎰	Bo–Bo	1957	Metrovick	C201-34 became B201-34 on being re-engined
D301–D305	0–6–0	1947	Inchicore	Formerly CIE 1000–4
E401–E419	0–6–0	1955	,,	
E421–E434	0–6–0	1961	,,	
F501–F503	B–B	1955	Walker Bros, Wigan	3ft gauge for West Clare Railway. At first numbered D31-3
G601–G603	0–4–0	1955	Deutz	
G611–G617	0–4–0	1962	,,	
K801	0–8–0	1954	MAK	Originally GNR no 800

All diesel-electric except E, F, G and K classes

NOTE: Early in 1973 it was decided to discontinue the use of prefix and suffix letters in favour of plain three-digit numbers. Thus the A class, for example, are now numbered 001–060.

In 1952, before the locomotive building programme was embarked upon, sixty diesel railcars were obtained from Park Royal, numbered 2601–60. They were very similar to a batch supplied by the same firm to the GNR and varied in accommodation, some being designed for main-line work and others for suburban services. More recently the tendency is for longer distance trains to be locomotive-hauled in the interests of increased passenger comfort.

The locomotive livery of the GSR was plain unlined grey, except for the 800 class which appeared in green. Under CIE it was initially decreed that all engines should be green, but this order was soon reversed after only a few engines had been dealt with, and thereafter the green livery was restricted to the 4-6-0s, Woolwich 2-6-0s and engines employed on the Dublin & South Eastern suburban services. A general reversion to black took place in 1954. The earlier diesels were painted green but classes A to G, of the 1953 programme were at first aluminium. This did not wear well and variations of bright green and black appeared. The American B class engines were at first grey and yellow, but a striking livery of black, gold and white is now universal.

From 1942 the engine numberplates dating back to McDonnell days were removed and replaced by painted numbers, but engines of the 400 class, together with some of the Woolwich 2-6-0s, received smokebox door numberplates, LMS fashion.

Most of the old GSWR coaching stock remained in use on the Great Southern for many years, including numbers of six- and even four-wheelers. Some old four-wheelers had a brief resuscitation in 1932 on the occasion of the Eucharistic Congress which was held in Dublin and attracted pilgrims from all over the world. Many extra trains had to be run, for which purpose almost any passenger vehicle capable of running was pressed into service. Many ancient coaches which were already laid aside for scrapping were hurriedly refurbished and repainted at Inchicore, some to be used perhaps not more than two or three times before being consigned once more to the scrap heap. Even so, there were still not enough coaches available, and the Army specials for the Curragh had literally to use cattle trucks.

However, the standard of comfort on the main line was very good, despite much old stock remaining in use. Pullman cars were introduced in 1926 and steel-bodied coaches were built at Inchicore in the mid 1930s. Nevertheless, still in daily use on the Cork–Rosslare boat express in 1955 was a fine Edwardian twelve-wheeled dining car, gas-lit and with clerestory roof, a beautiful connoisseur's period piece. Nowadays the general standard on CIE compares favourably with anything elsewhere in the British Isles.

In earlier days it was normal practice to provide three classes of passenger accommodation. The first company to dispense with second was the English Midland Railway in 1875 and the Great Southern did not do so until 1 September 1930. Second class had disappeared on the Midland Great Western as long ago as 1914 and on the Dublin & South Eastern Railway about 1921—both unusually early for Irish railways. In conformity with Great Britain the old third became known as second in 1956. Nowadays it is no longer referred to as such on CIE and the two classes comprise 'first' and 'standard', somewhat on the lines of the Russian 'soft' and 'hard' classes, although the latter description would hardly apply to the Irish 'standard', which is very comfortable indeed.

Coaching stock livery in early Great Southern days was a very dark purple-brown, almost indistinguishable from black, with straw lining, changed to a lighter shade (unlined) in 1927. In 1929 this was altered to chocolate and cream, very similar to the London & North Western Railway, and in 1933 to London Midland & Scottish crimson lake. In 1945 a change was made to dark green, with a light green top and waist bands, later altered to overall dark green. After this came a short period of unpainted aluminium for new stock, followed in 1952 by overall light green with or without a single white waistband. Nowadays the attractive black and orange with white lining-out as adopted on the diesel locomotives has become universal.

GREAT SOUTHERN RAILWAYS LOCOMOTIVE LIST

Class	Type	Former owning company	Loco numbers	Built	Withdrawn	Notes
A1	4-8-0T	GSWR	900	1915	1931	
			901	1924	1932	
B1	4-6-0	GSWR	500-2	1924-6	1955-7	Mixed traffic engines
B1A	4-6-0	GSR	800 *Maeve*	1939	1964	Preserved in Belfast Museum
			801 *Macha*	1939	1963	6ft 7in driving
			802 *Tailte*	1939	1957	wheels, 3 cylinders
B2	4-6-0	GSWR	400-9	1916-23	1930	400/4/8 original 4 cylinder design
B2A	4-6-0	GSWR	401/2/3/5-7/9	Rebuilt with 2 cylinders (401/6 with Caprotti valve gear)	1955-61	
B3	4-6-0	GSWR	362-7	1905-7	1928-31	5ft 2in wheels freight locos inside cylinders

Class	Type	Former owning company	Loco numbers	Built	Withdrawn	Notes
B4	4-6-0T	CBSCR	463-70	1906-20	1945-65	Standard CBSCR design from 1906 onwards
B5	4-6-0T	CBSCR	471	1893 (built as 4-4-0T rebuilt 1906)	1933	Smaller version of class B4
C1	4-4-2T	Proposed new GSR class for DSER section but never built				
C2	4-4-2T	DSER	455-7	1911-24	1955-9	
C3	4-4-2T	DSER	458-60	1893	1953-60	
C4	4-4-2T	GSWR	27/30-2	1900-1	1930-53	
C5	4-4-2T	WLWR	269-71/74	1896-7	1949-57	
C6	4-4-2T	CBSCR	479-81	1891-4	1930-5	Originally built as 4-4-0Ts
C7	4-4-2T	GSWR	37/38/317-20	1894-1902	1950-5	
D1	4-4-0	GSWR	341 *Sir William Goulding*	1913	1928	
D2	4-4-0	GSWR	321-3, 327-32	1904-5	1955-60	Express type 6ft 7in wheels
D3	4-4-0	GSWR	309/312	1903	1959	,, ,,
			324-6	1905	1927-8	
			327-32	1905-6		Later re-classified D2
D4	4-4-0	GSWR	333-40	1907-8	1955-9	Cross-country type 5ft 8½in wheels
			342-6	1936	1959-60	,, ,,
D5	4-4-0	MGWR	545-50	1902-5	1931 (549) 1955-9 (others)	
D6	4-4-0	MGWR	540-4	1909-15	1953-9	
D7	4-4-0	MGWR	536-9	1910-13	1950-3	
D8	4-4-0	DSER	454	1905	1949	
D9	4-4-0	DSER	450-3	1895-6	1929-40	
D10	4-4-0	GSWR	310/1/3/4 (also 309/12 see class D3)	1903	1957-9	
D11	4-4-0	GSWR	301 *Victoria* 302 *Lord Roberts* 303 *St Patrick* 304 *Princess Ena*	1900	1959-62	Names later removed

Class	Type	Former owning company	Loco numbers	Built	Withdrawn	Notes
D12	4-4-0	GSWR	305-7	1902	1957-9	
			308	1902	1933	
D13	4-4-0	GSWR	See note			
D14	4-4-0	GSWR	60-5	1891-5		Aspinall 6ft 7in express engines. No 93 rebuilt in 1893 as two-cylinder compound, later reconverted. Nos 88 and 89 later rebuilt with new framing straight cut away splashers and new cab. No 89 was classified D13 between 1925 and 1933. Some of the others later ran with Belpaire fireboxes and extended smokebox, but none were superheated
			85-9	1886		
			93-6	1885		
D15	4-4-0	WLWR	296	1896	1950	
			297	1896	1928	
			298	1897	1950	
D16	4-4-0	MGWR	530-5	1880-1	1949-53	5ft 8in wheels 'Achill' bogies. Rebuilt 1900-1 from 2-4-0
D17	4-4-0	GSWR	1/3/4/9/ 11/12/14/ 16/18/20/ 52-9, 97, 98	1883-90	1925 (53) 1949-59 (others)	Aspinall express design 6ft 7in driving wheels
D18	4-4-0T	CBSCR	477	1875	1930	Rebuilt from 2-4-0T
			478	1901	1934	
D19	4-4-0	GSWR	2/5/6/7/ 8/10/13/ 15/43-6	1877-80	1935 (46) 1945-57 (others)	McDonnell 'cross-country' class 5ft 8½in driving wheels
E1	0-4-4T	WLWR	279	1899	1953	
E2	0-4-4T	WLWR	295	1895	1954	
E3	0-4-4WT	GSWR	39/40/47-51/ 70-84	1879-87	1906-11 1925-45	(39/50/79/82/84) (others)
F1	2-4-2T	DSER	434-9	1901-9	1950-3	
F2	2-4-2T	DSER	428-33	1886-98	1925 (429) 1950-7 (others)	431-3 rebuilt from 2-4-0Ts
F3	2-4-2T	DSER	427	1896	1936	Former LNWR engine built at Crewe

Class	Type	Former owning company	Loco numbers	Built	Withdrawn	Notes
F4	2–4–2T	WLWR	267	1891	1935	
F5	2–4–2T	CMDR	491	1891	1934	Identical with class F4. Originally WLWR engine became GSWR 266, sold to CMDR 1914
F6	2–4–2T	GSWR	33–6/41/42	1892–4	1957–63	
G1	2–4–0T	DSER	423–6	1889–95	1926 (426) 1952–5 (others)	
G2	2–4–0	MGWR	650–68	1893–8	1954–63	
G3	2–4–0	WLWR	276	1892	1949	
			290	1893	1951	
			291	1893	1959	
			293	1894	1954	
G4	2–4–0	GSWR	21/22/26/	1873	1928	
			66–8	1876	1928	
G5	2–4–0T	CMDR	487	1865	1928	
			488	1867	1934	
			489	1881	1928	
G6	2–4–0T	CBSCR	482	1874	1930	
G7	2–4–0	DSER	422	1864	1928	
H1	0–6–4T	GSWR	203	1879	1940	
			205, 206	1880	1928	
H2	0–6–4T	GSWR	92	1881	1945	Combined engine and saloon latterly used as 'works cab' at Inchicore
I1	0–6–2T	GSWR	213	1903	1953	
		GSWR	214	1903	1949	
I2	0–6–2T	CMDR	490	1905	1935	
I3	0–6–2T	GSR	670–4	1933	1959–62	
J1	0–6–0	DSER	448	1897	1950	Originally 0–6–2T, rebuilt 1908
			449	1897	1940	
J2	0–6–0	MGWR	646–9	1904	1930–40	
J3	0–6–0	GSWR	211	1903	1949	Built as 0–6–2Ts, similar to 213 and 214 (Class I1). Rebuilt 1907
			212	1903	1959	

Class	Type	Former owning company	Loco numbers	Built	Withdrawn	Notes
J4	0–6–0	GSWR	257–64	1913–14	1959–66	
J5	0–6–0	MGWR	623–45	1921–4	1954–65	
J6	0–6–0	MGWR	619–22	1878	1945–9	Built for WDLR
J7	0–6–0	DSER	447	1891	1930	
J8	0–6–0	DSER	442	1904	1930	
			443	1905	1955	
			444	1910	1957	
			445–6	1905	1957	
J9	0–6–0	GSWR	249–52	1912	1961–5	
			351–2	1903	1964, 1955	
			353	1903	1931	Collision damage
			354	1903	1963	
J10	0–6–0T	MGWR	614–17	1881	1949–59	
			618	1890	1949	
J11	0–6–0T	GSWR	201/2	1895	1963, 1955	
			207–10	1887	1949–59	
			217–20	1901	1955–61	
J12	0–6–0T	GSWR	204	1879	1952	Built as 0–6–4T (similar to Class H1). Rebuilt 1914
J13	0–6–0T	GSWR	Negro	1876	1910	Originally 0–6–4Ts, numbered 201 and 202, rebuilt 1895, names added and numbers removed
			Jumbo	1876	1957	
J14	0–6–0	DSER	441	1901	1935	
J15	0–6–0	GSWR	101–200/223/29/32/ 240–3/253–6	1866–1903	1923–65	184, unrebuilt, preserved at Inchicore and 186, rebuilt, by Railway Preservation Society of Ireland, Belfast (both in working order)
J15A	0–6–0	GSR	700–4	1929	1955–63	
J15B	0–6–0	GSR	710–19	1934–5	1959–62	
J16	0–6–0	MGWR	563–8	1879–80	1950 (567) 1925–7 (others)	

Page 161 (*above*) Midland Great Western six-wheeled postal pick-up and sorting van with guard's brake compartment, no 27M, one of a pair built in 1908–9 for the Sligo & Westport mail trains and still in use in the 1950s; (*below*) these Drumm battery trains put in a good many years of useful service in the 1930s and 1940s on the busy Bray suburban line

Page 162 (above) Former Ulster Railway 0–4–2 as GNR no 106 Tornado. Built 1872 and scrapped 1906; (below) One of five neat little 4–4–0s built in 1915 for cross-country work, seen here at Enniskillen in 1953 after receiving the later blue livery with scarlet underframes and named Lough Derg. Although of distinctly Edwardian design, five more were built as late as 1948, which along with the large express engines of class VS, were the last 4–4–0s to be built, possibly in the whole world. All these came from the works of Beyer Peacock, which supplied many engines for the GNR over the years

Class	Type	Former owning company	Loco numbers	Built	Withdrawn	Notes
J17	0–6–0	MGWR	233	1901	1929	WLWR design identical with class J22
			234	1901	1950	
J18	0–6–0	MGWR	569–79	1876–95	1925–65	
			582–93			
J19	0–6–0	MGWR	594–613	1885–93	1925 (611) 1954–65 (others)	
J20	0–6–0	DSER	440	1899	1929	
J21	0–6–0ST	CBSCR	475	1887	1939	
			476	1890	1925	
J22	0–6–0	WLWR	235	1895	1927	
			236	1895	1951	
J23	0–6–0ST	CBSCR	474	1882	1925	
J24	0–6–0ST	CBSCR	472	1881	1940	
			473	1894	1935	
J25	0–6–0	WLWR	222	1900	1949	
			237	1897	1951	
			238	1897	1934	
			239	1897	1949	
J26	0–6–0T	MGWR	551–62	1891–4	1954–63	
J27	0–6–0ST	GSWR	Erin	1894	1930	Originally Waterford & Wexford Railway. Allocated GSWR no 300 but never carried
J28	0–6–0ST	GSWR	299	1892	1957	From Fenit Harbour Commission, originally named *Shamrock*
J29	0–6–0ST	GSWR	91	1881	1930	Originally 0–6–4T saloon engines similar to no 92 (Class H2)
J30	0–6–0T	GSWR	90	1875	1959	Preserved at Mallow
			99	1890	1931	
			100	1891	1959	
K1	2–6–0	GSR	372–91	1925–9	1955–62	
K1A	2–6–0	GSR	393–8	1930	1955–9	

K

Class	Type	Former owning company	Loco numbers	Built	Withdrawn	Notes
K2	2–6–0	DSER	461	1922	1965	Preserved at
			462	1922	1963	Inchicore. Inside cylinders
K3	2–6–0	GSWR	355–61	1903	1928 (355) 1955–60 (others)	Inside cylinders, built as 0–6–0s
K4	2–6–0	GSWR	368–71	1909	1928 (368/71) 1957 (369/70)	Inside cylinders
K5	2–6–0T	TCLR	Argadeen	1894	1957	,, ,,
L1	0–4–2WT	WTR	486	1909	1941	
L2	0–4–2ST	GSWR	Sambo	1914	1963	Works shunter at Inchicore
L3	0–4–2WT	WTR	485	1862	1930	
L4	0–4–2T	GSWR	Fairy	1894	1927	At first classified
(L5)			Sprite	1873	1927	L5. Used as stationary boiler at Inchicore until about 1934. These engines toured the system with the weekly pay carriage
L6	0–4–2T	TCLR	St Molaga	1890	1949	
M1 (later M2)	0–4–0T	DSER	Elf	1906	1931	Engine portions of former rail motors
			Imp	1906	1928	
M1	0–4–0 Sentinel	GSR	280/1	1927	1948	
M3	0–4–0ST	GSR	495	1920	1949	From Allman's Distillery, Bandon, 1930
unclassified	0–4–0	GSWR	Pat	1884	1963	Vertical boiler. Used on gantry at coaling stage, Cork Shed
N1	2–2–2WT	WTR	483	1855	1928	
			484	1855	1936	
P1	2–6–2T	GSR	850	1928	1955	
CC	0–6–6–0	CIE	CC1	1957	1958	Bulleid experimental turf-burning engine

During the height of the withdrawal period in the late 1950s, a number of engines were sold to Spain for scrap. They were shipped to San Juan de Nieva in 1958, and comprised B1 4–6–0 no 502, D10 4–4–0 no 313, D14 no 86, F6 2–4–2T nos 34 and 41, J8 0–6–0 no 445, J15 nos 107, 135 and 158, J18 nos 575, 576, 586 and 595, K 2–6–0 no 391, and K1 nos 395 and 397.

Narrow-gauge locomotives

Class	Wheel arrangement	Former owning company	Number
BN1	4–6–0T	West Clare	10C
BN2	4–6–0T	„ „	11C
BN3	4–6–0T	„ „	3C
BN4	4–6–0T	„ „	4C
DN1	4–4–0T	Cork & Muskerry	7K
DN2	4–4–0T	Cavan & Leitrim	1L–8L
DN3	4–4–0T	Cork & Muskerry	4K
DN4	4–4–0T	Schull & Skibbereen	1S, 2S
DN5	4–4–0T	„ „	4S
DN6	4–4–0T	Cork & Muskerry	1K, 2K
DN7	4–4–0T	„ „	8K
EN1	0–4–4T	„ „	5K, 6K (later 6S on ssr)
FN1	2–4–2T	Cork Blackrock & Passage	4P to 7P (later 10L to 13L on clr)
HN1	0–6–4T	Cavan & Leitrim	9L
IN1	0–6–2T	West Clare	5C, 6C
KN1	2–6–0T	Tralee & Dingle	4T, 7T
KN2	2–6–0T	„ „	1T, 2T, 3T, 6T, 8T
MN1	0–4–0T	Schull & Skibbereen	2S
PN1	2–6–2T	West Clare	2C, 4C, 8C, 9C
PN2	2–6–2T	Tralee & Dingle	5T

CHAPTER 15

GREAT NORTHERN RAILWAY

Ireland's second largest railway, with a main line connecting the two principal cities, Dublin and Belfast, and numerous secondary routes covering a considerable part of the area in the north and west known as Ulster, more particularly in the counties of Louth, Armagh, Monaghan, Fermanagh and Tyrone.

Principal constituents:
ULSTER RAILWAY   Incorporated 1836.
DUBLIN & DROGHEDA RAILWAY   Incorporated 1836.
DUBLIN & BELFAST JUNCTION RAILWAY   Incorporated 1845.
Opened in stages, finally completed throughout between Dublin and Belfast in 1855.

The GREAT NORTHERN RAILWAY as such was formed in 1876 as a result of the amalgamation of several companies, the chief of which were the three already mentioned together with the IRISH NORTH WESTERN and others. Additional absorptions in later years brought the total route mileage in 1922 to 617 miles.

Principal places served:
Dublin, Drogheda, Dundalk, Newry, Portadown, Lisburn, Belfast, Dungannon, Omagh, Strabane, Londonderry, Enniskillen, Bundoran.

The Great Northern was in many ways the most progressive and enterprising of all the Irish railways, and deservedly the most prosperous. The name Enterprise, given eventually to its best main-line train, was indeed aptly chosen and well justified. Its main line expresses were comparable with those of most English railways, and in one respect it was ahead of any of them, being the first to employ electric lighting exclusively; it never had any gas-lit coaches, although high-pressure calor gas was used for cooking in the restaurant cars after 1933, up to which time coal or coke had been employed.

It must inevitably be regarded as the principal trunk route in Ireland, as it linked the two major cities, Dublin and Belfast. The fact that in its later years these were destined to lie in two separate countries, one of them still within the British Empire, was particularly unfortunate from the railway point of view. One of the disadvantages most apparent to the traveller was the nuisance of customs examination at the frontier, with its consequent delays.

Other minor things of course cropped up from time to time, as I found for myself on one occasion in April 1948. I was breaking my journey at Dundalk and found that my train on the Londonderry line would be running one hour early owing to the fact that the date of commencement of 'summer time' was not co-ordinated between the two governments; this meant that my stay in Dundalk was curtailed. Another point was that charges for drinks in the restaurant cars also varied according to whether the train happened to be north or south of the border, being cheaper in the Free State owing to the lower excise rates, and this, with its obvious opportunities for 'fiddling', could be very irritating.

Whilst the Great Northern had no association with its larger namesake in England, it nevertheless had a number of similarities with it in outward appearances. Its coaches, which were finished in a grained mahogany livery from about 1900, strikingly resembled the English GNR's grained teak ones, and not only in livery. Some very handsome specimens with clerestory roofs might well have come from Doncaster just before or after World War I. One or two locomotive classes were also similar, particularly when the familiar initials GNR were embellished on the tank or tender, as was done in later years. The green livery of the engines was not unlike that of the English railway, although of a somewhat darker shade, and again was matched by the red-brown framing. The long chimney on the older engines also had a strong suggestion of Patrick Stirling.

In the 1950s during its last years as an independent company, it had the unique distinction of using four forms of motive power, ancient and modern. Steam was still the principal mode of operation, diesel traction had already arrived in the form of multiple-unit railcars (some time before they were adopted in Great Britain), electric traction was in use on the tramway system over the Hill of Howth, and last but not least, it owned the last horse-operated passenger branch in Great Britain and Ireland. In addition it ran road buses in the Free State, although it was prevented from doing so in Northern Ireland after that government's Road and Rail Traffic Act of 1935.

Amongst the earliest proposals for the construction of railways in Ireland was one for a rail connection between Dublin and Belfast. This was put forward in January 1825 by a proposed Leinster & Ulster Rail Company, which was to be created for the purpose of 'making rail roads between Dublin and the north, particularly Belfast, and the intermediate towns, with branches'. However, although farseeing, it was much too ambitious for the period and not surprisingly was stillborn. Another attempt was made in 1835, but again it was too large a project for one undertaking. Instead, two separate companies were promoted, the Ulster Railway at the northern end, which by an Act of 19 May 1836 was empowered to construct a 36 mile railway between Belfast and Armagh, and the 32 mile Dublin & Drogheda Railway, by an Act of 13 August 1836. The route of the latter was only decided after strong arguments between two opposing factions as to the respective merits of an inland route or one along the coast. The main advantage of the former was that it was two miles shorter, but against that it was more severely graded, whereas the coastal line could be constructed with nothing more severe than 1 in 160, and this was the one eventually decided upon.

Construction began in 1840 and the line was duly opened in 1844, the official ceremony taking place on 24 May, the Queen's birthday. At the same time Earl de Grey, the Lord Lieutenant, laid the foundation stone at Amiens Street of what was to be the southern terminus of the line, recourse having to be made in the meantime to a temporary platform. At the other end also, at Drogheda, the original station, with overall roof, was replaced some years later by the present one. At Amiens Street a grandiose edifice was put up, now known as Connolly. It is situated in a high position above the road frontage, at one time entailing a laborious climb with heavy luggage up a flight of steps, though nowadays there is an escalator.

Meanwhile the Ulster Railway had already completed its line as far as Portadown, the first section from Belfast to Lisburn having been opened on 12 August 1839, Lurgan being reached on 18 November 1841, Seago on 31 January 1842 and Portadown on 12 September 1842. This line was laid to gauge of 6ft 2in. The Royal Commission which had been appointed in 1846 to adjudicate on the gauge question laid down a universal measurement of 5ft 3in for the entire country, and the line between Belfast and Portadown had to be relaid accordingly. The Dublin & Drogheda Railway had been planned to 5ft 2in gauge, but this, too, had of course to conform to the slightly wider dimension.

The third step in the completion of the through line between the two cities was now inaugurated by an Act obtained in 1845 under the title of Dublin & Belfast Junction Railway, to provide the vital link of 63 miles. The Act also provided for a $16\frac{3}{4}$ mile branch from Dublin to Navan, opened on 15 February 1850, extended to Kells, $9\frac{1}{4}$ miles, on 11 June 1853, and to Oldcastle, $12\frac{3}{4}$ miles, on 17 May 1863. (It was closed almost exactly 100 years later, on 30 April 1963.) There had originally been a possibility that the through route between Dublin and Belfast might have taken a more inland course southwards from Armagh as an extension of the Ulster Railway, but by this time it had only reached Portadown and the powers for the construction of the line to Armagh had lapsed; they were revived later, but as a branch with an extension to Clones. The line from Portadown to Armagh was finally constructed and opened on 1 March 1848, then extended to Monaghan, 16¾ miles, 25 May 1858, and to Clones, another 12 miles, on 2 March 1863. The Clones & Cavan Extension, opened on 2 March 1863, took the line on to Cavan, 15¼ miles. Although built and operated by the Dublin & Enniskillen Railway, it had received, by way of financial assistance, £30,000 from the Ulster Railway and £20,000 each from the Dublin & Drogheda and the Dublin & Belfast Junction. At Cavan it made contact with the MGWR branch from Mullingar and in fact used the latter's station. In effect this formed a through route between Belfast and Dublin, albeit a very circuitous one. However no attempt was made to use it as such and in fact through travel was at times deliberately discouraged by one train being timed to depart a few minutes before the arrival of the other, a maddening practice not unknown in Great Britain even in the present day!

On the Dublin & Belfast Junction a major obstacle was the crossing of the River Boyne at Drogheda, which necessitated the construction of a large girder bridge. During the four years while the bridge was being built no through running between Dublin and Belfast was of course possible, although special trains for the Dublin International Exhibition of 1853 were allowed to cross the temporary wooden scaffolding at 4mph and with a load limited to 100 tons. The bridge was finally opened for normal traffic on 5 April 1855, completing the uninterrupted through route between the two cities.

Before the 1920s weight restrictions had to be imposed on traffic using the bridge and eventually reconstruction was decided upon. In 1930-2 a new viaduct was built virtually inside the old one and the running lines were interlaced, so that in effect the line was single across the bridge, which was then able to take the compound 4-4-0s introduced in 1932 for the accelerated Dublin-Belfast expresses.

Another large viaduct was necessary at Bessbrook, south of Goraghwood, where the railway passed close to the town of Newry (served by a branch). This consisted of eighteen masonry arches, and with a height from ground to track level of 137ft was the highest in Ireland.

North of the River Boyne at Drogheda a temporary station was built at Newfoundwell, pending construction of the bridge, and the line as far as Dundalk, 22 miles, was opened on 15 February 1849. Beyond Dundalk a further 10½ miles to a place called Wellington Inn, a temporary station not now identifiable, was opened on 31 July 1850. Meanwhile construction was proceeding southwards from the Ulster Railway at Portadown, reaching Mullaghglass on 6 January 1852. The last gap between here and Wellington Inn involved crossing difficult country embracing a western escarpment of the Mountains of Mourne, with steep gradients to the summit of the whole line, at mp 65½ from Dublin, as well as the Bessbrook viaduct. This section was opened on 10 June 1852, and the whole route was now complete except for the crossing of the Boyne at Drogheda.

The fourth largest constituent of the Great Northern, the Irish North Western, in conjunction with the Londonderry & Enniskillen, established through rail communication between Dublin and Londonderry, the third most important city on the ultimate Great Northern system. The link between Londonderry and Belfast was provided by the Portadown, Dungannon & Omagh Railway, and very broadly, the ultimate composition of the Great Northern Railway, between its three focal extremities of Dublin, Belfast and Londonderry, was in the shape of a letter Y.

The INWR was actually an amalgamation of the Dundalk & Enniskillen (originally incorporated as the Dundalk & Western Railway) and the Londonderry & Enniskillen, together with two other smaller systems. The first portion of the DER as far as Castleblayney was opened on 15 February 1849, at the same time as the Dublin & Belfast Junction reached Dundalk. Here the DER had its own station east of the DBJR main line, which it crossed on the level by the well-known Dundalk Square crossing, in later years used by the Dundalk Newry & Greenore Railway.

There was a mishap at the crossing in early days, and two more in 1944 and 1945, but accidents at this type of railway level crossing, with its obvious potential dangers, seem to have been very rare indeed. There are very few such crossings in Great Britain and Ireland, two of them, curiously enough, on the English Great Northern Railway at Newark and Retford (the latter recently replaced by a bridge), and another farther up the East Coast route on the North Eastern at Darlington, where the original Stockton & Darlington Railway crosses the main line to the north. In Ireland itself there is of course one at Limerick Junction.

Westwards from Castleblayney, the DER reached Ballybay on 17 July 1854, Newbliss the following year, Clones on 7 July 1858, and finally Enniskillen on 2 February 1859. The last 22 miles had been part of another projected railway, the Newry & Enniskillen, incorporated on 31 July 1845, but eventually were built in conjunction with the DER. The total distance from Dundalk to Enniskillen was 61½ miles.

A branch to Cootehill was opened on 18 October 1860, intended to go through to Cavan, but never completed, and later in GNR years another branch to Carrickmacross was opened on 31 July 1886. Cootehill and Carrickmacross both lost their passenger services in 1947 and were closed completely in 1960 and 1955 respectively.

The northern constituent of the INWR was the Londonderry & Enniskillen, incorporated in 1845 to construct the 60 mile line between these two centres. The first section, from Londonderry to Strabane, was opened on 19 April 1847, and to Omagh in 1852. From Omagh the railway was extended to Fintona on 15 June 1853 (although not officially authorised until the Act of the following year). Fintona itself was the terminus of a short branch, ¾ mile long. The main line was extended from Fintona Junction southwards to Dromore Road on 16 January 1854, and reached Enniskillen on 19 August 1854, four and a half years before the DER got there to complete the link. The route had originally been surveyed in 1837 by George Stephenson, but there was some difference of opinion with Sir John MacNeill, who was engineer for several other railways, as to the route to be taken between Strabane and Omagh; eventually George Stephenson's son, Robert, was called in as consultant and his route was adopted. There was also some argument as to the siting of the Londonderry terminus, the first station being somewhat to the south on the bank of the River Foyle, but the line was extended in 1850 to a new station just north of the Foyle Bridge, a much more convenient position.

The passenger service on the short Fintona branch was provided by a tram-type vehicle drawn by a horse and became famous in later years as the last to be so worked in the British Isles, though goods traffic was worked by steam. The vehicle, built in 1883, provided three classes (as was usual on the GNR until 1950, when second was abolished on the introduction of diesel railcars), first and second inside, and third on the open upper deck; in practice, as the journey was so short, lasting only a few minutes with a maximum speed of about 6mph, passengers rarely bothered to go upstairs except perhaps in fine weather.

The Londonderry & Enniskillen was a poor line financially but managed to eke out a precarious existence until 1859, when, with the DER, it became part of the through route between Dublin and Londonderry. Because of the financial advantages it was leased to the Dundalk & Enniskillen from 1 January 1860, and to make its title more appropriate this railway changed its name to Irish North Western by an Act of 7 July 1862.

Under an Act of 11 July 1861, the Enniskillen & Bundoran Railway was opened on 13 June 1866. This was a 35½ mile branch from Bundoran Junction, and served Bundoran and Ballyshannon, watering places on the west coast in Donegal Bay. It was worked by the INWR. A further Act, of 30 June 1862, in the name of the Enniskillen Bundoran & Sligo empowered an extension to the last-named town, which was already served by two other railways, but this line was never built.

Another line worked by the INWR was the Finn Valley, 13½ miles long, from Strabane to Stranorlar, opened on 7 September 1863. Constructed to the normal 5ft 3in gauge, it was in later years converted to 3ft and became part of the County Donegal system.

The Irish North Western Railway finally lost its identity on 1 April 1876, when it became part of the Great Northern, although some of its leased or worked lines retained their old identities for the time being. The new amalgamation brought together the Northern of Ireland (a short-lived concern formed in 1875 by the fusion of the Dublin & Drogheda and the Dublin & Belfast Junction), the Ulster Railway and other smaller lines to form the GNR.

The 4½ mile Belturbet branch, which left the Clones to Cavan Line at Ballyhaise, was opened by the Great Northern on 29 June 1885. It was joined at Belturbet two years later by the 3ft gauge Cavan & Leitrim Railway; the station was shared, the single platform accommodating each company's trains on either side with no physical connection, owing to the difference in gauge.

The Portadown Dungannon & Omagh Railway provided the missing link in a shorter route between Belfast and Londonderry, 100½ miles as against 146½ via Clones (the distance by the BNCR route was only 95 miles). The first section, the Portadown & Dungannon Railway, 13½ miles, was authorised by an Act of 1847, but owing to delays was not opened until 5 April 1858. In August 1858 a further Act incorporated the Portadown, Dungannon & Omagh and enabled the remaining 27 miles to Omagh, already served by the Londonderry & Enniskillen, to be opened in September 1861.

A branch from Dungannon to Cookstown, 14¼ miles, was promoted in 1874 jointly by the PDOR and the Ulster Railway, but was not ready until after absorption by the Great Northern. It was opened on 28 July 1879. Cookstown now had two separate stations, having been served since 1856 by the Belfast & Northern Counties Railway, and it thus enjoyed the competing services of rival concerns into Belfast. Passenger services ceased in 1956; the line beyond Coalisland was closed completely but the Dungannon–Coalisland section remained open for goods until January 1965.

Another branch was that to Ardee, 4¾ miles long, from Dromin Junction on the Dublin main line. There had previously been a proposal to construct a steam tramway to serve the sizeable little township, but this had been opposed by the GNR, which by an Act of 27 June 1892 was empowered to build the branch, opened on 1 August 1896. Although Ardee lost its passenger service in 1934, the branch is still open for goods by virtue of the fact that it now comes under CIE administration.

The Castleblayney Keady & Armagh Railway was the final outcome of the ambition of the Midland Great Western to extend northwards into GNR territory by extending its branch from Navan to Kingscourt, itself the cause of some friction between the two railways. A bill had been passed in 1900 authorising the construction of such a railway under the title of Kingscourt Keady & Armagh Railway. It was strongly backed by the MGWR but naturally opposed by the GNR, which had had a bill for a line between Castleblayney and Armagh rejected by Parliament. Eventually terms were agreed; the MGWR abandoned its claim, the Kingscourt extension project was not proceeded with, and the GNR took over part control of the renamed Castleblayney, Keady & Armagh line. Construction was started from the north end, and after some difficulties with the contractors the 8 mile section to Keady was opened on 31 May 1909, and the $10\frac{1}{4}$ miles thence to Castleblayney, joining up with the Dundalk to Clones line, on 10 November 1910. In 1911 the nominally independent CKAR lost its identity, being absorbed by the Great Northern. This was one of the most short-lived lines in the whole country; the Castleblayney–Keady section, was completely closed as early as 1923. The Armagh section lost its passenger service in 1932, but the line survived for goods until the wholesale closures of 1957.

In the Belfast area there was the Dublin & Antrim Junction Railway, curiously named in that it was over 100 miles from Dublin. It left the Great Northern main line at Lisburn, $7\frac{1}{2}$ miles out of Belfast, and ran northwards to Antrim Junction, $20\frac{1}{4}$ miles; it was at first worked by the Ulster Railway. At Antrim Junction it made connection with the Belfast & Northern Counties.

In Belfast itself, the Belfast Central Railway, incorporated on 25 July 1864, provided for connecting lines between the three separate railways serving the city, and the construction of a central station, a total of $5\frac{3}{4}$ miles of line. Further Acts of 5 July 1865 and of 31 July 1868 authorised extensions and tramway construction totalling $6\frac{1}{4}$ miles, as well as working arrangements in conjunction with the Ulster, Belfast Holywood & Bangor, Belfast & Northern Counties, and Belfast Harbour Commissioners. It involved the construction of a bridge over the River Lagan to enable the Ulster Railway to gain access to the Belfast & County Down on the east side of the river. There were two small intermediate stations, but never any proposal for a central one. The Belfast Central Railway became part of the GNR system in 1885.

The major part of the eventual Great Northern system lay almost entirely to the west of the main line between Dublin and Belfast. Unfortunately this extensive network has now been completely closed and abandoned, leaving a large area of the north-west of the country, including several counties, Donegal, Tyrone, Fermanagh and Monaghan, completely without rail communication. This holocaust took place for the most part during 1957, so far as passenger services were concerned; one or two sections remained open for goods a year or two longer. The main Londonderry line via Portadown and Omagh did not succumb until 1965.

As to the lines east of the main line, Newry, situated at the head of Carling-ford Lough, was already a port of some importance before railways came on the scene, after which it became an obvious target for the promoters. The Newry & Enniskillen, incorporated on 31 July 1845, was intended to provide a through route by way of Armagh and Clones, but actually only achieved the construc-tion of the first section as far as Armagh, and a further Act of 17 August 1857 changed its name to the Newry & Armagh Railway. The parts beyond Armagh were in the event built by the Ulster Railway as far as Clones; the Dundalk & Enniskillen (later Irish North Western) continued as far as Enniskillen.

The first section of the line from Newry, the 3½ mile link to Goraghwood, where it crossed the main line of the Dublin & Belfast Junction, was opened on 1 March 1854, but receipts were poor, no dividend could be paid to the shareholders, and there was little prospect of any until the railway could be extended to Armagh. This was through somewhat hilly country, and involved two tunnels, one about 400 yards long and the other just one yard short of a mile, 1,759 yards, actually the longest in the whole country. The Newry & Armagh was absorbed by the GNR in 1879.

This line was notorious in being the scene of the Armagh accident on 12 June 1889, the worst in the history of Irish railways. The death roll was eighty, over a quarter of them children. As a result of this accident legislation was passed making it compulsory to fit continuous automatic brakes on passenger trains.

Armagh was finally reached on 25 August 1864, at first with a temporary station, but six months later the line joined up with the Ulster Railway, whose station it now used, subject to a rental. The passenger service between Armagh and Goraghwood ceased in 1933, the section to Markethill being closed com-pletely, but thence to Goraghwood remained open for goods traffic until 1957.

Extension southward to Newry was promoted by an independent company, the Newry Warrenpoint & Rostrevor, incorporated on 27 July 1846. In fact the railway only actually got as far as Warrenpoint, 7 miles from Newry, the line being opened on 28 May 1849. It remained an independent concern until 4 June 1886, when it passed into the hands of the GNR.

Banbridge, another little town north of Newry, nearer Belfast, with a considerable linen industry, was first reached on 23 March 1859 by a 6¾ mile branch from the main DBJR line at Scarva by a concern with the grandiose title of Banbridge Newry Dublin & Belfast Junction Railway, incorporated on 20 August 1853, leased to the DBJR and taken over by the GNR in 1876. Another line, the Banbridge Lisburn & Belfast Railway, authorised on 14 June 1858, left the main line of the Ulster Railway at Lisburn, and got to Banbridge,

17 miles distant, on 13 July 1863. It was worked by the Ulster Railway. The Banbridge Extension Railway, authorised on 28 June 1861, was planned as a 12 mile line to Ballyroney, but although work was actually started it was not completed until GNR days, and was not opened until 14 December 1880.

By the end of the century the GNR was casting envious eyes at Newcastle, a pleasant resort on the coast of Dundrum Bay, with which the Belfast & County Down Railway was enjoying a lucrative traffic. Newcastle being only 10 miles from the Great Northern railhead at Ballyroney, both companies now proposed to bridge the gap. The Great Northern would have liked its own complete line into Newcastle, but the BCDR for its part would have been prepared to build the railway itself and obtain running powers over the GNR to Scarva. Eventually a compromise was reached, under which each company would build its own line as far as Castlewellan and join up there, the Great Northern having running powers over the BCDR into Newcastle station, now to be operated on a joint basis, and the County Down being afforded the doubtful benefit of running powers at Ballyroney, which it never in fact used. These plans were authorised by an Act of 30 July 1900, and the line opened on 24 March 1906. Incidentally the through running gave Newcastle the distinction of being one of the few places in Ireland served by two competing railways.

Some of the lines east of the main line suffered drastic closures even before those of the west during that dark period of the later 1950s. Newcastle lost its train services in 1955, and Banbridge was cut off from rail communication in 1956. The branch from Goraghwood to Newry and Warrenpoint survived until 1965, when it was completely closed, at the same time as the Londonderry line, leaving the Great Northern north of the border consisting only of the Belfast main line and the connecting branch to Antrim.

The 3½ mile Howth branch, leaving the main line 4¾ miles out of Dublin to serve the residential suburbs of Sutton and Howth, was sanctioned as early as 1845, and opened on 30 July 1846. Initially the main purpose was to promote the harbour there as a port for services to Great Britain, but this never materialised. However, even in early days the line had a reasonably frequent service for the benefit of Dublin businessmen who had their homes at Howth. This it still does, some trains working through over the former DSER Bray line south of the city. The Howth branch is now one of the very few remnants, and the only one with a passenger service, of the formerly complex Great Northern system, apart from the Dublin to Belfast main line.

Howth (Norse for 'head') is actually a rocky promontory whose summit, Slievemartin, is 560ft above sea level. It is 2 miles long and 1½ miles wide, and is joined to the mainland by a low spit of land of comparatively recent formation

Great Northern Railway Company (Ireland).

PORTRUSH ELECTRIC TRAMWAY COUPON.

44

This through Ticket is issued subject to the conditions and regulations referred to in the Time Tables, Bills, and Notices of the respective Companies on whose Railways, Tramways, Coaches, or Steamboats it is available; and the holder, by accepting it, agrees that the respective Companies are not to be liable for any loss, damage, injury, delay, or detention caused or arising off their respective Railways, Tramways, Coaches, or Steamboats. The contract and liability of each Company are limited to its own Railways, Tramways, Coaches and Steamboats.

189

CRUMLIN STATION,

Third Class Fare, 1s. 6d.

This Ticket entitles Holder to travel once in each direction

Portrush to Giant's Causeway and Back

within One Month.

*Issued with*_____ _____ Class Ticket,

*No.*_____ to PORTRUSH.

_____ Booking Clerk.

Printed by JOHN FALCONER, 53 Upper Sackville-street, Dublin.

Great Northern Railway Company (Ireland).

44

189

CRUMLIN STATION,

Third Class Fare, 1s. 6d.

Portrush to Giant's Causeway and Back.

*Issued with*_____ _____ Class Ticket,

*No.*_____ to PORTRUSH.

_____ Booking Clerk.

GNR paper ticket for through travel on Portrush Electric Tramway before which it was an island. The harbour, built between 1807 and 1810, was once a packet station, but was gradually superseded by Kingstown (now Dun Laoghaire). The town is a pleasant resort with one of the lowest rainfalls in the whole of Ireland.

With sightseers in mind the Great Northern planned a tramway around the hill, but owing to the gradient this would have been difficult with steam working. In the 1890s, when electric trams were already an established fact, an independent concern known as the Clontarf & Hill of Howth Company already had plans for such a line, but eventually it was left to the GNR to proceed with the scheme which ultimately materialised. The tram route left the GNR Howth branch at Sutton and rejoined it at its Howth terminus, being basically in the shape of a U, the total length being 5¼ miles. It was of 5ft 3in gauge, as was the Dublin United Tramway, unusually wide for an electric tramway. The Sutton to Summit section was opened on 17 June 1901, and Summit to Howth in 1 August 1901. The summit was 407ft above sea level, with a ruling gradient of 1 in 20, but it had ½ mile at 1 in 16½.

It was operated by conventional double-deck open-top tramcars, taking current at 550 volts from overhead wires and running almost entirely on re-served track consisting of ordinary bullhead rail. There were ten of these cars and a service vehicle, the sheds and the powerhouse being at Sutton.

By the late 1950s it was one of the last tramway services still operating in Great Britain and Ireland, and although its eventual closure seemed inevitable, it came with untoward suddenness. It was announced by the CIE on 14 May 1959 that closure would take place in a fortnight's time, and this was duly carried out.

The outbreak of World War I in 1914 came at the time of highest prosperity for the company, but the effects of the conflict were soon felt. The government assumed control from 1 January 1917 and guaranteed the company equivalent earnings to those of 1913; this arrangement lasted until 17 August 1921 and the company received £3 million in compensation for enforced lack of track maintenance and deterioration of rolling stock.

The Great Northern was the principal railway sufferer in the complications resulting from the splitting of the country. Its system was divided, rather more in the north, but with a considerable mileage in the Free State, and its lines crossed the border in no less than seventeen places, all involving customs examination. The routes chiefly affected, apart from the Dublin to Belfast main line, were Portadown–Clones–Enniskillen, and the Bundoran branch; each crossing entailed halts and delays at two customs stations, one on either side of the border. After 1947 non-stop trains between Dublin and Belfast were made possible by luggage examination at the termini.

During the 1920s road competition began to appear, at first from very small concerns, even one-man operations. They were able to buy surplus wartime lorries or passenger-carrying vehicles cheaply and run them where they pleased, there being no restrictions. The Great Northern weathered this unwelcome competition well, mainly by running its own buses and road goods vehicles to points which the railway did not itself reach, and of course in sensible conjunction with its rail services, with which the private operators tended to compete. In 1932 the Road Transport Act was passed in the Free State and made compulsory the licensing of all road operators; restrictions were imposed so that unwarranted competition was discouraged or not allowed. Unfortunately this did not apply in the north, and the Road and Rail Traffic (North Ireland) 1935 Act laid the seeds of disaster for the Great Northern. It was no longer allowed to run its own bus services, the fleet being bought out by the new Northern Ireland Transport Board, which proceeded to use it in direct competition instead of as feeder services as had been promised.

Specimen GNR tickets

After a period of comparative financial stability during the war years, owing to the traffic increase in wartime and restrictions on private motoring, the situation again deteriorated and reached a crisis by 1950, when the whole line was threatened with imminent closure. The position was saved by the creation of the Great Northern Railway Board, with the financial backing of the governments of each country, albeit somewhat reluctant in the case of Northern Ireland, with five members of the board from each. The purchase price was £4½ million. This took effect from 1 September 1953 and for the next five years the railway continued as virtually a joint line, unique in that it was owned by the national undertakings of two different countries.

The board was disbanded on 1 October 1958, and what remained of the railway was divided between the two national concerns, CIE and UTA, geographically with regard to the line itself, track, stations and station property, while movable assets such as locomotives and rolling stock were apportioned in equal numbers. This final dismemberment of what had once been a progressive and efficient railway was sad indeed.

Page 179 (above) The last main-line engines for the Great Northern were five three-cylinder 4-4-0s built in 1948, the last express engines of their type in Great Britain and Ireland. No 207 Boyne, seen here at Howth Junction in 1960, was one of the engines allocated to CIE when the locomotive stock was divided in that year. Note the initials indicating new ownership on the buffer beam, number, name and livery remaining unchanged; (below) the crack train on the GNR was the Enterprise express between Belfast and Dublin. For a period in the early 1950s it ran through between Belfast and Cork by arrangement with CIE and is here seen emerging from Phoenix Park Tunnel, Dublin, behind no 800 Maeve, one of the three large 4-6-0s built in 1939, the last new engines for the Great Southern. This tunnel, less than half a mile long, is one of the very few in the whole country, none of which exceed a mile in length

Page 180 The Great Northern was unique during its final independent years in the 1950s in employing four forms of motive power. Apart from steam and diesel railcars it also operated the Hill of Howth electric tramway, as depicted above, whilst the short Fintona branch, horse-worked to the end, was well known and much photographed in its last days. Both of these views, however, date back to the 1930s

As a step toward effecting economies, apart from the widespread closures which were to follow, it was proposed to change to diesel traction, a decision already taken on its own lines by CIE. It was now planned to order over 100 diesel locomotives but these never materialised, as they were simply not required, owing to the extensive closures from 1955 onwards.

LOCOMOTIVES AND ROLLING STOCK

At the time of its formation in 1876 the Great Northern naturally inherited a large variety of locomotives, including some diminutive 2–2–0Ts from the decrepit Londonderry & Enniskillen Railway, and 2–2–2s, 2–4–0s and 0–4–2s from the Ulster Railway, the Irish North Western, the Dublin & Drogheda, and the DBJR.

Unlike the other constituents the Ulster Railway engines were named, and were also distinctive in having outside frames, much favoured by some English railways, notably the Great Western, the Midland and the North Eastern, but almost unknown in Ireland on the broad gauge, though the NCC had a few such 2–4–0s. Ulster engines had 100 added to their numbers by the Great Northern, becoming nos 101–41, the other railways' engines being numbered below 100 and including, in addition to the above, a few 0–6–0s and one or two tank engines. Most of these old acquisitions had gone by the early part of the twentieth century.

Not many new engines appeared during the first few years of the GNR, just a few 0–6–0s and 2–4–0s from Sharp Stewart and Beyer Peacock. The latter firm was to supply very many of the Great Northern's locomotives, right to the end of its existence.

The company's workshops were situated at Dundalk, where both the Dublin & Belfast Junction and the Irish North Western had previously established their headquarters. For the first few years there had been a separate southern and northern division, the latter with its own locomotive superintendent, J. Eaton, but these were amalgamated about 1880 under the superintendency of J. Park; he was succeeded in 1895 by C. Clifford, who had originally been with the INWR. Clifford's place on retirement in 1911 was taken by G. T. Glover, who came from the North Eastern. The last two steam locomotive superintendents were G. B. Howden, appointed in 1923, and H. R. McIntosh, in 1939.

Park's first express engines were a couple of 4–2–2s, no 88 *Victoria* and 89 *Albert*, which appeared in 1885 from the works of Beyer Peacock; they were forerunners of a type which was to gain much favour on several English railways, notably the Midland and the Great Western. They were however the

L

BELFAST—DUNGANNON—OMAGH—LONDONDERRY.

STATIONS	WEEK-DAYS																SUNDAYS					
		RC	X	RC		SO	SX	SO	SX	SO		RC	X			WSO						
	a.m.	a.m.	a.m.	a.m.	no'n	p.m.	p.m.	p.m.	p.m.	p.m.	p.m.	p.m.	p.m.	p.m.	p.m.	p.m.	a.m.	a.m.	p.m.	p.m.	p.m.	p.m.
BELFAST ......dep.	7 45	8 25	..	1115	12 0	1 55	2 10	2g15	..	..	..	5 0	..	5 35	7 30	9 40	..	10 0	1245	5 5	8 10	9 0
Lisburn .... "	7 58	8 41	..	1130	..	..	..	..	..	..	..	5 16	..	cS	7 45	9 55	..	1017	1 3	5 21	8 25	9 24
Lurgan .... "	8 17	8 58	..	1147	1227	..	..	..	..	..	..	5 33	..	6 7	8 9	1021	..	1038	1 23	5 45	8 42	9 44
Portadown ....arr.	8 25	9 7	..	1156	1235	2 30	2 40	2g45	..	..	..	5 41	..	6 15	8 17	1029	..	1046	1 31	5 53	8 50	9 52
Dublin.......dep.	..	..	..	9 0	..	..	..	..	..	..	..	2 30	..	..	..	6 25	..	..	1020	..	6 0	7 0
Portadown ..arr.	..	..	..	1136	..	..	..	..	X	X	..	5 14	..	..	..	8 57	..	..	1242	..	8 25	9 41
Portadown ....dep.	8*29	9 11	..	12 9	1 0	2 34	2 43	2g48	2*55	3* 0	..	5 48	5 57	6*25	8 23	1045	..	1049	1 35	6 3	9 2	10 23
Annaghmore .... "	8*41	..	..	..	1 13	..	..	..	3* 8	3*13	..	..	6 9	6*38	8 36	1058	..	11 1	1 47	6 15	9 14	10 35
Trew and Moy .. "	8*48	..	..	..	1 21	..	..	..	3*16	3*21	..	..	6 17	6*46	8 44	11 6	..	11 9	1 53	6 23	9 22	10 43
Dungannon ....arr.	8*56	9 37	..	1234	1 30	3 0	3 8	3g13	3*25	3*30	..	6 14	6 26	6*55	8 53	1115	..	1118	2 2	6 32	9 30	10 52
" ....dep.	——	9 43	9*54	1240	..	——	3 11	3 16	3*45	3*40	..	6 17	6*34	——	8 56	..	..	1123		..	9 32	
Donaghmore .... "	STOP	..	10* 0	..	..	STOP	x	x	3*54	3*49	..	..	6*41	STOP	9 2	..	..	1134	Commences 24th June	..	9 36	Commences 24th June.
Pomeroy .... "	..	..	10*13	cS	..	..	x	x	4* 7	4* 2	..	6s35	6*54	..	9 15	..	..	1146		..	9 50	
Carrickmore .... "	..	..	10*23	..	..	..	x	x	4*19	4*14	..	..	7* 4	..	9 25	..	..	1158		..	10 0	
Sixmilecross .... "	..	fw	10*29	..	..	..	x	x	4*27	4*22	..	..	7*12	..	9 32	..	..	12 6		..	10 7	
Beragh .... "	..	..	10*33	..	..	..	x	x	4*32	4*27	..	..	7*17	..	9 38	..	..	1211		..	10 12	
Omagh ....arr.	a.m.	1028	10*45	1 26	..	p.m.	4 0	4 3	4*45	4*40	..	7 9	7*30	..	9 50	..	..	1224		..	10 24	
" ....dep.	8 18	1035	..	1 33	..	1 50	4 5	4 6	..	..	5 20	7 19	..	..	9 58	..	..	1228		..	10 29	
Newtownstewart dep.	8 33	1051	..	..	..	2 5	4 19	4 20	..	..	5 37	7 36	..	..	1014	..	..	1245		..	10 46	
Victoria Bridge .. "	8 42	..	..	..	..	2 14	4 30	4 30	..	..	5 49	7 45	..	..	1023	..	..	1256		..	10 56	
Sion Mills .... "	8 47	..	..	cS	..	2 19	4 34	4 34	..	..	5 55	7 50	..	..	1028	..	..	1 1		..	11 1	
Strabane ......arr.	8 54	11 6	..	2 3	..	2 26	4 41	4 41	..	..	6 2	7 57	..	..	1035	..	..	1 8		..	11 8	
Strabane ....dep.	..	1120	..	2 35	..	..	5 35	5 35	..	..	..	8 10	..	..	..	..	..	..	..	..	12 30	..
Letterkenny .arr.	..	1232	..	3 54	..	..	6 47	6 47	..	..	..	9 15	..	..	..	..	..	..	..	..	1 35	..
Strabane ....dep.	..	1120	..	2 40	..	..	4 50	4 50	..	..	6 10	8 0	..	..	..	..	..	..	..	..	..	..
Stranorlar ...arr.	..	1212	..	3 32	..	..	5 33	5 33	..	..	6 50	8 40	..	..	..	..	..	..	..	..	..	..
Donegal .....arr.	..	1 9	..	4 30	..	..	6 43	6 43	..	..	7†50	..	..	..	..	..	..	..	..	..	..	..
Killybegs.....arr.	..	2 35	..	6 0	..	..	7 50	7 50	..	..	9† 0	..	..	..	..	..	..	..	..	..	..	..
Strabane ......dep.	8 58	1111	..	2 12	..	2 30	4 45	4 45	..	..	6 15	8 2	..	p.m. 9 20	1038	..	1220	1 10	..	..	11 17	..
Porthall......... "	9 5	..	..	..	..	2 36	..	..	..	..	6 21	..	..	9 26	..	..	..	..	..	..	..	..
St. Johnston .... "	9 14	..	..	..	..	2 45	..	..	..	..	6 29	..	..	9 35	..	..	..	..	..	..	..	..
Carrigans .... "	9 20	..	..	..	..	2 50	..	..	..	..	6 34	..	..	9 40	..	..	..	..	..	..	..	..
LONDONDERRY arr.	9 30	1135	..	2 35	..	3 2	5 5	5 5	..	..	6 45	8 25	..	9 52	11 0	..	1250	1 35	..	..	11 40	..

*—One Class only. †—Saturdays only. **cS**—Calls on Saturdays. **fw**—Calls on first Wednesday of each month. **g**—Does not convey passengers for Portadown or Dungannon. RC—Restaurant Car. SO—Saturdays only. **s** and **SX**—Saturdays excepted. **WSO**—Wednesdays and Saturdays only. **X**—Calls at certain Public Road Level Crossings on request. **x**—Calls on request to pick up passengers for stations beyond Omagh.

26

LONDONDERRY—OMAGH—DUNGANNON—BELFAST.

STATIONS	WEEKDAYS																	SUNDAYS			
					RC	'	SO	X	RC			RC					SO				
	a.m.	a.m.	a.m.	a.m.	a.m.	a.m.	p.m.	p.m.	p.m.	p.m.	p.m.	p.m.	p.m.	p.m.	p.m.	p.m.	p.m.	a.m.	p.m.	p.m.	p.m.
LONDONDERRY dep.	..	6 50	7 15	..	9 35	1015	..	..	1225	1 35	..	3 50	..	5 20	..	6 45	1110	9 30	..	..	6 20
Carrigans .... "	..	7 4	..	..	..	1032	..	..	..	1 49	..	..	..	5 43	..	6 55	1123	..	..	..	..
St. Johnstone ...... "	..	7 10	..	..	..	1040	..	..	..	1 55	..	..	..	5 48	..	6 59	1128	..	..	..	..
Porthall............ "	..	7 18	..	..	..	1053	..	..	..	2 5	..	..	..	5 56	..	7 6	1136	..	..	..	..
Strabane ....arr.	..	7 23	7 37	..	9 58	1058	..	..	1248	2 10	..	4 13	..	6 1	..	7 11	1141	9 53	..	..	6 43
Killybegs........dep.	..	..	..	..	..	..	..	..	9 25	..	..	1230	..	..	..	3 50	..	..	..	..	..
Donegal .... "	..	..	..	..	..	..	..	..	1034	..	..	1 42	..	..	..	5 0	..	..	..	..	..
Stranorlar....... "	..	..	6 45	8 45	8 45	..	..	..	1129	1 20	..	2 40	..	..	..	6 5	..	..	..	..	..
Strabane ....arr.	..	..	7 28	9 30	9 30	..	..	..	1220	2 0	..	3 25	..	..	..	6 53	..	..	..	..	..
Letterkenny ....dep.	..	..	..	..	8 45	..	..	..	1115	..	..	2 35	..	..	..	5 30	..	..		..	..
Strabane ....arr.	..	..	..	..	9 48	..	..	..	1225	..	..	3 49	..	..	..	6 46	..	..		..	..
Strabane ....dep.	..	..	7 41	9 35	10 3	..	..	..	1255	2 30	..	4 20	..	6 12	..	7 15	1148	9 56	Commences 24th June.	..	6 45
Sion Mills .... "	..	..	7 48	9 44	..	..	..	..	1 1	2 37	..	..	..	6 20	..	7 23	1156	10 3		..	6 52
Victoria Bridge ..... "	..	..	7 53	9 50	..	..	..	..	1 6	2 45	..	..	..	6 25	..	7 27	1159	10 8		..	6 57
Newtownstewart .. "	..	..	8 2	10 0	..	..	..	..	1 16	2 56	..	..	..	6 36	..	7 37	arr.	10 19		..	7 8
Omagh ....arr.	..	..	8 17	1015	1033	..	..	..	1 32	3 12	..	4 50	..	6 52	..	7 50	..	10 34		..	7 23
" ....dep.	6*35	..	8 30	..	1046	..	..	1255	1 40	..	..	5 0	5*15	..	..	8 2	..	10 38		..	7 28
Beragh .... "	6*49	..	8 45	..	..	..	..	1* 8	..	..	..	..	5*29	..	..	8 15	..	10 52		..	7 42
Sixmilecross .... "	6*54	..	8 50	..	..	..	..	1*12	..	..	..	..	5*34	..	..	8 19	..	10 56		..	7 46
Carrickmore .... "	7* 2	..	8 59	..	..	..	..	1*29	..	..	..	..	5*43	..	..	8 27	..	11 5	..	..	7 55
Pomeroy .... "	7*14	..	9 12	..	cM	..	..	1*41	..	..	..	..	5*57	..	..	8 37	..	11 18	..	..	8 7
Donaghmore .... "	7*27	..	9 26	..	..	..	..	1*54	..	..	..	..	6* 9	..	..	8 48	..	11 28	..	..	8 20
Dungannon ....arr.	7*35	..	9 32	..	1132	..	..	2* 0	2 27	..	..	5 45	6*15	..	..	8 54	..	11 41	..	..	8 25
" ....dep.	7 55	.	9 42	..	1137	..	1240	2* 1	2 31	..	4 46	5 48	6 35	..	8*25	8 58	..	11 43	2 26	8 15	8 27
Trew and Moy ..... "	8 4	.	9 51	..	..	..	1249	2*10	2 40	..	4 55	..	6 43	..	8*34	9 5	..	11 52	2 34	8 24	8 35
Annaghmore .... "	8 12	.	9 59	..	..	..	1258	2*18	2 48	..	5 3	..	6 51	..	8*42	9 12	..	12 0	2 42	8 32	8 43
Portadown ....arr.	8 24	..	10 11	..	12 1	..	1 11	2*30	3 0	..	5 15	6 13	7 3	..	8*55	9 22	..	12 12	2 55	8 45	8 55
Portadown .....dep.	8 56	..	..	..	1242	..	..	..	3 34	..	..	6 47	..	..	..	..	..	12a45		..	..
Dublin..........arr.	1115	..	..	..	3 0	..	..	..	6 15	..	..	9 20	..	..	..	..	..	3a20		..	..
Portadown ....dep.	8 30	..	10 16	..	1210	..	1 20	2f58	3 8	..	5 21	6 20	7 38	..	9 4	9 28	..	12 14	Runs to Warrenpoint.	8 58	9 5
Lurgan .... "	8 40	..	10 27	..	1221	..	1 31	..	3 19	..	5 32	6 30	7 48	..	9 14	9 38	..	12 24		9 8	9 16
Lisburn .... "	9 2	..	10 48	..	..	..	1 50		..	..	5 52	6 49	8 12	..	..	9 53	..	12 43		9 28	9 38
BELFAST ....arr.	9 13	..	11 0	..	1255	..	2 5	3f30	3 55	..	6 5	7 0	8 25	..	9 40	10 5	..	12 55		9 40	9 50

*—One Class only. a—Commences 24th June. **cM**—Calls on Mondays. f—Commences 25th June. **RC**—Restaurant Car. **SO**—Saturdays only. **X**—Calls at certain Public Road Level Crossings on request.

27

Specimen pages from June 1956 issue of GNR timetable, one of the last to appear before dissolution, shows County Donegal Railway connections. All of these lines except the main portions of the railway between Belfast, Portadown and Dublin are now closed only ones ever to run in Ireland, and for a few years they worked on the Limited Mail between Dublin and Belfast. They were scrapped and replaced in 1904 by a couple of 4–4–0s which took the same names and numbers.

In 1885–9 Park turned out some 4–4–0s with 5ft 7in wheels for cross-country working, and in 1892 he adapted this type with larger wheels for express duties. With sundry variations and progressive enlargements this was to remain the only wheel arrangement ever used by the company for main-line work to the end of steam.

The general design of locomotives introduced by Park and continued by his successors was extremely neat and simple, and up to World War I presented a very attractive appearance in a livery of rich green with red-brown underframes, not unlike the Great Central. Oblong nameplates with red background were placed on the side of the boiler barrel. Unfortunately all this was discarded in Glover's time; the names were removed and the livery became a sombre black, relieved only by a single red line, giving the engines a very plain utilitarian appearance, only counterbalanced to some extent by the very neat outlines. There were no embellishments, such as copper-capped chimneys or brasswork, and the decorative Beyer Peacock maker's plates combined with the splasher beading were taken off. A few of the top link engines after 1939 received a bright blue livery with red framing, and the policy of naming was reintroduced to a small degree with the compounds in 1932.

Apart from the latter, and their 1948 successors, all engines (with two minor exceptions) had inside cylinders and had what perhaps can best be described as a strictly Edwardian appearance. They were largely 4–4–0s for express and intermediate work, 0–6–0s for freight and miscellaneous duties, and 4–4–2Ts and a few older 2–4–2Ts for suburban and branch work. There were a few other tank engines, including only three 0–6–0Ts, one of which was an outside-cylinder crane engine used for shunting at Dundalk works, the only one of its kind ever to run in Ireland.

ENGINES OF CONSTITUENT COMPANIES SURVIVING IN 1930

Number	Former owning company	Type	Built	Withdrawn
37	Irish North Western	0–6–0	1876	1948
40	Dublin & Belfast Junction	0–6–0	1872	1937
41	,, ,, ,,	0–6–0	1872	1934
137	Ulster Railway	0–6–0	1872	1938
138	,, ,,	0–6–0	1873	1948
193	Irish North Western	0–6–0	1871	1948
194	,, ,, ,,	0–6–0	1873	1948
195	Belfast Central	4–4–0T	1878	1950

Number	Former owning company	Type	Built	With-drawn
203	*	{ 0–4–0ST outside cylinders }	1904	1930
204	*	0–6–0T	1903	1930
119	No 1 until 1921	0–6–0T	1887†	1937
5	Stationary boiler at Dundalk works until 1929. Scrapped 1931	4–4–0T	1889	1921

* Purchased from contractors on completion of Castleblayney Keady & Armagh Railway.
† First engine built at Dundalk works. Originally 4–4–0T. Rebuilt as 0–6–0T in 1921.

GNR MAIN LOCOMOTIVE LIST IN 1930

A few miscellaneous renumberings took place after this time, and later numbers are shown in brackets. The renumbering by the UTA took place in 1960. Those taken over by the CIE retained their Great Northern numbers until withdrawal.

Official classifica-tion	Type	Engine numbers	Years of construction	Withdrawal dates or other particulars
H	2–4–0	84–7	1880–1	1932
P	5′ 6″ 4–4–0	88, 89	1904 replacements of 4–2–2s built 1885	1956
P	5′ 6″ 4–4–0	51–4, 104, 105	1892–1905	1950–6
P	6′ 6″ 4–4–0	72, 73, 83 (26), 82 (27)	1892–5	1957–9
PP & PPs	6′ 6″ 4–4–0	12, 25, 42–6, 70, 71, 74 (UTA 42), 75–7, 106, 107, 129	1896–1911	1957–9
Qs QLs	6′ 6″ 4–4–0 6′ 6″ 4–4–0	120–5, 130–6 24, 113/14, 126–8, 156/7	1899–1904 1904–10	{ 1932 (114) others 1951–63. 131 preserved by CIE
S	6′ 6″ 4–4–0	170 Errigal 171 Slieve Gullion 172 Slieve Donard (UTA 60) 173 Galtee More (UTA 61) 174 Carrantuohill	1913 major re-construction in 1938–9	1965 171 preserved in working order by Railway Preserva-tion Society of Ireland
S2	6′ 6″ 4–4–0	190 Lugnaquilla (UTA 62) 191 Croagh Patrick	1915 Major re-construction in 1938–9	1959–65

Official classification	Type	Engine numbers	Years of construction	Withdrawal dates or other particulars
		192 *Slievenamon* (UTA 63) (names given on reconstruction)		
U	5′ 9″ 4–4–0	196 *Lough Gill* (UTA 64) 197 *Lough Neagh* 198 *Lough Swilly* 199 *Lough Derg* 200 *Lough Melvin* (UTA 65) names added 1949–50	1915	1959–65
A	0–6–0 Power class A	28–33, 64 (67), 60, 61, 67–9, 79 (69), 80, 81, 145, 146, 149 150	1882–91	1928–61 No 31 sold to SLNCR in 1928, and the second no 69 sold to SLNCR in 1940
AL		29, 32, 35, 36, 55–9, 140, 141	1883–6	1957–61
B		26, 27, 62, 63, 66 (27, 149), 34	1877–80	1925–38 No 149 sold to SLNCR in 1931
PGs	0–6–0 Power class B	10, 11, 100–3, 151	1899–1904	1960–4
QGs		152–5	1903–4	1963
NQG NQGs	0–6–0 Power class C	9, 38, 39, 112	1911	1959–64
SG SG2		15, 16–18 (UTA 38–40) 19, 175, 176 (UTA 43) 177–81, 182/3 (UTA 41/2) 184	1913–25	1960–3
LQGs	0–6–0 Power class D	78 (119), 108–10, 158–64	1906–11	1959–64
		6 (UTA 30), 7 (UTA 31), 8, 13 (UTA 32), 14, 20 (UTA 33), 47, 48, 49 (UTA 36), 96, 97 (UTA 37), 117, 118, 201 (40 UTA 34), 202 (41 UTA 35)	1920–1	1959–65
T T1	4–4–2T	1–5, 21, 30, 62–6, 115, 116, 139, 142–4, 147 (67), 148 (69), 185–9	1913–29	1959–64

Official classification	Type	Engine numbers	Years of construction	Withdrawal dates or other particulars
JT	2–4–2T	90–5	1897–1902	1955–63 No 93 preserved in Belfast Museum
RT	0–6–4T	22, 23, 166, 167 (UTA 22–5)	1908–11	1960–5
QGT QGT2	0–6–2T	98, 99, 168, 169	1904–11	1957–60
—	0–6–0T Crane, outside cylinders	31 (CIE 365A)	1927	1964

The 4–4–0s nos 25, 26 and 124, 0–6–0s 36 and 41 and 2–4–2T 90 were sold for scrap together with a number of others from the CIE and shipped to Spain in 1958, where they were cut up at San Juan de Nieva.

Many railways in the British Isles experimented with steam railmotors in the early 1900s. The Great Northern obtained four totally enclosed cars from North British in 1905, and three more by Manning Wardle in 1906. The Coachwork was by British Electrical Engineering. They worked on local services around Dublin and Belfast. On withdrawal in 1914–16 the engines were removed and the coach bodies converted to tri-composite brake carriages.

NEW ENGINES AFTER 1930

Official classification	Type	Engine numbers	Years of construction	Withdrawal dates or other particulars
V	4–4–0 3 cylinder compound	83 *Eagle* 84 *Falcon* 85 *Merlin* 86 *Peregrine* 87 *Kestrel*	1932	1959–61 No 85 preserved in Belfast Museum
UG	0–6–0	78 (UTA 45), 79 (UTA 46) 80, 81, 82 (UTA 47) 145, 146 (UTA 48) 147, 148, 149 (UTA 49)	1937 1948	1960–5
U	5′ 9″ 4–4–0 1915 design	201 *Meath* (UTA 66) 202 *Louth* (UTA 67) 203 *Armagh* 204 *Antrim* 205 *Down* (UTA 68)	1948	1960–5

Official classifica-tion	Tppe	Engine nvmbers	Years of construction	Withdrawal dates or other particulars
VS	4-4-0 3 cylinder simple	206 Liffey 207 Boyne 208 Lagan (UTA 58) 209 Foyle 210 Erne (UTA 59)	1948	1959-65

With the exception of nos 78-82 constructed at the company's own works at Dundalk in 1937, all these new engines were built by Beyer Peacock.

The largest locomotive shed was at Adelaide, Belfast, where in 1934 for instance, there were stationed about 80 of the locomotive stock of some 200 engines comprising examples of practically all classes. Dublin, Amiens Street, had 25 engines, and Dundalk, headquarters of the system, thirty-three. Smaller sheds of some importance were, with permanent allocations:

> Portadown (14)
> Londonderry (16)
> Drogheda (10)
> Newry (8)
> Enniskillen (7)
> Clones (8)

There were also small sheds, such as Bundoran and Banbridge, and some of the shorter branches accommodated one or two engines overnight, supplied from the parent depot.

Great Northern coaching stock, nearly all of which was built at Dundalk, was generally speaking adequate and progressive, as good as anything to be found in other parts of Ireland, although somewhat behind many English railways. Third class tended to be on the austere side, but against this the railway retained a very comfortable and reasonably priced second class, as did the Northern Counties Committee and the BCDR, for many years after it had gone out of general use in Great Britain. Bogie coaches first appeared as early as 1889, and gradually increased in number; no more six-wheeled vehicles were built after 1896, but their use on secondary services continued until after World War II. Vestibuled trains did not come until 1911, but the railway started refreshment services in 1895, at first only on the main line and for first- and second-class passengers. Between the wars there was often some sort of refreshment to be had, even if only a tea tray, on several of the longer distance cross-country services. The Great Northern pioneered electric lighting in 1896, and it never used gas.

The only diesel locomotive it ever owned was no 800, a mixed-traffic diesel-hydraulic 0–8–0 supplied by a German firm in 1954, which eventually went to CIE. However, the GNR was early in the field with diesel railbuses and railcars. The first were a couple of railcars built at Dundalk works in 1932, A and B, the first a diesel-mechanical and the second diesel-electric. Railcar C, which followed in 1934, had the engine and driving compartment articulated from the coach body to reduce vibration in the passenger coach, but had the disadvantage that it needed turning. Railcar sets C2 and C3, which appeared in 1935, consisted of two cars back to back, only one power bogie, the leading one according to direction of travel, being in use at a time. D and E, which came out in 1936, had two bodies articulated to a central power bogie with six coupled wheels, and F and G, which followed in 1938, had four wheels coupled hydraulically.

Concurrently with these railcars, some railbuses were built for use on branches with very light traffic; these were of ordinary bus construction and, in fact, the first one was converted from a road bus, and was remarkable in having pneumatic tyres adapted with a steel rim for rail running. In all, four railbuses were put into service between 1934 and 1936.

In 1950 the Great Northern introduced the modern multiple-unit railcar, with its much wider potentialities not only for cross-country and intermediate passenger service, but for main-line operation as well. Indeed, quite soon some sets were built specially for working the star train, the Enterprise express. While for lengthy journeys a locomotive-hauled train is far more suitable, none the less the multiple-unit railcar has secured an established place in the passenger transport of the United Kingdom and it should not be forgotten that it originated with the enterprise of that regrettably now defunct railway, the Great Northern of Ireland.

CHAPTER 16

DUNDALK NEWRY & GREENORE
RAILWAY

This little railway was entirely English-owned throughout its existence, being a small offshoot of the LNWR and in turn of its successors, the LMS and British Railways.

Incorporated 1873. Opened 1876.

Route mileage: 26½ miles.

Principal places served:
  Greenore (in conjunction with steamer services), Newry, Dundalk.

Closed 1951.

The origins of the DNGR lay in the aspirations of the LNWR to extend its operations across the Irish Sea. It had already inherited from its constituent, the Chester & Holyhead, its own steamer services between Holyhead and Kingstown (Dun Laoghaire), which had been started by the Chester & Holyhead in 1848, and jointly with the Lancashire & Yorkshire it operated steamers between Fleetwood and Belfast; moreover from 1872 it shared in the Belfast services via Stranraer and Larne, through the Portpatrick & Wigtownshire Railway, of which it was one of the four joint owners. At the same time the Dundalk & Enniskillen Railway was interested in developing the port of Greenore for services to England in conjunction with the LNWR, which was mainly why it changed its title in 1862 to Irish North Western.

  There were proposals in 1863 for the setting up of an independent concern, the Dundalk & Greenore Railway, with the financial backing of both the English and Irish North Western companies, and for a rival scheme promoted by interested parties in Newry, including the other railways already serving the town, the Newry & Armagh and the Newry, Warrenpoint & Rostrevor, which wanted access from their district to Greenore via Carlingford rather than via Dundalk. Eventually agreement was reached between the two projects, the DGR and the Newry & Greenore, by Act of 28 July 1863, under which the two schemes would proceed separately but with joint construction, ownership and management of the railway and harbour works at Greenore. In the event the Newry & Greenore was unable to raise the necessary capital, and the financial responsibility of building the railway and harbour at Greenore fell entirely to the LNWR, working in conjunction with the DGR and the INWR.

An Act of 14 July 1870 empowered the LNWR to operate steamer services between Holyhead and Greenore, and other points on Carlingford Lough, which included Warrenpoint and Greencastle on the County Down side, but there were no harbours, only piers, at these places. The INWR in turn found itself in financial difficulties and unable to implement its part of the arrangement under which it would have provided the rolling stock for the DGR, and it was left to the LNWR to take over all responsibility for running the line. The opening ceremony eventually took place on 30 April 1873, steamer services to and from Holyhead starting on 1–2 May. The terminus of the DGR at Dundalk was at Quay Street, in the eastern part of the town, but to give connection with the main line of the Dublin & Belfast Junction trains were run through over the INWR using Dundalk Square crossing to a junction to the west of it, where they reversed into a joint INWR and DBJR station, later replaced in GNR days by a new one slightly to the north, and this arrangement lasted through the history of the DNGR.

Greenore station consisted of a single platform with an overall roof, and the railway built a fine hotel nearby. Later it added a golf course in an attempt to increase the attractiveness of the town as a holiday resort, instead of being merely a point of transit on a journey between England and Ireland. The company also had its own reservoir, water and eventually electricity supplies, and sewage system.

The Newry & Dundalk having failed to materialise, the DGR, by Act of 21 July 1873, was authorised to build the railway, and at the same time its name was changed to Dundalk Newry & Greenore Railway; it was opened on 1 August 1876. It had its own station at Newry, Bridge Street, but made end-on connection with the GNR between the two stations, the Great Northern one being at Edward Street. This enabled the Great Northern to run through boat expresses between Belfast and Greenore, over the DNGR, with trains supplied by the latter but worked through by Great Northern engines.

The Greenore–Newry route was a very scenic one, amongst the best in Ireland, running along the west side of Carlingford Lough and, in fact, so close to the shore that it was damaged on several occasions during severe gales.

The eastern side of the lough was overlooked by the Mountains of Mourne, whilst to the west was a smaller range of hills. This stretch of line also included the wrought-iron Essmore bridge; engineering works on the DNGR were not numerous, but there were two considerable viaducts, Castletown and Bally-mascanlon, and a smaller one, Riverstown, on the Dundalk section.

The boats used on the Holyhead–Greenore service in earlier days were paddle steamers, *Edith*, *Countess of Erne*, *Eleanor*, *Earl Spencer* and *Isabella*, which were replaced in later years by more modern ships. The last new one was a very fine two-funnelled turbine steamer *Curraghmore*, later renamed *Duke of Aber-corn*.

The DNGR unfortunately never fulfilled expectations. The fault lay to some extent with the London & North Western itself in that although the intention was to foster traffic between England and Ireland, particularly the north-west,

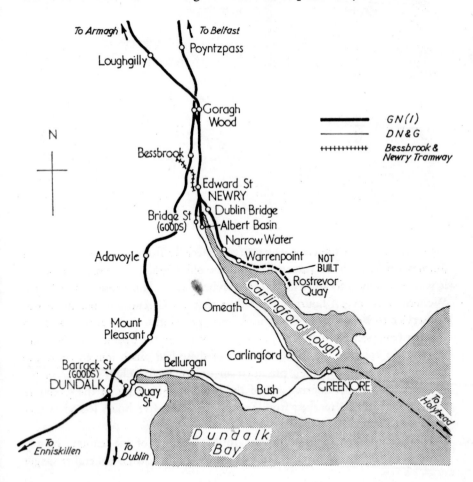

DNGR paper ticket

the service was not sufficiently attractive, especially from the point of view of journey times, to divert patronage from the older established routes, to which it was definitely inferior. The direct Holyhead to Dublin route of the North Western, was several hours quicker than that via Greenore. Then there was the service to Belfast from Fleetwood, operated jointly by the North Western and the Lancashire & Yorkshire, and yet another on the opening of Heysham Harbour in 1904 by the Midland; both of these had much longer sea routes than via Greenore but they provided an uninterrupted night's sleep on the steamer. Even Londonderry, one of the principal objectives of the Greenore route, could still be reached from London in about five hours less via either Dublin or Larne.

Things improved to some extent around the turn of the century, mainly through the efforts of Sir Frederick Harrison, who became general manager of the LNWR in 1893, but better timings and publicity failed to secure any lasting benefit, and the railway became increasingly dependent on its cargo and cattle transhipments, apart from its local traffic which was never very extensive. World War I brought to an end nearly all holiday traffic and the line was taken over by the government in 1917. The steamer passenger service was not resumed until 1920, and then only in a somewhat halfhearted manner. Cattle traffic continued to provide a profitable source of revenue, though the overall loss in 1923 was £25,000; and the passenger service was never resumed after the 1926 general strike. By this time of course ownership of the railway had passed from the LNWR to the newly formed LMS.

The partition of Ireland in 1921 also produced its problems, as the DNGR was one of those railways which found itself partly in the northern province and partly in the Free State. The border cut across the railway between Newry and Omeath, the customs points being at the latter place and at Greenore.

Specimen DNGR tickets

In order to achieve economies negotiation was opened with the Great Northern for the latter to take over the working of the line, which it did on 1 July 1933, and this resulted in some temporary improvement. Within two years the annual loss was reduced to £10,000, but at the end of World War II it had risen to £35,000, largely owing to the loss of much of the cattle traffic, although this did not cease entirely.

In 1948 ownership passed into the hands of the British Transport Commission, which in 1950 decided that it would not subsidise the railway after the end of that year; the period of grace was later extended for another twelve months. This was just at the time when it was being proposed that the GNR should be taken over by the two Irish governments. Both of these, however, refused to include the DNGR and the railway was closed accordingly on 31 December 1951. Such were the legal difficulties arising from the fact that it was an English-owned railway whose lines ran in two different countries in Ireland, that the final winding up did not take place until July 1957.

Recently freight traffic at Greenore has been so heavy that there have been serious suggestions of restoring the line between there and Dundalk, where it would join the Great Northern line north of the river to avoid the reconstruction of Castletown viaduct.

LOCOMOTIVES AND ROLLING STOCK

The DNGR engines were all of one class, built at Crewe and of pure North Western design, although not exactly like anything to be found on the parent system, being a cross between Ramsbottom's DX 0–6–0 tender engines and F. W. Webb's 0–6–0 'special tanks'; the DNGR locos were similar to the latter but had 5ft 2in driving wheels in place of 4ft 6in. They bore the unmistakable stamp of a genuine Crewe product, from the pattern of the chimney to the distinctive design of the numberplates, and of course Webb's black livery.

The first three, 1 *Macrory*, 2 *Greenore* and 3 *Dundalk*, were built at Crewe in 1873, followed by 4 *Newry* and 5 *Carlingford* in 1876, when the Newry section was opened, and finally by 6 *Holyhead* in 1898. The latter was not new, being reconstructed from a DX 0–6–0 built in 1867 as no 900, but later renumbered 3204 and later still 1855.

No 5 was scrapped in 1928, but the others were still in existence at the closing of the line, although nos 2 and 4 had been out of use for some years, lying in Dundalk yard in a state of dereliction. All were broken up at Sutton, Dublin, in May 1952 except no 1, which was sent to Belfast with a view to preservation, but unfortunately this did not materialise. After the Great Northern took over the working of the line it used its own 2–4–2Ts on the passenger trains, but the surviving saddle tanks were not affected in any way and kept their DNGR numbers and identity to the end. The Great Northern also used a couple of its railbuses on some services.

The coaching stock was also typically LNWR, with its distinctive chocolate and white livery (perpetuated under Great Northern control), mostly six-wheelers, but there were a few bogie vehicles for the through Belfast boat trains. All three classes were provided, first, second and third.

There are some engine nameplates in Clapham Museum, and fortunately one of the six-wheelers has found a permanent resting place in Belfast Museum, now the only large tangible relic of what was once an offshoot of the 'premier line'.

CHAPTER 17

BELFAST & NORTHERN COUNTIES RAILWAY

Latterly known as the NORTHERN COUNTIES COMMITTEE (MIDLAND RAILWAY) *after absorption by the* MIDLAND RAILWAY *in 1903. Mostly 5ft 3in but also sections of 3ft gauge. Principal railway in the north-east with an almost complete monopoly of the counties of Londonderry and Antrim.*

Principal constituents:

BELFAST & BALLYMENA RAILWAY   Incorporated 1845. Opened 1848 (renamed BELFAST & NORTHERN COUNTIES RAILWAY 1860).

LONDONDERRY & COLERAINE RAILWAY   Incorporated 1852. Opened 1853 (acquired by BNCR 1871).

BALLYMENA BALLYMONEY COLERAINE & PORTRUSH JUNCTION RAILWAY   Incorporated 1853. Opened 1855 (acquired by BNCR 1861).

CARRICKFERGUS & LARNE RAILWAY   Incorporated 1860. Opened 1862 worked by BNCR.

Other subsequent additions include the DERRY CENTRAL line, the Cookstown branch, and narrow-gauge systems.

In 1903 the BELFAST & NORTHERN COUNTIES RAILWAY was acquired by the MIDLAND RAILWAY of England, which became part of the LMS in 1923.

Route mileage in 1922: 5ft 3in gauge—201 miles.

3ft gauge—64 miles.

Principal places served:

Belfast, Larne (in connection with steamer sailings to Stranraer), Ballymena, Coleraine, Portrush, Londonderry.

After the absorption of the Waterford Limerick & Western by the Great Southern & Western in 1901, the Belfast & Northern Counties became the fourth largest railway in Ireland, with a route mileage of 265, of which 64 miles were 3ft gauge. It enjoyed an almost complete monopoly of the area it served, the north-east, in the counties of Antrim and Londonderry. However, the city of Londonderry was also reached by the Great Northern, one of the few instances of direct competition between rival routes. There were one or two smaller towns which were also served by both railways from Belfast, namely Cookstown and Antrim, and these were moreover the only points of physical contact between the BNCR and the rest of the Irish railway system, apart from the docks and street connections at Belfast and the bridge at Londonderry.

Again, like most major railway systems, the BNCR grew up very largely by amalgamation and absorption of a number of lines which started as independent concerns. The nucleus of the railway was the Belfast & Ballymena, between which two points there were proposals for rail communication as early as 1836. These came to nothing but the project was revived in 1844, and on 21 July 1845 an Act of Parliament authorised the construction of the Belfast & Ballymena Railway. The first sod was cut near Whitehouse on 16 November 1845 by the tenth Viscount Massereene, and the line was opened to Greenisland and Ballymena, 33¼ miles, together with an extension from Greenisland to Carrickfergus, 2¾ miles, and a 1¾ mile branch to Randalstown, on 11 April 1848.

At what ultimately became the other end of the system, the Londonderry & Coleraine Railway, originally incorporated on 4 August 1845, but dissolved and reincorporated on 23 May 1852, was opened as far as Limavady, 19 miles, on 1 October of that year for goods traffic and on 20 December for passengers. The railway reached the west bank of the River Bann at Coleraine in July 1853 from Limavady Junction and the 3¼ miles to Limavady then became a branch; the distance from the junction to Coleraine was another 17 miles. Later the Limavady branch was extended to Dungiven, another 10¼ miles, in July 1883, by a separate company, the Limavady & Dungiven Railway, which although worked by the Belfast & Northern Counties, was not actually absorbed until February 1907, by which time the BNCR had itself been taken over, in 1903, by the Midland Railway of England. Much of the line between Coleraine and Londonderry runs alongside the shores of Lough Foyle and by the open sea, with fine stretches of sand on the beach below; there are two short tunnels.

The missing link in the eventual through route between Belfast and Londonderry was provided by the independent Ballymena Ballymoney Coleraine & Portrush Junction Railway, incorporated on 8 July 1853 and opened on 7 November 1855. This made end-on connection with the Belfast & Ballymena and provided another 34¼ miles of the through route to the watering place of Portrush, on the northern coast. At Coleraine it was within a short distance of the terminus of the Londonderry & Coleraine Railway but on the other bank of the

Page 197 (above) Dundalk Newry & Greenore saddle-tank no 2 *Greenore*, built at Crewe in 1873. The LNWR design will be noted; (*below*) some of the LNWR saddle-tanks remained at work until the closure of the DNGR in 1951 although the GNR took over the working of the line in 1933. This illustration shows a train running over Dundalk Square crossing in 1950, where the DNGR crossed the GNR main line at right angles, with 2–4–2T no 90. The second coaching vehicle is one of the Crewe six-wheelers still painted in LNWR livery

Page 198 (*above*) A handsome GNR clerestory roof coach seen at Belfast in 1950, in many ways reminiscent of Doncaster, although the Irish railway had no actual connection with its English namesake; (*centre*) old GNR six-wheelers at Belturbet in 1948; (*bottom*) the LMS Northern Counties Committee, together with some other Irish railways, notably the Great Northern and the Belfast & County Down, maintained three classes right through to the age of the diesel railcar in the 1950s. A tri-composite compartment suburban coach seen here at Belfast in 1948

River Bann, and until this was bridged five years later through passengers between Belfast and Londonderry had to change trains and be ferried across. It was not until 1860 that the connecting line, authorised on 19 April 1859, was opened on completion of the bridge in November 1860, which established through rail communication between the two cities. The line to Portrush was then regarded as the branch, although from a traffic point of view it was, and still is, more important, having more through expresses than Londonderry to and from Belfast, at any rate whilst the rival Great Northern route was still in operation. Very shortly after the opening of the bridge in January 1861, the Portrush company was acquired by the Belfast & Northern Counties Railway, the title by which the Belfast & Ballymena had been known since 15 May 1860. The Londonderry & Coleraine Railway was not taken over by the BNCR until 24 July 1871, although it had been leased since 1860.

This original bridge over the Bann was 435ft long with sixteen fixed spans and two opening ones to allow shipping access to Coleraine itself. It was replaced in 1924 by a new one several hundred yards downstream, consisting of eleven spans with a rising bascule section 85ft wide between the central piers. This involved a diversion of the approaches on either side of the river, the old ones being abandoned except for a short section serving Coleraine Harbour, which had been opened in January 1892; this line was closed in 1966.

Branching off the LCR at one time was what must have been the shortest-lived railway ever. This was a 4½ mile line from Magilligan to the northern coast at Magilligan Strand, opened in 1854 and believed to have been worked by horse traction. It was unremunerative from the start, and the service appears to have lasted only for about a year. It appeared in Bradshaw in 1855, but never again, and it seems likely that it closed in that year.

The original Belfast & Ballymena already included a branch eastwards from Greenisland as far as Carrickfergus, as part of the original system. In 1860 another company was formed by an Act dated 15 May, the Carrickfergus & Larne Railway, to connect Belfast with Larne, one of the nearest points to the Scottish coast, and which provided a short sea crossing of only 36 miles to Stranraer Harbour, far less than any of the other established routes between Great Britain and Ireland.

The new line, 14¾ miles from Carrickfergus, was completed and opened on 1 October 1862, and a steamer service inaugurated at the same time; this still operates in connection with train services both from Glasgow and London. The new railway was worked from the first by the Belfast & Northern Counties but was not absorbed until 1 July 1890.

Two other harbour extensions were made in addition to that to Coleraine: Portrush Harbour Tramway, financed by the BNCR and the Portrush Harbour

M

Commissioners, incorporated on 23 June 1864, and opened in June 1866; and the Carrickfergus Harbour Junction Railway, in June 1887.

A disadvantage of the working of express trains on the Belfast–Coleraine section lay in the fact that all trains had to reverse at Greenisland, 6¾ miles out of Belfast. They would sometimes be taken over the section by any engine available and the main-line locomotive would be attached at Greenisland for the main part of the journey, or the latter engine would work throughout, using the turntable at Greenisland and running tender-first between there and Belfast. Powers had been obtained as long ago as 1872 for a direct cut-off, but it was not until 1931 that this major operation was finally undertaken. It involved the construction of a new direct loop, 2¾ miles in length, and included the building of what was then the longest reinforced-concrete viaduct in the British Isles, 630ft, with a maximum height of 70ft and three main arches, each with a span of 89ft. It cost £250,000, of which £80,000 was contributed by the Government of Northern Ireland for the relief of unemployment. It was the last important new railway construction in Ireland, and took nearly three years, being finally opened on 17 January 1934 by the Duke of Abercorn, in a train hauled by engine no 90 which suitably bore his name.

This enabled the most important express trains to be speeded up very considerably. The best train was the North Atlantic Express, one of Ireland's very few named trains, leaving Portrush at 8.10 am and returning at 5.15 pm, calling only at Ballymena; it covered the 67½ miles to Portrush in 80 minutes, no mean achievement for that time on a route which was largely single line, even with light loads of five coaches. The peak of express running was reached in 1938, with a 60mph timing of 31 minutes for the 31 miles between Ballymena and Belfast, and an overall timing of 73 minutes.

With the exception of the 4½ mile branch to Ballyclare, off the original Belfast & Ballymena, opened in November 1884, the remaining portion of the BNCR lay to the west of the main line between Antrim and Coleraine.

The short branch of the Belfast & Ballymena to Randalstown was in November 1856 extended to Cookstown, a town of some 5,000 inhabitants. It lies just inside County Tyrone, the only place on the BNCR system not in the counties of Londonderry and Antrim. The point of divergence of the original Randalstown branch now became known as Cookstown Junction.

Cookstown is about 35 miles due west of Belfast as the crow flies, but the distance by rail was 53½ miles owing to a wide detour around Lough Neagh, the largest lake in the British Isles, covering 153½ square miles, and 80 miles in circumference.

When the Great Northern built its line to Cookstown in 1879, it was, like the BNCR's, a dead-end branch; each company had its own station, one beside the other, but there was physical connection between the two lines. The distance from Belfast by the Great Northern was 54½ miles, slightly longer than the BNCR but not enough to make the two routes uncompetitive. Each company normally operated about four trains daily and one on Sundays, but only one of these on each line was a through train to and from Belfast, the others being branch trains with connections at Cookstown Junction and Dungannon respectively.

In the 1880s two more independent railways were promoted which were worked by the BNCR and in due course became part of it. The Derry Central Railway, 29½ miles, left the Cookstown branch at the intermediate point of Magherafelt and ran northwards to join the main line of the BNCR at Macfin, 4¾ miles short of Coleraine. It was opened in February 1880 and acquired by the BNCR in September 1901. The Draperstown Railway also diverged at Magherafelt, which now became the junction of four lines, and this one ran westwards for 8 miles to terminate at Draperstown, bounded by mountain ranges on three sides, Slieve Gallion to the south, and the Sperrin Mountains to the north and west. This railway was opened in July 1883 and acquired by the BNCR in July 1895.

None of these branches ever enjoyed a great amount of traffic and all were naturally single line, as was indeed most of the system, including much of the main line itself. Sections which were doubled were from Belfast to Greencastle, in November 1862, and on to Greenisland in the following September; Greencastle to Doagh in November 1875, the section thence to Dunadry having already been done three years earlier; and Dunadry to Cookstown Junction, in February 1877, and on to Ballymena in July 1878. This was as far as doubling ever got on the main line to Portrush and Londonderry. However, some of the station passing loops are arranged and signalled for two-way running so that, with automatic tablet-catching apparatus on the engine, an express could take the through road without slackening speed. The signals, by the way, were of the somersault pattern. On the Larne line beyond Greenisland doubling was extended as far as Carrickfergus in April 1897, but it was not until 1929 that this got as far as Whitehead, and never beyond.

The main terminus at York Road, Belfast, headquarters of the railway, was a fine building with an imposing façade, but it was severely damaged in the air raids of April and May 1941, when most of the company's offices were destroyed along with many valuable records of the railway's history. The building also embodied a fine hotel, named the Midland; this was used as a hostel for US forces later in the war, but reopened to the public in January 1946.

The station is situated some distance from the city centre (although handy for Donegal Quay, where the boats from Heysham, Liverpool and Ardrossan berth). It was however reached by the Belfast street trams in 1872, then horse-worked but later electrified, and these actually entered the station by a spur line, as they also did at Queens Quay, the Belfast & County Down station. The tramway system was abandoned in the 1950s and replaced by buses.

There is still quite a busy local and commuter service, mostly on the Larne line, but also to Ballymena, which now has a population of some 15,000, and there are also business expresses from Portrush. Nowadays the whole service is worked by multiple-unit diesel railcars.

Until May 1955 there were the usual three classes of accommodation; the BNCR was probably the first railway in Great Britain and Ireland to convey third-class passengers by all trains, which it did as early as October 1862, ten years before the Midland, the first railway in England to do so.

The BNCR was also not backward in other respects regarding the comfort of its passengers. Third-class carriages had overall roofs by 1856, restaurant cars were introduced in June 1898, and steam heating, perhaps a little behind the times, in December 1906. The modern corridor stock of the NCC was of a very good standard, many of the vehicles having all three classes. The bombing raids of April and May 1941 resulted in the loss of twenty coaches, which were hastily replaced by LMS vehicles from Derby, suitably regauged.

In conjunction with the railways in Great Britain the company operated steamer services between Belfast and Fleetwood and Barrow from the 1850s onward, and when the Midland opened Heysham Harbour in 1903, at the same time as it took over the BNCR, it ran its own ships between Belfast and Heysham. This service still survives.

On the opening of the line to Larne Harbour in 1862 a service to Stranraer was initiated, but it was withdrawn in 1864 and not restored until 1872, when the Larne & Stranraer Steamboat company was established, jointly operated by the Midland, LNWR, Caledonian, Glasgow & South Western, Portpatrick & Wigtownshire and of course the BNCR itself. This service also still operates.

The BNCR, or Northern Counties Committee as it became, was also early in the field of road transport. Steam goods wagons were already in use by 1902, and in April of that year the company started running its own omnibuses to serve the area between Greenisland and Whiteabbey. In May 1906 a road motor was inaugurated between Cushendall and Parkmore on the narrow-gauge line from Ballymena. The railway also by this time had its own sightseeing char-à-bancs, as they were then called, early versions, quite unenclosed, of the modern motor coach. Other bus services followed, including a replacement of the Port-stewart Tramway by buses in January 1926. In 1930 the railway had taken over most of the privately owned bus services in its area. By 1935 the fleet had grown

Seals of all undertakings directly connected with the N.C.C.

Seals of constituent companies

to 130 buses and 60 lorries, when these were transferred to the newly formed Northern Ireland Road Transport Board.

In August 1934 air services began between Belfast and Glasgow, and Belfast, Liverpool and London, operated by Railway Air Services. This organisation was taken over by British European Airways in February 1947.

During the war an extension of an RAF runway at Ballykelly, between Coleraine and Londonderry, to accommodate larger aircraft, had to be built right across the main line—Britain's one and only rail-air level crossing. The signalling is operated by a lever frame in a signal box on the up side, interlocked with the control tower at the airfield. As at an ordinary road crossing, trains have right of way except in an emergency.

Two steam railmotors had been introduced by the Midland Railway in 1905 for local trains out of Belfast, nos 90 and 91, but these lasted only until 1913. The first experiment in non-steam rail traction was made in 1924, when a road bus was fitted with flanged wheels and tried out between Coleraine and Portrush, and in January 1933 the first Leyland petrol-engined bogie railcar was built at York Road shops. The second unit, which appeared in 1934, was diesel engined, as were subsequent ones; it could run with two trailers, one at each end, and had provision for first-class passengers. Two more appeared in 1937 and 1938.

In 1925 a Sentinel railcar was also tried out (together with a Sentinel shunting locomotive) but these also were apparently unsatisfactory and both were out of service by 1930 and scrapped in 1932. The shunter had the number 91, and the railcar 401, in the coaching stock list. However, these were early experimental versions; later versions produced by the Sentinel company were successful and were used, on other railways, until the coming of the diesel railcar and shunter.

It was on 1 July 1903 that the Midland Railway of England, in its constant effort to widen its sphere of operation, amalgamated with the Belfast & Northern Counties, Ireland's fourth largest railway. For many years the line retained its old characteristics, the only noticeable alteration being the change of title; the railway was now known as the Midland Railway, Northern Counties Committee, as the Act provided for the operation of the railway by a committee of management sitting in Belfast.

It was not until the English grouping of 1923 when the railway became LMS (NCC), that the real Midland influence began to manifest itself, more especially in the adoption of Midland—or LMS—crimson-lake livery for engines and coaching stock, and in the gradual 'Midlandisation' of the engines, many of which were then built at Derby. Although by the 1930s the line had in many ways assumed the guise of a miniature edition of the Midland, it never went in for clerestory coaches which were such a distinctive feature of the parent company.

Then, when the railways of Britain were nationalised on 1 January 1948, the NCC became the 'Railway Executive, Northern Counties Committee', but this arrangement, involving two state-owned concerns, was not to last for long. The formation of the Ulster Transport Authority, embracing all railways and road interests in Northern Ireland, resulted in the purchase of the NCC on 1 April 1949 from the British Transport Commission for the sum of £2,668,000.

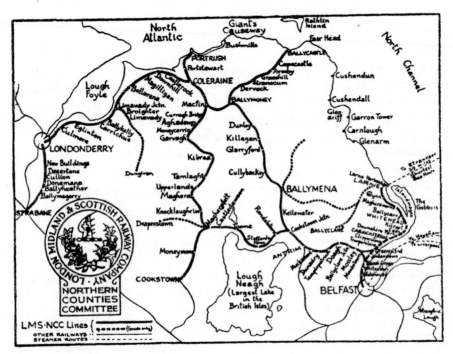

Official map of NCC system, 1939

LOCOMOTIVES AND ROLLING STOCK

When the original Belfast & Ballymena became the BNCR in 1860, it possessed nineteen engines; ten of these had been built in 1847, five by Bury, with that firm's typical bar frames and haystack fireboxes, and five by Sharp Brothers, to their own quite different design. One of each batch was an 0–4–2 for goods work, and the other four were 2–2–2 passenger engines. Most of them were scrapped in the 1870s, but one lasted until 1902. The principal remaining engines were six 2–4–0s and two 0–6–0s from Sharp Stewart in 1856–7; these had long working lives, most of them lasting not only into Midland but even into LMS ownership, four of the 2–4–0s until 1924, and one 0–6–0, no 19, until 1933.

When the Ballymena, Ballymoney, Coleraine & Portrush Railway was amalgamated with the BNCR in 1861 it had four 2–2–2s of Sharp design and two Fairbairn 2–2–2WTs. These became BNCR 20–5, and only one survived the turn of the century, this being 2–4–0 no 20, scrapped in 1906.

The Londonderry & Coleraine engines, taken over in 1861 (though the line was nominally independent for another ten years), were a very miscellaneous collection; details of them are either very obscure or unknown. They became BNCR nos 26–34 and included five Sharp 2–2–2WTs. Most of the LCR engines were scrapped by 1880, though one 0–4–2 lasted until 1889 and a 2–4–0 until 1901.

Additions to the BNCR stock between 1861 and 1876 consisted of ten 2–4–0s for passenger work, eight of them with double frames, and a few 0–6–0s, all built by either Beyer Peacock or Sharp Stewart. These were long-lived engines, 0–6–0 no 36 of 1863 and 2–4–0 no 41 of 1872 both being at work until 1933.

The most interesting phase of development however began in 1876 with the appointment as locomotive superintendent of Bowman Malcolm at the very early age of twenty-two. It is possibly unique in the railway world for one so young to obtain such an important position, and he held if for a record forty-six years, until 1922. He was succeeded by W. K. Wallace and died on 3 January 1933.

Malcolm was responsible for several interesting designs, particularly in the field of compounding, which was a popular subject for experiment among British railways around the turn of the century. Only four however adopted it to any extent and these followed three different systems. F. W. Webb on the LNWR went in at first for three-cylinder designs with uncoupled wheels, and later three- and four-cylinder coupled engines. On the Midland Johnson's three-cylinder 4–4–0s on the Smith principle were perpetuated with modifications by his successor, Deeley, and built in considerable numbers after the grouping. The North Eastern, on the other hand, adopted the Worsdell von Borries two-cylinder system, and it was this which was adopted by Malcolm on the BNCR. The most obvious characteristic of a von Borries compound to an observer was its two exhaust beats per revolution of the driving wheels, in place of the normal four (or six for a three-cylinder engine). Acceleration from starting seemed to be slow, the engine moving quite a distance before the first exhaust came from the chimney. The engines had two inside cylinders of unequal size, except for the narrow-gauge tanks, which had outside cylinders.

On the BNCR and NCC nothing but compounds were built between 1890 and 1908, after which a reversion to simples was made for broad-gauge engines, although narrow-gauge compounds appeared until 1920, when the last was built, and some of them continued in service until 1950. Unfortunately none have been preserved, although one von Borries still exists in the shape of NER *Aerolite* in York Museum.

Mr Malcolm's broad-gauge engines were nearly all 2–4–0s or 4–4–0s, but there were also a couple of 0–6–0s. The 4–4–0s included two very fine machines built in 1895 as 2–4–0s but converted shortly afterwards; their 7ft driving wheels were the largest ever used in Ireland. One was eventually converted to simple, but the other remained compound until scrapped in 1944.

The only other Irish railways to try compounds were the County Down, which had a few engines, the GSWR which experimented with a 4–4–0 and an 0–6–0, and of course the GNR, which in 1932 built five very fine 4–4–0s, the last compounds for any railway in the British Isles.

A noticeable feature of the NCC locomotive stock was the almost complete absence of tank engines (by contrast all the narrow-gauge engines were tanks); this continued until the appearance of the 2–6–4Ts in 1946. Apart from a few 2–2–2WTs in the early days, the only ones up to that time were four 2–4–0STs (originally 2–4–0 side tanks) built in 1883, nos 25 and 47–9, one 0–4–0ST for shunting, no 42, scrapped in 1925, and a similar engine built at Belfast in 1914, no 16. There were also two of the standard LMS Jinties, nos 18 and 19, transferred in 1944 from England, and suitably regauged.

Although a few of the compound engines had received names during Malcolm's reign, it was not until 1930 that a general policy of naming express passenger engines was undertaken. However, this was not fully implemented so far as the 4–4–0s were concerned, being discontinued after 1934 when a few had still to be dealt with (the allocated names are shown in brackets), though names were given to the new 2–6–0s as they appeared until the war years, when two of the last to come out were never named. These engines, fifteen in all, were built between 1933 and 1940, some at Derby and some at Belfast, and were introduced for express working to Portrush and Londonderry. They bore unmistakeable signs of LMS parentage, with such features as Fowler chimneys, cabs and tenders.

The last main-line engines, and in fact the last steam engines, were the 2–6–4Ts which came out between 1946 and 1950, built at Derby but erected in Belfast. Although designed by H. G. Ivatt, they were very similar to the LMS Fowler 2–6–4Ts of 1927, so as to be standard with the 2–6–0s, but they had 6ft driving wheels for express working. They were the last steam engines in use on the UTA, as late as 1970, although in the end only on freight working, and one of them has been preserved in working order by the Irish Railway Record Society.

Until 1923 the livery of BNCR engines was 'invisible green', in effect really black, but which in certain lighting conditions assumed a greenish hue. Under the LMS all engines, passenger and freight, were painted in Midland lake, and incidentally kept in sparkling condition. During the war years this was changed to black. The last engine to be turned out in red was 4–4–0 no 81 *Carrickfergus Castle* in 1941, which was repainted at the Dundalk works of the GNR, where under wartime conditions and after the severe air raid on Belfast in that year some NCC engines had to be sent for overhaul.

The 2–6–4Ts which started to appear in 1946 were at first painted in the current LMS livery for express types, black with a maroon border separated by a single straw coloured line.

After the formation of the UTA, 2–6–0 no 90, 4–4–0 no 80 and 2–6–4T no 5 appeared in a green livery, but this was soon superseded by black lined red and yellow.

All through the NCC period coaching stock was Midland crimson-lake with the usual gold lining out. The UTA adopted a green livery.

Locomotive exchanges between railways were rare in Ireland. One of the few occurred in August 1935 when 2–6–0 no 96 was sent for trials on the Great Northern in exchange for GNR 4–4–0 no 170.

NCC LOCOMOTIVE STOCK IN 1929, WITH SUBSEQUENT ADDITIONS

Note: certain engines appear more than once in the table, with cross references, owing to subsequent rebuilding and renumbering.

Names in brackets were allocated but never carried, the 1930 naming programme not being fully implemented.

Classes A and D carried their names previous to 1930.

Class	Type	No	Name	Built	With-drawn	Notes
A	4–4–0	20		1905		Rebuilt to U2 no 84
	compound	33	*King Edward VII*	1902		Rebuilt to A1
		34	*Queen Alexandra* (renamed as below)	1901		,,
		58		1907		,,
		59		1906		,, U2 no 86
		63	*Ben Bradagh*	1905		,, U2 no 87
		67		1908		,, U2 no 85
		69		1904		,, A1
A1	4–4–0	33	*Binevenagh*	1902	1949	
	simple	34	*Knocklayd*	1901	1950	
	rebuilt	58	*(Lurigethan)*	1907	1954	

Class	Type	No	Name	Built	With-drawn	Notes
	from	62	*Slemish*	1903	1954	No 4 until 1930
	compound	64	*Trostan*	1905	1954	
		65	*Knockagh*	1905	1950	
		66	*Ben Madigan*	1905	1954	
		68	*Slieve Gallion*	1908	1947	
		69	*Slieve Bane*	1904	1954	
B1	4–4–0 compound	60	*County Donegal*	1897	1946	Rebuilt to B3 simple in 1932
		61	*County Antrim*	1897	1946	,, ,,
B3	4–4–0 simple	21	*County Down*	1892	1940*	Rebuilt from 2–4–0 compound class C
		24	*County Londonderry*	1898	1947	Rebuilt from 4–4–0 compound class B
		28	*County Tyrone*	1890	1938	Rebuilt from 2–4–0 compound class C
C	2–4–0 compound	56		1895	1942	
C1	2–4–0 compound large boiler	51		1892	1938	
		52		1892	—	Rebuilt 1931 to 4–4–0 class U1 no 4
		57	*Galgorm Castle*†	1895	1938	Rebuilt from class C
D	4–4–0 compound 7′ 0″	55	*Parkmount*	1895	1944	
D1	4–4–0 7′ 0″ rebuilt from compound	50	*Jubilee*	1895	1946	
E	0–6–0 compound	53		1892	1934	
		54		1892	1944	
F	2–4–0 simple	23		1885	1942	
		45		1880	1938	
F1	2–4–0 simple large boiler	46		1880	1938	
G	2–4–0 double-framed	8		1878	1930	
		11		1873	1933	
		41		1872	1933	
G1	2–4–0 double-framed large boiler	6		1873	1931	
		10		1876	1931	

* Reinstated 1941 and withdrawn again 1947.
† Name carried by 4–4–0 no 3 previous to 1931.

Class	Type	No	Name	Built	With-drawn	Notes
J	2–4–0ST	25		1883	1934	
	rebuilt	47		1883	1932	
	from	48		1883	1933	
	2–4–0T	49		1883	1934	
K	0–6–0	30		1880	1938	
K1	0–6–0	7		1873	1934	
		31		1878	1947	
		32		1870	1933	
		38		1867	1929	
		43		1875	1938	
		44		1876	1938	
L	0–6–0	19		1857	1933	
		36		1863	1933	
L	0–6–0T	18		1926	1956	Late LMS 7456 Trans 1944
		19		1928	1963	Late LMS 7553 Trans 1944
N	0–4–0ST	16		1914	1951	
U1	4–4–0	1	Glenshesk	1897	1947	Rebuilt from B1 compound no 59
		2	Glendun	1897	1947	Rebuilt from B1 compound no 62
		3	Galgorm Castle*†	1890	1946	Rebuilt from B1 compound 2–4–0 no 33
		4	Glenariff	1892	1949	Rebuilt from C1 compound no 52. Renumbered 4A in 1947
U2	4–4–0	70	(Portmuck Castle)	1914	1956	Rebuilt from class U
		71	Glenarm Castle	1914	1956	,, ,, ,,
		72	(Shane's Castle)	1922	1961	,, ,, ,,
		73	(Carn Castle)	1922	1956	,, ,, ,,
		74	Dunluce Castle	1924	1961	Preserved in Belfast Museum
		75	Antrim Castle	1924	1956	
		76	Olderfleet Castle	1924	1960	
		77	(Ballygalley Castle)	1924	1956	
		78	Chichester Castle	1924	1960	
		79	Kenbaan Castle	1925	1956	
		80	Dunseverick Castle	1925	1961	
		81	Carrickfergus Castle	1925	1957	

* Renamed Glenaan in 1931.
† Galgorm Castle nameplate transferred to 2–4–0 no 57.

Class	Type	No	Name	Built	With-drawn	Notes
		82	Dunanie Castle	1925	1956	
		83	Carra Castle	1925	1956	
		84	Lissanoure Castle	1905†	1961	Rebuilt from class A no 20
		85	—	1908	1960	Rebuilt from class A no 67
		86	(Craiggore)	1906	1960	Rebuilt from class A no 59
		87	Queen Alexandra	1905	1957	Rebuilt from class A no 63
V later VI	2–6–0	90	‡Duke of Abercorn	1933	1956	
		91	‖The Bush	1933	1956	
		92	§The Bann	1933	1957	
		93	¶The Foyle	1933	1965	
		94	The Maine	1934	1965	
		95	The Braid	1934	1964	
		96	Silver Jubilee	1935	1961	
		97	Earl of Ulster	1935	1965	
		98	King Edward VIII	1937	1965	
		99	King George VI	1938	1965	
		100	Queen Elizabeth	1939	1955	
		101	Lord Masserene	1940	1956	
		102		1940	1956	
		103	Thomas Somerset	1942	1959	
		104		1942	1965	
WT	2–6–4T	1 to 10		1947	1968–70	No 4 preserved in working order by Railway Preservation Society of Ireland
		50 to 57		1949 –50	1968–70	
Sentinel	0–4–0	91		1925	1932	
Sentinel railcar		401	(Carriage stock)	1925	1932	
Diesel mech- anical shunt- ing loco- motives	0–4–0	16		1951		
	0–6–0	17		1937		
	0–4–0	20		1945		
	0–6–0	22		1934		Originally LMS 7057
Diesel electric locomotive	2–2–2–2	28		1945		Built for BCDR

† Carried works plate 'LMS–NCC 1929 Belfast' after rebuilding.
‡ Original intended name was Earl of Ulster.
‖ Original intended name was Sorley Boy.
§ Original intended name was Richard de Burgh.
¶ Original intended name was John de Courcy.

CHAPTER 18

NORTHERN COUNTIES COMMITTEE NARROW GAUGE LINES

Four 3ft gauge lines, all independently built, which were ultimately owned by the London Midland & Scottish Railway (Northern Counties Committee).

BALLYMENA CUSHENDALL & RED BAY RAILWAY Incorporated 1872, completed as far as Retreat by 1876, but never extended beyond. Taken over by BELFAST & NORTHERN COUNTIES in 1884. Passed into hands of MR (NCC) in 1903.

Route mileage: 16½ miles.

Principal places served:
  Ballymena, Parkmore (never reached Cushendall, its main objective, on the Antrim coast).

Closed completely by 1940.

BALLYMENA & LARNE RAILWAY Incorporated 1874. Opened 1877–8. Taken over by BELFAST & NORTHERN COUNTIES RAILWAY in 1889. Passed into hands of MR (NCC) in 1923.

Route mileage: 30 miles.

Principal places served:
  Larne, Ballymena, Ballyclare.

Closed in sections and completely by 1950.

BALLYCASTLE RAILWAY Incorporated 1878. Opened 1880. Taken over by LMS (NCC) in 1924. Ownership transferred by BRITISH RAILWAYS in 1948 to ULSTER TRANSPORT AUTHORITY.

Route mileage: 16¼ miles.

Principal place served:
   Ballycastle (watering place on Antrim coast).

Closed 1950.

PORTSTEWART TRAMWAY   Small steam tramway at Portrush connecting the town with the BNCR station. Opened 1882. Acquired by Belfast & Northern Counties Railway 1897. Passed into hands of MR (NCC) in 1903, and LMS (NCC) in 1923.

Length: 1¾ miles.

Closed 1926.

The Ballymena Cushendall & Red Bay was in fact the oldest 3ft gauge railway in Ireland, most of which were built after the Tramways Act of 1883. It was incorporated on 18 July 1872 and was conceived as a mineral line to serve the Vale of Cushendall in County Antrim, where there were considerable iron ore deposits, the exploitation of which was then being developed. The railway left the Belfast & Northern Counties at Ballymena and climbed over the high ridge of the Antrim Mountains, attaining a summit level of 1,045ft, the highest on any Irish railway and the only one exceeding 1,000ft.

   The first section from Ballymena to Cargan, 11¾ miles, was opened on 26 May 1875, and on to Retreat, another 4¾ miles, on 8 October 1876. This was as far as it got, and the railway belied its name in that it never reached either Red Bay or Cushendall, on the coast of the North Channel of the Irish Sea. It had been hoped to ship some of the iron ore from Red Bay to England, but instead this traffic was routed via Ballymena and Larne. Running over wild moorland country, it was one of the most heavily graded lines in Ireland, with an almost continuous ascent for 15 miles, including an unbroken stretch of 3 miles, mostly at 1 in 37 or 1 in 39, easing slightly to 1 in 60. In October 1884 it was taken over by the BNCR.

   At first only freight traffic was carried, but the BNCR decided to run a passenger service, as far as Knockanally on 5 April 1886, extended to Parkmore on 27 April 1888. The passenger service operated until 1 October 1930 and freight traffic ceased from Rathkenny to Retreat on 17 April 1937, the line being closed completely in 1940.

The railway had three engines, nos 1–3, 0–4–2STs built by Black Hawthorn in 1874, works nos 301–3. The coaches were bogie saloons with wrought-iron gated-end vestibules.

Like the BCRBR, the Ballymena & Larne came into being before the 1883 Act, being incorporated on 7 July 1874. This provided for the construction of a through main line between Larne Harbour and Ballymena, 25¼ miles, together with a 2¾ mile branch to Ballyclare (later extended to Doagh, another 2 miles). The section from Larne Harbour to Ballyclare was initially opened for freight traffic only, on 1 August 1877, and was followed by completion of the main line to Ballymena, which left the branch at Ballyboley, on 24 April 1878, when passenger services were inaugurated. The last bit from Ballyclare to Doagh was opened on 1 May 1884, and meanwhile a connection with the Red Bay railway had been put in at Ballymena in September 1880 to enable through freight traffic to be operated.

In July 1889 the BLR was, like the BCRBR, taken over by the BNCR. The line ran parallel with the BNCR along the causeway between Larne Town and Harbour, and at Ballymena it had its own platform at the Northern Counties station. There were running sheds at both Larne and Ballymena, in the latter case shared with the BNCR.

Passenger services ceased on the Doagh line in 1930, the section from Ballyclare being closed completely in 1933, and the remainder of the branch in 1950, at the same time as the main line between Ballyboley and Larne, the portion between Ballyboley and Ballymena having already been closed in 1940.

The locomotive stock consisted of two 2–4–0Ts, nos 1 and 4, built by Beyer Peacock in 1877 and 1880, works nos 1687 and 1828, very similar to the standard type used on the Isle of Man Railway, and still to be seen there today. There were also three 0–6–0Ts, nos 2, 3 and 6, again by Beyer Peacock in 1877 (1700 and 1701) and 1883 (2304). No 5 was an 'odd man out' in more senses than one. It was the only one of its kind, a 2–6–0ST, and was built by Beyer Peacock in 1880, works no 1947; in latter days at any rate it seems to have been the regular engine for the Doagh branch.

The coaching stock comprised the usual first- and third-class bogie vehicles, mainly of the compartment type. Of particular interest were three built by the NCC at Belfast in 1930 for use on the through Larne–Ballymena boat express, which covered the 25¼ mile journey non-stop in one hour, probably the fastest narrow-gauge schedule in Ireland, although it is doubtful whether the actual speeds equalled those on the Cork Blackrock & Passage Railway. These vehicles were vestibuled corridor coaches with steam heating, electric lighting and lavatory accommodation, in effect, up to normal main-line standards.

Page 215 (above) NCC (former Belfast & Northern Counties Railway) two-cylinder compound no 33 King Edward VII at Ballymena in 1930, typical of the Worsdell von Borries compounds built in considerable numbers by B. Malcolm over many years; (below) two-cylinder compounds were also built for the 3ft gauge sections of the NCC. This view, taken at Belfast in 1948, shows one mounted on a transporter for conveyance to Ballymoney for work on the Ballycastle line

Page 216 (*above*) The last new engines for the NCC were eighteen mixed-traffic 2–6–4Ts very similar to the LMS Fowler engines of the parent company, but with 6ft wheels. They were built at Derby, as were some other engines after the Midland had absorbed the BNCR in 1903. Standing with no 8 (built in 1946) is one of the earlier NCC experiments in railcars, no 3, built in 1937; (*below*) mixed train on the narrow gauge. Ballymena Cushendall & Red Bay Railway, Ireland's first 3ft gauge line, at Parkmore about 1907. The engine is 0–4–2ST no 102, built in 1874, which ran until 1923

Their life was short on this service, as it ceased in 1933, but they were ultimately disposed of to the County Donegal.

The Ballycastle Railway was incorporated on 22 July 1878 and opened in October 1880. It ran from Ballymoney on the BNCR main line, where it had its own bay platform at the latter's station, to Ballycastle, 16¼ miles away on the coast. Ballycastle is the only town of any size in this most north-easterly part of the county, and was in early times a landing place for settlers from Scotland, the fifteen miles or so across the North Channel to the Mull of Kintyre being the closest proximity between the two countries. Eventually Ballycastle became a popular holiday resort with something approaching 3,000 inhabitants, nowadays easily reached from Belfast by road, but at the time of the opening of the railway made much more accessible in consequence.

The original locomotives were three 0-6-0STs from Black Hawthorn in 1879, works nos 554, 555 and 513, no 1 *Dalriada*, 2 *Countess of Antrim* and 3 *Lady Boyd*. No 3, which was slightly smaller, was a contractor's engine bought by the Ballycastle in 1882.

These sufficed until 1908, when two much bigger engines were built by Kitson, works nos 4565-6. They were 4-4-2Ts, and became nos 3 and 4, the old no 3 being scrapped at the same time. There was a shed at Ballycastle, large enough for all three 0-6-0STs or the two 4-4-2Ts, but the timetable necessitated one engine remaining overnight at Ballymoney in any case. The train service normally consisted of four trains each way daily and one on Sundays, with more during the holiday season.

Unlike the other two lines, the Ballycastle was never taken over by the BNCR. It was absorbed by the NCC on 11 August 1924, in a somewhat moribund state, having been closed since the previous December. It was eventually closed by the UTA on 3 July 1950, under its widespread scheme of closures.

Portstewart lies 3 miles to the west of Portrush and is a seaside resort with a population of about 4,000. It was served by a station 1¾ miles distant on the BNCR Portrush branch, and to give more convenient access a 3ft gauge tramway along the public road was opened in June 1882; this was known as the Portstewart Tramway.

Trips were made mainly in connection with the main-line trains, and the tramway found itself unable to pay, its traffic being purely local; it was in danger of closing but was acquired by the Belfast & Northern Counties as a useful adjunct to its own system, in June 1897. As successors to the BNCR, the Midland Railway in 1903 and the LMS in 1923 were content with this arrangement until 1926, when it was decided to substitute a bus service, and the tramway was closed on 31 January.

Originally there were two tram engines, nos 1 and 2, built by Kitson in 1882

N

and 1883 (works nos T56 and T84). No 3 followed in 1901 (no T302), and is thought to have been the last of its kind, at any rate built by Kitson.

On the closure of the line no 3 was sold to a contractor at Castlerock, and was still to be seen well into the 1930s. Nos 1 and 2 are both preserved, being amongst the very few engines of this type to survive. After being stored at Belfast for several years, during which time they still bore the legend MR.NCC, no 1 was sent to Hull museum and fortunately escaped severe damage in an air raid during the war, whilst no 2, now repainted in BNCR green livery, has a permanent resting place in Belfast Museum.

It is not certain what the original passenger vehicles were like, but two double-deck bogie cars with open decks were obtained in 1899; they were sold for garden shelters when the tramway was closed.

Although part of a large organisation, the NCC narrow-gauge lines produced their share of amusing anecdotes like other small concerns, as 'The Mystery of the Missing Wagon' shows. On an occasion between the wars a wagon disappeared from a goods train between Ballymena and Larne. The make-up of the train had been checked at the beginning of the journey, but on arrival at Larne there was one wagon less, although the train and all its couplings were still intact. This discrepancy could not be explained, and eventually the most obvious solution was accepted, namely, that there must have been an error in the counting at Ballymena.

That, however, was not the end of the story, as some days later the missing wagon was discovered amongst some bushes at the foot of a place called Ballynashee, which means 'the place of the fairies', on whom the responsibility was now placed by some local credulous believers in the supernatural. How these fairies, or even the local leprechauns, accomplished the arduous task of uncoupling with a shunting pole was not explained. But perhaps the crew of the train knew more than they cared to tell. Quite possibly the missing wagon had contained some cases of Irish whiskey, but this does not seem to have been recorded.

LOCOMOTIVES AND ROLLING STOCK

The BNCR locomotives were all of one basic type, two-cylinder compound 2-4-2Ts built on the Worsdell von Borries principle to the design of Bowman Malcolm. The first two came from Beyer Peacock in 1892, works nos 3463-4, 69 and 70 in the BNCR list, renumbered 110 and 111 in 1897. Four more followed at intervals under the Midland regime, no 112 in 1908, 113 in 1909, 103 in 1919, all built at Belfast, and finally 104 in 1920, reputed to have been mainly constructed at Derby, although like the others it carried a works plate 'MR-NCC

Makers   Belfast 1920'. Nos 112 and 113 later became 101 and 102, and these, together with 104, were again renumbered 41–3 in 1939–42 to make way for the new 2–6–0s then appearing, whilst 111 became 44. No 110 was in 1931 rebuilt as a 2–4–4T, the only engine of this wheel arrangement ever to run in the British Isles.

Coaching stock, of first, second and third class, was of the compartment type, both bogie and six-wheelers, but these vehicles were replaced to a large extent by those from the Ballymena & Larne when that railway ceased passenger working in 1933.

NCC NARROW-GAUGE LOCOMOTIVE STOCK—SUMMARY

Original owner and number		BNCR numbers	NCC numbers	Type	Disposal
BCRBR	1	60, 101	101A	0–4–2ST	Scrapped 1923
	2	61, 102	102A	0–4–2ST	„ 1923
	3	62, 103	103	0–4–2ST	„ 1909
BLR	1	63, 104	104	2–4–0T	Scrapped 1918
	4	64, 105	105	2–4–0T	Sold 1928 to CVBT
	2	65, 106	106	0–6–0T	Scrapped 1933
	3	66, 107	107	0–6–0T	„ 1931
	6	67, 108	108	0–6–0T	„ 1932
	5	68, 109	109	2–6–0ST	„ 1934
BR	3	—	113	4–4–2T	„ 1946
	4	—	114	4–4–2T	„ 1942
BNCR	69	69, 110	110	2–4–2T later 2–4–4T	„ 1946
	70	70, 111	111, 44	2–4–2T	„ 1950
NCC	112		112, 102, 42	2–4–2T	„ 1950
	113		113, 101, 41	2–4–2T	„ 1950
	103		103	2–4–2T	„ 1938
	104		104, 43	2–4–2T	„ 1950

The 2–4–2Ts worked on all three railways, and were latterly the only type still in use. Some transfers of the older engines took place, such as 106 and 108 to the Ballycastle from 1930 to 1932, and 113 and 114, which were really too heavy for that line and went to Larne, where they were stationed for a number of years.

The livery on the BNCR was dark green, changed to crimson-lake after the take-over by the Midland in 1903. During this period they were lettered NCC on the tank sides. Nos 41 and 44 survived to be fully repainted in UTA lined black, complete with new insignia.

CHAPTER 19

GIANT'S CAUSEWAY TRAMWAY

A 3ft gauge electric tramway (originally steam-worked for a short time).

Opened 1883.

Route mileage: 8 miles

Principal places served:
Portrush, Bushmills, Giant's Causeway, a famous natural rock formation on the Antrim coast.

Closed 1949.

This small 3ft gauge system, the Giant's Causeway Portrush & Bush Valley Railway & Tramway Company, to give it its full title, possessed the distinction of being the first electric railway in Great Britain and Ireland, a claim sometimes disputed in favour of the small Volk's line along the seafront at Brighton. Both were opened in 1883, the latter forestalling the Giant's Causeway by a few weeks so far as electric operation was concerned, but whereas the Volk's line was of quite short length, only performing the function of an alternative to a walk along the promenade, the other was a fully fledged railway—or tramway—8 miles long. It connected the important watering place of Portrush, on the Antrim coast, served by the Belfast & Northern Counties Railway, with Bushmills, 6 miles to the east and a little inland, and Giant's Causeway, again on the coast. The latter is named after its extraordinary rock formations consisting of vertical basaltic columns of amazingly symmetrical form, which are mainly hexagonal but some have anything between five and nine sides. Similar formations are found at Fingal's Cave, on the island of Staffa, 80 miles away, and off the west coast of Scotland, where Mendelssohn found inspiration for his well known 'Hebrides' overture. Legend has it that the Ossianic giant Finn McCoul was responsible for the existence of both of these geological freaks of nature, for which no scientific explanation seems really satisfactory.

The chief promoters of the Giant's Causeway line were two brothers, Arthur and William Traill, the elder of whom was chairman of the company until his death in 1915 and was succeeded by his brother, who died in 1933.

The line as far as Bushmills was incorporated in 1878 and was opened on 29 January 1883, at first with steam operation. Owing to delays in completion of the hydro-electric plant, electric working had to be postponed and did not begin until 28 September 1883. The last 2 miles from Bushmills to Giant's Causeway were authorised by an Act of 6 August 1885, and opened on 1 July 1887. As conductor rails were planned, they could not be used at Portrush, where the track ran through the main street, and so two steam engines were obtained for this portion. As it turned out, they had to be used over the whole route for the first few months.

Specimen ticket of Giant's Causeway
Tramway

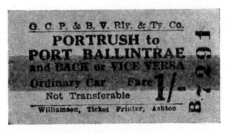

Electric power was provided by water turbines on the River Bush, at Bushmills; more powerful ones were installed later, but this was still not sufficient, even with an auxiliary station at Portrush, during heavy traffic, and the steam locomotives had to be used to supplement the electric cars. After 1915 the power was increased again and steam working almost entirely dispensed with.

The conductor rails, 1½ft above ground level, had to be placed at the far side of the road from the public highway, along which the tramway ran for most of its length (the Causeway extension was on private property). This was never a satisfactory arrangement. It was obviously dangerous in spite of the low voltage, and gaps had to be left at accommodation crossings; where these were too wide to be bridged by the collector shoes at each end of the car or trailer, the driver had to rely on momentum to take him across. In 1899 current collection was converted to the overhead trolley system and this enabled electric working to be continued through the streets of Portrush.

The tramway suffered from the usual road competition during the 1930s, but the company continued to operate at a small profit during the war. By 1949 however the track was in a bad state of repair, and with falling receipts it was decided that the company could not continue without assistance from the

Ulster Transport Authority, which was not forthcoming. It was therefore closed on the 30 September 1949 and all the assets—track, generating equipment, and rolling stock—auctioned at Belfast eighteen months later.

So the first electric railway in Great Britain and Ireland came to its end after 66 years of operation. Its smaller contemporary, Volk's Railway at Brighton, is still in use at the time of writing, 1972.

LOCOMOTIVES AND ROLLING STOCK

The first two steam engines were of the conventional enclosed tram-type of the period, with vertical boilers, built by Wilkinson of Wigan in 1883. One of these was called *Wartrail*. Two slightly larger machines appeared later, no 3 *Dunluce Castle* in 1886 and no 4 *Brian Boroimhe* in 1896. Of the originals, no 2 was withdrawn in 1899 and no 1 in 1910. Nos 3 and 4 were kept in reserve after 1915 and finally sold in 1930 to Mr R. Faris, a contractor in Portstewart, for use in a stone quarry, where no 4 at least, stripped of its cab, was still to be seen for several years afterwards. The livery was green.

The original passenger stock consisted of seven cars, two first-class saloons, two open firsts, and three third-class opens, some of them being powered vehicles, but it is not certain which ones were actually fitted with motors from the start. First class was discontinued in 1923.

There were eventually six motor cars and twelve trailers, all four-wheelers, several of them open vehicles with toast-rack seating, but there were also a few saloons for use during the winter season when traffic was light anyway, and during inclement weather. The very ornate decorations of the earlier cars were retained on some vehicles right to the end, and as very few new vehicles had been obtained since the turn of the century, the trains eventually presented an almost incredibly vintage appearance in their last years. In fact, one car, no 9, was substantially rebuilt as late as 1945, and emerged, complete with clerestory roof and decorative embellishments, in a style which could only be described as Victorian, most pleasing in appearance (or possibly not, according to one's taste).

The livery was red and cream. There were also a few goods vehicles. The workshop and sheds were situated at Portrush.

CHAPTER 20

BELFAST & COUNTY DOWN RAILWAY

A not inconsiderable system of lines covering most of the county of Down, lying to the east and south of Belfast. Incorporated 1846. Opened in sections between 1848 and 1861, together with later extensions.

Principal constituents:
DOWNPATRICK DUNDRUM & NEWCASTLE RAILWAY   Opened 1869 absorbed by BCDR 1881.
BELFAST HOLYWOOD & BANGOR RAILWAY   Incorporated 1860. Opened 1865, absorbed by BCDR 1884.
Whole railway taken over by Ulster Transport Authority in 1948.

Route mileage: 80 miles.

Principal places served:
Belfast, Holywood, Bangor, Donaghadee, Ballynahinch, Downpatrick, Ardglass, Newcastle.

With the exception of the line between Belfast and Bangor, which still retains a busy residential service, the whole railway was closed by the ULSTER TRANSPORT AUTHORITY *in 1950.*

Like many of the smaller Irish railways, this was very much a self-contained system having little contact with any other railway. It lay entirely within the confines of County Down, in which it had an almost complete monopoly. This county, lying to the south and south-east of Belfast, is one of the six which now comprise Ulster.

The railway mania of the mid 1840s saw the first proposals in the county for railway construction, which culminated in an Act of 20 January 1846 for a line from Belfast to Downpatrick, the county town. In the ruins of the ancient cathedral are reputed to lie the bones of Saint Patrick, the patron saint of Ireland. The present cathedral, embodying the chancel of the old one, was built in 1790. There were also to be branches to Holywood, Donaghadee, and Bangor, in all a total route mileage of 45 miles. The initial section completed was from Belfast to Holywood, opened on 2 August 1848. The first parts of what was to be the main line, from Belfast to Comber and on to Newtownards, were opened on 6 May 1850. From Comber the main line continued southwards to Ballynahinch, opened on 10 September 1858, and to Downpatrick, on 23 March 1859.

Ballynahinch itself was actually on a $3\frac{1}{4}$ mile long branch, from what became Ballynahinch Junction on completion of the line to Downpatrick. The New-townards branch was extended to Donaghadee on 3 June 1861. At this time Donaghadee was envisaged as the principal Irish port for a service to Port-patrick in south-west Scotland, and indeed a fine harbour was constructed there and opened in 1863. After only two years of operation, however, the route was abandoned in favour of the Larne–Stranraer crossing, and the high hopes of the importance of Donaghadee were never realised; it remains to this day a pleasant but small seaside resort with a population in 1962 of only some 3,200.

It was also the intention to reach Bangor, a much larger seaside township on the shores of the Belfast Lough, within potentially easy reach of Belfast, being only 13 miles distant direct, by a branch line leaving the Donaghadee line at Conlig, but this would have been a much more circuitous route and was never built. Instead, a new railway came into being, the Belfast Holywood & Bangor, incorporated on 25 May 1860, in effect an extension of the BCDR branch from its existing terminus at Holywood. This was opened on 1 May 1865, public services commencing seventeen days later, and on 22 August in the same year the Holywood branch was taken over by the new BHBR. In 1873 the company was leased to the BCDR, but regained its independence in 1876, at the same time obtaining running powers to work its trains into the original company's terminus at Queens Quay, Belfast. Previously it had had its own separate station alongside, but these were eventually merged into one in 1884, in which year the BHBR finally lost its identity, being taken over by the BCDR on the 1 September of that year. What originally started as a short branch of the Belfast & County Down eventually became in effect its main line, with a busy commuter and seaside traffic, although still officially regarded as a branch. It is the only part of the BCDR to survive to this day.

In July 1861 an Act authorised the construction of the Downpatrick & Newry Railway, a 31 mile extension from the former terminus southwards to join the Newry Warrenpoint & Rostrevor Railway, but this was never completed.

The scheme was superseded by an Act of 10 August 1866, the Downpatrick Dundrum & Newcastle Railway, opened on 25 March 1869, and worked by the BCDR, which purchased the line in 1881.

Another branch from Downpatrick to Ardglass, known as the Downpatrick Killough & Ardglass Railway, worked from its inception by the parent company, was authorised on 31 May 1892. In the same year an avoiding line was constructed to enable trains from Belfast to Newcastle to dispense with the necessity of reversing at Downpatrick, which was a terminal station. Passengers for Downpatrick had to detrain at the exchange platform into the Ardglass branch local, which ran into the main terminal station.

Newcastle (population about 3,700 in 1962), a very popular seaside and golfing resort, was the southernmost extremity of the BCDR. The Great Northern was by this time casting its sights in this direction to secure some of the lucrative traffic being enjoyed by the BCDR, it having already reached Banbridge in 1863 by direct route from Belfast and Ballyroney in 1877, within $10\frac{1}{2}$ miles of Newcastle. As a counter measure, the BCDR sought to build its own line to join up with the GNR at Ballyroney, but eventually a compromise was reached under which the GNR would extend its line as far as Castlewellan and the BCDR construct its own branch to that point, over which the Great Northern would have running powers into Newcastle. These plans were provided for in an Act of 30 July 1900, and the through route was opened on 24 March 1906. This final extension brought the total mileage of the BCDR system up to 80 route miles.

Newcastle consequently received the rare distinction in Ireland of being in effect a jointly operated station, although actually owned by the County Down, and moreover the town itself was one of the very few in the country served by two rival railways.

The link at Castlewellan was one of the three connections which the Belfast & County Down had with other railways. The BCDR system in Belfast was situated on the east side of the River Lagan, the other two railways, the GNR and the NCC, both being on the west side.

There was however a connecting line from the GNR system from Belfast Central Junction, near its terminus at Great Victoria Street, through the city and over the river, by which transfer of stock and freight traffic could be made. Although it never carried a regular passenger service it was frequently used by the GNR for excursion traffic to Bangor. It joined the BCDR at Ballymacarrett Junction, whence diverged the 'main line' and the Bangor 'branch' about half a mile out of its main Queens Quay terminus. This connection was closed on 12 August 1965. There was also a short branch line down to Donegal Quay through the streets into the docks area, over which it was possible to reach the NCC system at York Road, but it was entirely unsuitable for passenger traffic.

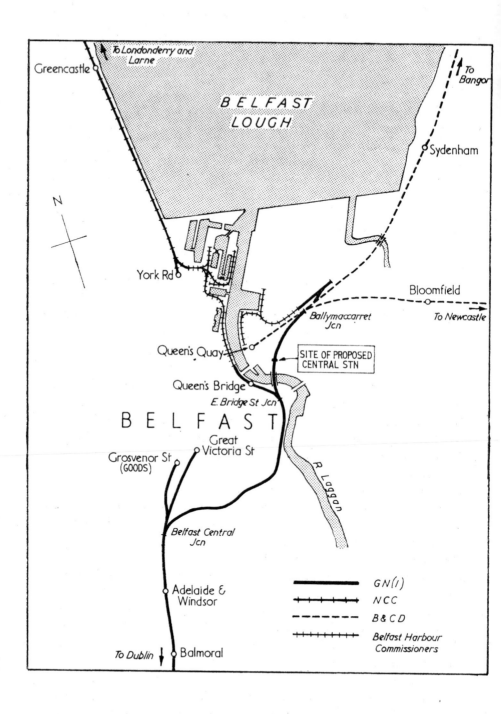

To Londonderry and Larne

Greencastle

BELFAST LOUGH

To Bangor

Sydenham

York Rd

Ballymaccarret Jcn

Bloomfield

To Newcastle

Queen's Quay

SITE OF PROPOSED CENTRAL STN

Queen's Bridge

E. Bridge St Jcn

B E L F A S T

Great Victoria St

Grosvenor St (GOODS)

R. Laggan

Belfast Central Jcn

Adelaide & Windsor

To Dublin

Balmoral

GN(I)

NCC

B & C D

Belfast Harbour Commissioners

These links were closed some years ago and as the lines to Newcastle have also been abandoned, the one remaining section of the BCDR, to Bangor, is now isolated. Queens Quay terminus is an imposing station, with five platforms (most no longer required), which was rebuilt in 1910–14. It has a large concourse and was also served by electric trams from the city, which ran right into the station itself until replaced by buses in 1954. The railway maintained its own well-equipped workshops for the upkeep of its thirty engines, most of which were quartered in a commodious engine shed, although two or three would inevitably be outstabled at the ends of the branches.

The BCDR was a busy line by Irish standards, especially on the Bangor section, which is double track throughout, the rest being for the main part single. The Bangor line still carries a busy commuter service and the only comparable ones in Ireland are on the old DSER and GNR lines out of Dublin, and to a smaller extent the GNR and NCC out of Belfast. Bangor's population in 1962 was around 24,000, many of whom work in Belfast, and this popular seaside resort also attracts considerable excursion traffic, although not so much as formerly. The railway probably reached its peak of prosperity between the wars and during World War II, after which decline set in rapidly.

The finances of the company received a crippling blow by a bad accident at Ballymacarrett Junction on 10 January 1945, a collision between two trains causing the deaths of twenty-three passengers and injury to twenty-four others. The resulting £75,000 paid in compensation was a sum the company could ill afford, and it never really recovered. Oddly enough, there had been a somewhat similar accident at the same site on 13 May 1871.

The final story in its demise however was dealt by the newly formed Ulster Transport Authority, which took over control in 1948. This body's very strong anti-rail bias resulted in the early closure of nearly the whole of the system, only the Bangor line being spared in view of its heavy business traffic, the only remnant of what was once a fascinating and indeed, to those who knew it, a 'happy' system. On 16 January 1950 the main line beyond Comber was completely closed, except for the Newcastle–Castlewellan section operated jointly with the GNR. The BCDR however withdrew its own service from 24 April 1950, although the Great Northern continued to run its trains into Newcastle until May 1955. The Ballynahinch and Ardglass branches also closed in January 1950, followed by the Donaghadee branch on 24 April of that year.

LOCOMOTIVES AND ROLLING STOCK

The earliest BCDR engines were mainly of the 2–2–2, 2–2–2WT, 2–4–0T and 0–4–2 wheel arrangements, together with half a dozen 2–4–0STs, taken over

		A.M.	A.M.	A.M.	A.M.	A.M.	A.M.	A.M.✱	NOON	P.M.	P.M.	P.M.	P.M.	P.M.	P.M.	P.M.	P.M.	P.M.	P.M.
Belfast (Queen's Qy).	dep.	7 0	7 30	7 45	8 31	9 20	1030	1050	12 0	1210	1215	1250	1 11	1 15	1 32		1 50	2 12	2 15
Bloomfield	,,		7 34		8 35	9 24	1035				1219	1254	1 15	1 19	1 36			2 16	2 19
Neill's Hill	,,		7 36		8 37	9 26	1038				1222	1257	1 17	1 22	1 39			2 19	2 22
Knock	,,		7 38		8 39	9 28	1040				1224	1259	1 20	1 25	1 41			2 21	2 24
Dundonald	,,	7 12	7 43		8 44	9 33	1045				1229	1 4	1 25	1 30	1 46			2 26	2 30
Comber	arr.	7 17	7 48	7 57	8 49	9 38	1050	11 2		1223	1234	1 9	1 30	1 35	1 52		2 4	2 31	2 35
Comber	dep.	7 18	7 51			9 40	1052			1225	1235				1 54			Stop	2 37
Newtownards	,,	7 30	8 7			9 49	11 4			1235	1245				2 2				2 48
Ballygrainey	,,						1115								C				3
Millisle Road Halt	,,	7 40	8 24			10 6	1124			1254					2 21				3
Donaghadee	arr.	7 47	8 25			10 7	1125			1255					2 22				3 5
Comber	dep.			7 58			11 3					1240			2 5				
Ballygowan	,,			8 7			1113					1249			2 16				
Shephard's Halt	,,											1252							
Saintfield	,,			8 14			1120					1255			2 25				
Ballynahinch Jct.	,,			8 20			1126					1 1			2 33				
Creevyargon Halt	arr.			8 25			1130												
Ballynahinch	arr.			8 29			1135					1 9			2 42				
Ballynahinch	dep.			7 55			1115					1250			2 20				
Creevyargon Halt	,,			7 58			1118												
Crossgar	dep.			8 28			1133					1 10			2 41				
King's Bridge Halt	,,						B					1 15			D				P.M.
Downpatrick	arr.			9 38			1145					1 20			2 51				
Downpatrick	dep.			8 50			1150					1 30		3 5	3 30				
Ballynoe Halt	,,			8 55			1158					1 38		3 13	3 38				
Bright Halt	,,			9 2			12 2					1 42		3 17	3 42				
Killough	,,			9 5			12 7					1 47		3 22	3 47				
Ardglass	arr.			9 10			1210					1 50		3 25	3 50				
Downpatrick	dep.			8 43			1138								2 56				
Tullymurry	,,			8 51			1149								3 4				
Dundrum	,,			9 0			1158								3 13				
Newcastle	arr.			9 7			12 6	12 57							3 20				
Newcastle	dep.			9A40			1213												
Castlewellan	arr.			9 47			1220												

✱ These Trains run via the Loop Line, the connections from and to Downpatrick being made by the Branch Trains.

		P.M.	P.M.	P.M.	P.M.✱	P.M.	P.M.	P.M.	P.M.	P.M.	P.M.	P.M.	P.M.	P.M.	P.M.
Belfast (Queen's Qy.)	dep.	3 22	4 45	5 12	5 40	5 48		6 14	6 18		6 47	7 55	8 55	1015	11 5
Bloomfield	,,	3 27		5 16		5 52			6 22		6 51	8 0	8 59	1019	1110
Neill's Hill	,,	3 30		5 19		5 56			6 25		6 54	8 3	9 2	1022	1113
Knock	,,	3 32		5 21		6 2			6 28		6 56	8 5	9 4	1024	1115
Dundonald	,,	3 37	E	5 25					6 33		6 56	8 10	9 9	1029	1120
Comber	arr.	3 42	4 58	5 30		6 7		6 28	6 38		6 8	8 15	9 14	1034	1125
Comber	dep.	3 44		5 31		6 9		6 40				8 20	9 17		1126
Newtownards	,,	3 55		5 41		6 21		6 52				8 31	9 20		1134
Ballygrainey	,,	4 5	K			6 31		7 2				C			1144
Millisle Road Halt	,,	4 14		5 58		6 39		7 9				8 48			1153
Donaghadee	arr.	4 15		5 59		6 40		7 10				8 50			1155
Comber	dep.	Stop	4 59	Stop		6 29			6 42			8 17			
Ballygowan	,,		5 9			6 38			6 52			8 27			
Shephard's Halt	,,					6 41									
Saintfield	,,		5 17			6 46		7 0				8 35			
Ballynahinch Jct.	,,		5 24			6 51		7 5				8 42			
Creevyargon Halt	arr.					6 55		7 10				F			
Ballynahinch	arr.		5 33			6 59		7 15				8 50			
Ballynahinch	dep.		5 0									8 30			
Creevyargon Halt	,,														
Crossgar	dep.		5 33		6 10			6 58				8 51			
King's Bridge Halt	,,		D					7 3				D			
Downpatrick	arr.	P.M.	5 42	P.M.	6 20			7 9				9 0			
Downpatrick	dep.	6 25		5 50	6 25										
Ballynoe Halt	,,	6 33		5 58	6 33			6 32							
Bright Halt	,,	6 37		6 2	6 37										
Killough	,,	6 42		6 7	6 42			6 42							
Ardglass	arr.	6 45		6 10	6 45										
Downpatrick	dep.	5 47			6 13							9F 5			
Tullymurry	,,	5 54										F			
Dundrum	,,	6 3			6 32							9F20			
Newcastle	arr.	6 10			6 40							9F27			
Newcastle	dep.			6 45	6 45										
Castlewellan	arr.			6 52	6 52										

✱—These Trains run via the Loop Line the connections from and to Downpatrick being made by the Branch Train.

Specimen timetable of BCDR main line in April 1940

from the Belfast Holywood & Bangor in 1884. Most of these had been gradually replaced by about the turn of the century with more modern types, chiefly tank engines of the 2–4–2T and 4–4–2T variety. Some of the former were two-cylinder Worsdell von Borries compounds, later rebuilt as 4–4–2Ts, and lasted in this form until 1920.

There were also some 2–4–0 tender engines on the same compound principle very similar to others on the Belfast & Northern Counties Railway, and one 2–4–0 simple, no 6, built by Beyer Peacock in 1894, which lasted until the end of steam. In common with many other railways in the British Isles, three steam railmotors were experimented with in 1905–6, which remained intermittently in traffic until 1918. From 1901 onwards the company maintained a stock of thirty engines until the decline began in the 1950s. And a fascinating and varied collection they were, consisting for instance in 1930 of no less than eleven different classes:

Wheel arrangement	Numbers
0–4–2T	2, 9
2–4–2T small tanks	27, 28
2–4–2T large tanks	5, 7
4–4–2T small	1, 3, 11, 12, 13, 15, 17, 18, 19, 20, 21, 30
4–4–2T large	8, 16
4–6–4T	22, 23, 24, 25
0–6–4T	29
0–6–0 small	26
0–6–0 intermediate	14
0–6–0 large	4, 10
2–4–0	6

With the exception of the two 0–4–2Ts, all these had been built by Beyer Peacock, which supplied all the firm's engines from 1891 onwards. The oldest engine remaining in the above list was 0–6–0 no 26, built in 1892.

The largest engines, the four 4–6–4Ts of 1920, were confined to the Bangor line, but they tended to be sluggish and very heavy on coal. Surprisingly for such a modern design they were not superheated. When further engines were required in 1921, more of the well-tried 4–4–2T type were obtained, the only one which could be described as in any way standard.

This stock remained almost static from 1930 onwards; only one more steam engine was to be built, a large 4–4–2T (similar to nos 8 and 16), which came out in 1945, and was destined to have a life of only eleven years. This was no 9, taking the number of the 0–4–2T, which became no 28 for a year or two on the scrapping of the 2–4–2T.

There were also two experimental diesel engines, which appeared in 1933 and 1937 from Harland & Wolff, the well-known Belfast firm. The first one appeared as D1, and the second should have been D2 but instead came out as 28, numbered in the steam stock, and D1 was later renumbered 2, both taking the place of the two 0-4-2Ts, which were then scrapped.

The BCDR, right to the end of steam working, never abandoned the excellent practice of allocating two pairs of drivers and firemen permanently to each engine. This almost invariably resulted in much rivalry between the various teams in keeping their charges well up to scratch and the engines usually pre-presented a very well-kept appearance, as well as having better mechanical efficiency. The livery was a very pleasing rich dark green, lined out in black and white, very reminiscent of the old Great Central. It can still be seen in Belfast Museum, where 4-4-2T no 30 has been restored to its former condition.

On absorption by the UTA in 1950 all surviving engines were renumbered by the addition of 200 to avoid confusion with the NCC, with which there was some interchange, some of the BCDR engines going over to York Road, whilst some NCC 2-6-4Ts were tried out on the Bangor line; transfer was effected by means of the Belfast Central Railway, Lisburn and Antrim. All the BCDR engines carried their new numbers between 201 and 230 except nos 2, 5, 6, 7, 10, 26, 27 and 28, but apart from redundancy occasioned by closure of most of the system, the writing was already on the wall when diesel multiple-units first appeared on the Bangor line in 1951. They gradually replaced the steam trains, which were right to the end largely composed of six-wheelers. At the same time second class was abolished, three classes having persisted right up to that time. The new diesel trains provided first- and third-class accommodation only.

In early 1954 the local trains were entirely operated by multiple-units, in-cidentally the first service in the British Isles to be so worked, although steam excursions from the GNR continued for a while. The BCDR engines had been allowed gradually to run down, without any major repairs being effected, and they accumulated in the old steam shed, never to run again. They were sold for scrap in 1956.

CHAPTER 21

ULSTER TRANSPORT AUTHORITY
and NORTHERN IRELAND RAILWAYS

ULSTER TRANSPORT AUTHORITY
State-owned organisation formed to take over on 1 October 1948 the railways (NCC and BCDR) and road transport undertakings wholly within Northern Ireland. Assumed control also, on 1 October 1958, of that part of the Great Northern Railway within Northern Ireland.

NORTHERN IRELAND RAILWAYS
New organisation created to be responsible from 1 April 1968 for the railway system only.

A bill introduced by the Stormont Parliament in 1947 authorised the establishment of the Ulster Transport Authority, to take over the Northern Counties Committee, Belfast & County Down Railway, and the Northern Ireland Road Transport Board. The Great Northern, with its principal main line between Dublin and Belfast crossing the border, retained its independent status until 1 October 1958, when that part of the railway lying in the north—by this time reduced to a shadow of its former self—became part of the UTA, the southern part being transferred to CIE.

The UTA took over from the NCC and BCDR 340 route miles of railway, 90 locomotives, 440 carriages, 4 railcars and about 3,000 wagons, together with 988 buses and 924 lorries. The sorry story of the UTA's subsequent anti-rail policy, which was soon to eliminate rail-borne goods traffic, all diverted to lorries, and retain only the most important lines of the system, which even the new government could not dispense with, meant the disappearance of the remainder of the NCC minor lines and all the BCDR branches; the routes surviving were the GNR line to Dublin, the NCC lines to Larne, Portrush and Londonderry and the BCDR Bangor line. The GNR line to Londonderry was closed even though it followed a completely different route from the NCC one.

The earliest closures had already occurred before World War II. The first to go were the Draperstown branch, which lost its passenger service on 1 October 1930, Limavady–Dungiven likewise on 31 January 1933, and the short Bally-clare branch in 1938. All of these were retained for goods traffic until 1950, when they were closed entirely. The other branches, Limavady Junction to Limavady, Cookstown, and the Derry Central line, kept their passenger services until 1950, but these also were retained for goods until 1955–6, except for part of the Derry Central as far as Kilrea, which remained open through from Cookstown Junction until 1959.

A further reorganisation took place on 1 April 1968. The road interests were now separated by the creation of Northern Ireland Railways Limited, which assumed responsibility for the railways only. Road transport was now taken over by the Northern Ireland Transport Holding Company, this again being divided into two parts, Ulsterbus, for the passenger road services, and Northern Ireland Carriers, for the lorries. The NIR was divided into four regions: the Midland Region (Belfast–Ballymena and Larne), North West Region (Bally-money–Portrush and Londonderry), Southern Region (Belfast–Portadown and the border) and Down Region (Belfast–Bangor).

The first chairman of the NIR was Major F. A. Pope, who came from the NCC, and under his direction the fortunes of the remaining railways in the north took a marked turn for the better. There was a complete change in the general attitude towards maintaining such as remained of the system, and plans were made for some expansion and improvement rather than further retraction. There was even a small profit shown during the first year of operation. The recent regrettable 'troubles' in this divided country have of course not helped the situation.

But even under these difficulties plans have been going ahead for a major reconstruction in Belfast itself, so as to concentrate services at a central station. The line of the Belfast Central Railway, connecting the former GNR and BCDR systems, will be reopened and a new bridge built over the River Lagan. This will enable all services except those on the Larne line, which will continue to use York Road, to be diverted to a new station, Belfast Central, to be built in the Mayfields area. Diversion of the NCC trains from Londonderry via what was a secondary branch between Antrim and Knockmore Junction, Lisburn, will involve the upgrading of the line to main-line standards, and although this will increase the length of the route and journey time to some extent, this should be more than offset by the advantage of interchange facilities and a station more conveniently situated near the centre of the city. Fortunately the generous width of the original Ulster Railway road bed and bridges, built to a gauge of 6ft 2in, will enable a third track to be laid alongside the two GNR main lines between Belfast and Knockmore Junction. The link between Antrim

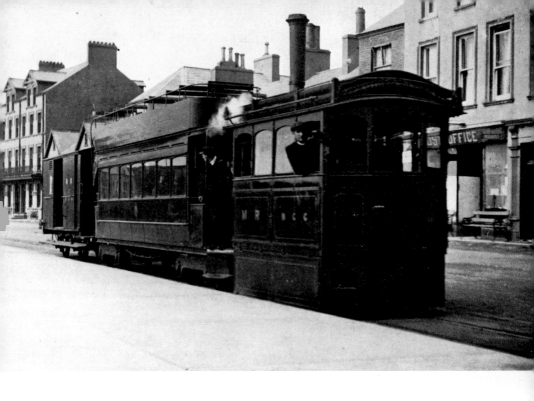

Page 233 (above) Portstewart Tramway train, 5 May 1920; (below) the Giant's Causeway Portrush & Bush Valley Tramway

Page 234 (*above*) The Belfast & County Down Railway in the last days of steam. Train about to leave Queen's Quay terminus in 1950 with one of the four large 4–6–4Ts, formerly no 23 but now renumbered 223 by the UTA. This was (and still is) a very busy suburban line with a good residential service. Until dieselisation (see below) the trains were mostly composed of six-wheelers with separate provision for first-, second- and third-class passengers; (*below*) new style train at Bangor in 1953, by which this important but only surviving section of the old BCDR is now entirely operated

and Greenisland will no longer be used by passenger trains, but will be retained to provide access to the Larne line and York Road repair shops.

Other recent developments have included reconstruction of the station at Portadown, opened on 5 October 1970, on a new site near the business part of the town, and a new station at Craigavon West, opened on 12 October 1970, to serve the new residential estate which has grown up there.

The widening of the lines between Belfast and Lisburn is in direct contrast to what would have been a retrograde step farther down the line during the last years of UTA, when it was proposed to single several miles of the track south of Portadown on the Dublin main line—Ireland's most important trunk route. Fortunately CIE, which was jointly responsible for the operation of the route, made strong objections, and the idea was dropped.

Since dieselisation many of the through trains between Belfast and Dublin have been worked throughout by CIE engines and men, as the UTA had no main-line diesels of its own, having gone over entirely to railcar operation. Even the Enterprise express was worked by a railcar set, but eventually it was decided this was hardly good enough for Ireland's 'crack train' and that a reversion should be made to locomotive-hauled stock. For this purpose a new eight-coach train, inclusive of a restaurant/bar, was built by British Rail at Derby in 1970—painted in a new livery of maroon and blue, with a narrow white intervening band—and three 1,350hp Bo-Bo diesel-electric locomotives were built at Doncaster, to work it on the push-and-pull principle, one at either end. In the winter a formation of five cars is sometimes sufficient, worked by one engine only, with a driving cabin in the coach at the other end. These new engines are numbered 101-3 and named *Eagle*, *Falcon* and *Merlin*, commemorating three of the former GNR compounds.

CIE also works a certain number of through goods trains between Dublin, Belfast and Londonderry, the only freight now conveyed by Northern Ireland Railways.

As a last minute note of interest, the unfortunate troubles of Northern Ireland since 1969 have spread to the railways and there have been instances of deliberate sabotage, like those of the 1920s. The GNR main line near the border has been the subject of such incidents, and on 15 August 1973 CIE diesel locomotive no B201 was blown to pieces by a bomb.

CHAPTER 22

LONDONDERRY & LOUGH SWILLY RAILWAY

Extensive 3ft gauge system from Londonderry through the northern parts of County Donegal. Incorporated 1852, but construction slow and first trains did not run until 1863. Originally built to 5ft 3in gauge, but converted to 3ft in 1885. Steam-worked throughout its existence.

Later constituents:

LETTERKENNY RAILWAY Incorporated 1860. Opened 1883, constructed to 3ft gauge. Absorbed by L & LSR in 1887.

CARNDONAGH EXTENSION RAILWAY Opened 1901.

LETTERKENNY & BURTONPORT EXTENSION RAILWAY Opened 1903. Worked by L & LSR although with nominally separate engines and rolling stock. Very spectacular line through one of the wildest mountainous parts of the country.

Total mileage: 99 miles.

Principal places served:

Londonderry, Buncrana, Carndonagh, Letterkenny, Burtonport.

CARDONAGH EXTENSION RAILWAY *Closed 1935.*

BURTONPORT EXTENSION *Closed 1940, partly reopened 1941, finally closed 1947.*

Remainder of railway closed 1953.

The Londonderry & Lough Swilly Railway was one of three Irish railways which started life as a standard 5ft 3in line and was later converted to 3ft gauge. The other two were the Cork Blackrock & Passage and the Finn Valley, which eventually became part of the County Donegal system.

Whilst the headquarters of the L & LSR were in Londonderry itself, the greater part of the system lay in County Donegal. This is the most north-westerly region of the whole country, and lies in what became the Free State, now the Republic of Ireland. In true Irish fashion, the most northerly point in the whole island, Malin Head, is situated in what is commonly referred to as Southern Ireland; and incidentally the most northerly point on any Irish railway was on the Londonderry & Lough Swilly system. The present County Donegal corresponds very closely to what was from the fifth to the eleventh century one of the seven separate Kingdoms of Ireland, known as Ailech.

From the middle of the nineteenth century, when the population of the county had reached a maximum of nearly 300,000, it fell sharply in consequence of the famine of the 1840s. Consequently a century later it had dropped to less than half this number, largely scattered over the bleak mountainous countryside. There are no towns of any size, Letterkenny being the largest, with a present population of something over 4,000, followed by Buncrana with about 3,000, and Ballyshannon, 2,500, and then Bundoran and the county town, Donegal itself, with less than 1,500 each. There are no natural resources apart from peat, largely used locally as fuel, and virtually no industries.

Against such a background there was obviously little to attract the railway promoter; there were one or two schemes put forward during the period of the Railway Mania of 1845, but not surprisingly nothing came of them, and until the 1860s the county remained devoid of any rail communication, a position to which it has unfortunately reverted today.

The origin of the L & LSR lay in the passing of an Act in 1852 authorising the construction of a line from Derry to Carrowan, $8\frac{3}{4}$ miles out, on the shores of Lough Swilly, under the title of the Lough Foyle & Lough Swilly Railway, but a further Act of 26 June 1853 amended the name to the Londonderry & Lough Swilly Railway. This was its title to the end of its existence as an actual railway, and in fact it still exists as such, although its operations are now confined to road services.

Even after the 1853 Act had been passed construction did not begin until 1860, and the first train did not run until 31 December 1863. The terminus was at Farland Point, on what became a short branch, very soon abandoned, off the through line to Letterkenny, and the line was built to 5ft 3in gauge.

An Act of 22 July 1861 authorised the company to extend its line along the eastern shores of Lough Swilly to Buncrana, a popular seaside resort, only 12 miles from Londonderry, and considerable excursion traffic eventually developed. This was by far the most profitable part of the system, and the last to retain a passenger service.

An extension northward from Buncrana to Carndonagh, another $18\frac{1}{4}$ miles, was planned in 1883, after the passing of the Tramways Act, which provided for substantial assistance in light railway construction, but it was deferred for the time being. It was eventually opened on 1 July 1901, but was the shortest-lived section on the system, being closed as early as November 1935.

The Buncrana and Carndonagh line left that to Letterkenny at what later became known as Tooban Junction. This line was originally a separate company, the Letterkenny Railway, incorporated on 3 July 1860, although it was again many years before construction began. It was not ready for opening until 1883 and was built to 3ft gauge, the Lough Swilly line to Buncrana having up to that time been broad-gauge. As an alternative to having a permanent mixed-gauge line between Londonderry and Tooban Junction, the L & LSR, which undertook to work the Letterkenny Railway, made the bold decision to convert its own line to 3ft standards. This involved of course the acquisition of new engines and stock, and the conversion was effected in 1885; two years later the L & LSR absorbed the Letterkenny Railway, bringing its total route mileage up to 31 miles.

At Letterkenny it was eventually joined by the Strabane & Letterkenny Railway, worked by the County Donegal and opened in 1909. Thus here was another of the few towns in Ireland served by competitive routes, and not unnaturally relations between the two lines were never too cordial. Although there was actual physical connection at Letterkenny by means of a transfer siding, the companies had their own separate stations, alongside each other.

The last addition to the L & LSR system was again a separate company, the Letterkenny & Burtonport Extension, a straggly line 49¾ miles long in all, which pursued a necessarily tortuous way around the mountains of the wildest part of County Donegal, and finished up at the small fishing port of Burtonport, which possesses a good harbour on the north-west Atlantic coast. Fishing is its only industry, but it provided a lucrative business for the new railway. The line was opened on 3 March 1903. Burtonport is in fact only 28 miles from Letterkenny as the crow flies, but very little traffic could have been expected from the intermediate stations, most of which were anything up to four miles away from the places they served, very small communities in any case.

Roads in this area were extremely scarce and of very poor quality, so that for many years the railway enjoyed a virtual monopoly of such traffic as there was. There were a few connecting buses of a sort, but one can only speculate on what sort of vehicles they were, or how they managed on the crude highways. I have tickets in my collection bearing such inscriptions as 'Sweeney's Car DUNGLOE RD TO DUNGLOE Fare 1 shilling, 28lb luggage free', and 'Sterritt's Car convey one passenger, DUNFANAGHY RD TO DUNFANAGHY and return. 28lb luggage free', no fare specified.

The 74½ miles between Derry and Burtonport was the longest through narrow-gauge journey in the British Isles and occupied over four hours, usually with about a quarter of an hour at Letterkenny, but was a fascinating experience for the enthusiast. First-class travel was most desirable, as third class was distinctly spartan, with wooden seats. Travellers in winter must have found it decidedly chilly, as trains were never steam heated. Incidentally the L & LSR once operated all three classes, but second was abolished in 1929.

The major engineering feat on the line was Owencarrow viaduct, and on two occasions trains were partly blown off in hurricane winds, to which this part of the country is particularly prone. The first was on 22 February 1906, when two coaches were derailed, but without serious results. On 30 January 1925 however two coaches were blown off and fell upside down on to an embankment of rocks, part way across, with four fatal casualties.

For a time the railway possessed its own steamer, which it acquired in 1923 from the Lough Swilly Steamship Co; the 140 ton *Lake of Shadows*, built in 1905, lasted until 1934, and there were also some smaller motor vessels.

The headquarters of the system were at Londonderry, the workshops and locomotives being at Pennyburn, a short way out of the terminus. At this point the railway crossed a fairly busy street on the level, a source of some contention and argument over the years, and the scene of more than one fatal accident.

The terminal station, at Graving Dock, was a barn-like structure with stone walls, austere in the extreme, the sort of building one would pass without a second glance, and about as unlike a railway station as one could imagine, only recognisable by the large hand-painted board on the roof: 'Lough Swilly Railway'. It was also a considerable distance from the city centre, to which however there was rail connection for the transfer of traffic over the lines of the Londonderry Harbour & Railway Commissioners. In early years there was another station at Middle Quay, on the riverside, much nearer to the centre of things, over which passenger trains were worked—incidentally without parliamentary authority—by the L & LSR and later by the Harbour engines, but this arrangement came to an end in 1887, after which the more inconvenient premises at Graving Dock served as the terminus. Between 1897 and 1919 a 4ft 8½in gauge horse tramway operated between the station and Foyle bridge.

One cannot with truth describe the Lough Swilly as a 'happy' line, at least that was the impression I got when I paid my first visit in 1930, when economic difficulties had already begun to manifest themselves, and the future of the line seemed in jeopardy. Curiously enough, on later occasions, in 1937 and particularly on three more visits between 1948 and 1953, when its days were definitely numbered, the staff seemed more cheerful, perhaps as a result of their doubts having been resolved.

In 1930 however I did not receive the same open-armed welcome to which

I was treated on nearly every other Irish railway at that time. Mr Napier, the loco superintendent, gave me permission to visit the shed and works at Penny-burn and to take photographs, but somewhat grudgingly, I recollect. Having no 17, the old 0–6–0T, brought out from the back of the shed for photography seemed quite out of the question, at any rate with 'him' around, as the driver on duty put it; however, I managed to induce the latter, with the aid of a little palm-greasing, to do this for me around midday, when 'he' was away for lunch, albeit with fearful glances over the shoulder, in case 'he', from whose offices the shed yard was visible, should return unexpectedly.

Mr Napier was almost the last of a long succession of some twenty locomotive superintendents; some of them held the post for a very short time but he was in office from 1919 to 1951.

Specimen tickets of L & LSR

In its heyday the L & LSR was one of the most prosperous of the Irish narrow-gauge lines; in 1902, for instance, it made a profit of £11,627 and declared a dividend of 7 per cent. However, by the early 1930s economic difficulties were making themselves felt. The Carndonagh Extension was closed first, in 1935, and the rest of the system was already threatened when World War II delayed closure for a few more years. Road competition was the cause and, in fact, the Lough Swilly was already running its own bus services. The Burtonport Extension was closed on 3 June 1940, but the section from Letterkenny to Gweedore had to be reopened on 3 February 1941 and passengers were again carried from March 1943 until 6 January 1947, when it was closed finally. Services on the Buncrana line continued intermittently until September 1948, but excursions were subsequently run at weekends until final closure on 8 August 1953.

The Londonderry to Letterkenny line, which was finally closed on 1 July 1953, had nominally worked only a goods service after 1940, but the make-up of the train included a brake coach in which passengers were in fact carried, if they so desired, and were prepared to accept the somewhat indefinite timings, slow running and delays incurred by shunting at intermediate stations.

LOCOMOTIVES AND ROLLING STOCK

The original complement of 5ft 3in gauge engines consisted of two o–6–oTs, nos 1 and 2, built in 1862 by Fossick & Hackworth; two o–6–oSTs, nos 3 and 4, came from R. Stephenson in 1864, and two further o–6–oTs, nos 4 and 5, from Sharp Stewart in 1876 and 1879, by which time no 3 had been sold, and its number taken by the original no 2, the earlier no 4 in turn becoming no 2. When the gauge was converted to 3ft in 1885 two of the five remaining engines were sold to the Cork & Bandon Railway. The first 3ft gauge engines were three o–6–2Ts from Black Hawthorn, nos 1–3, which arrived in 1883. They were named *J. T. Macky*, *Londonderry* and *Donegal*, and they lasted until 1911–13. No 4 was o–6–oT *Innishowen*, also by Black Hawthorn in 1885. It eventually became no 17 and lost its name, but remained as spare engine at Pennyburn for many years, still being in the works yard out of service in 1937, and not broken up until 1940. Nos 5 and 6 were small 2–4–oTs, obtained secondhand in 1885 from the Glenariff Iron Ore & Harbour Co, having been built by R. Stephenson in 1873. They were scrapped about 1900.

In 1899 there appeared two much larger engines than any previously seen on the line, a couple of 4–6–2Ts, forerunners of what was to be the most numerous type on the Lough Swilly. They were nos 5 and 6, built by Hudswell Clarke, and were followed by nos 7 and 8, from the same makers, in 1901. No 7 had the distinction of working a Royal Train in 1903, and received the name *Edward VII* in consequence, but this was later removed. Two more 4–6–2Ts came from Kerr Stuart in 1904, nos 9 *Aberfoyle* and 10 *Richmond*. They were the last engines to receive names and they also lost them some time prior to 1930. The last two 4–6–2Ts, nos 13 and 14, came from Hawthorn Leslie in 1910. Nos 5 and 6 were renumbered 15 and 16 in 1912, no 9 was scrapped in 1928, and no 7 in 1940, but the remainder lasted to the end of the railway's existence, being cut up in 1953 and 1954.

For the opening of the Burtonport Extension, Andrew Barclay & Sons delivered four 4–6–oTs, nos 1–4. Although this line was worked throughout by the L & LSR it was the practice to allocate certain engines to the Burtonport line, and these were accordingly lettered L & BER although numbered in the Lough Swilly stock; 4–6–2Ts nos 13 and 14 later became L & BER engines in exchange for 4–8–4Ts 5 and 6.

The last four locomotives were remarkable machines. Nos 11 and 12 were big 4–8–0s, built by Hudswell Clarke in 1905. Although intended for the L & BER, a maker's photograph shows one of these carrying the inscription L & LSR on the tender. In later pictures the tenders appear to be blank, and whether either of them actually bore the letters L & BER, as did the other engines specially allocated, is uncertain. Nos 5 and 6 were 4–8–4Ts from the same firm in 1912, the last new engines the company ever had. They were massive machines by narrow-gauge standards, with a weight of 58¼ tons, and would not have been out of proportion if built for 5ft 3in gauge operation.

These four engines were unique in a number of respects. With the exception of a couple of 4–8–0Ts on the GSWR they were the only eight-coupled steam engines to run in Ireland, and both the 4–8–0s and the 4–8–4Ts were the only examples of these wheel arrangements ever to run in the British Isles.

The 4–8–0s spent practically all their working lives on the Burtonport line; no 12 lasted to the end, but no 11 was withdrawn in 1933. After the 4–8–4Ts had been exchanged for two 4–6–2Ts, they worked mainly to Buncrana on excursion trains.

Although specific engines were nominally confined to the Burtonport line, it somewhat naturally followed that there were occasions when they were to be found on the Lough Swilly proper, and vice versa. Indeed after 1913 the practice of lettering specific engines L & BER ceased, but no 4 was still thus adorned to the end in 1953, and in the old green livery, much faded and shabby, but apparently not having received a repaint for at least forty years. The original 'pea green' livery had been replaced by plain black by the 1920s, but no 12 was running in 1937 in a dark shade of grey, unlined. After about this time some engines reappeared in green with yellow lining out, and in place of the letters L & LSR was a diamond-shaped emblem enclosing the bare initials LSR.

This railway had the distinction of being entirely steam operated to the end; although the neighbouring County Donegal pioneered the introduction of diesel railcars, they were never taken up by the Lough Swilly.

The coaching stock comprised both six-wheelers and bogies, somewhat austere, mostly third class, with a few composites comprising first- and second-class accommodation, until the latter was abolished in 1929. Like the locomotives, those coaches allocated to the Burtonport line and the wagon stock, were lettered L & BER but in this case numbered in a separate series duplicating those carried by the purely L & LSR vehicles, and the coaches, at any rate, seem to have been kept fairly strictly to their own sphere of operation.

It is the greatest pity that the preservation movement came just too late to save a Lough Swilly engine for a museum, particularly one of the 4–8–4Ts or the 4–8–0 no 12. The numberplate of the latter, and possibly those of nos 5 and 6, may still be in existence in private hands, but apart from these no tangible remains of any of these remarkable engines have survived for posterity.

CHAPTER 23

COUNTY DONEGAL RAILWAY

The most extensive 3ft gauge system in Ireland, traversing the southern half of County Donegal, and, like the L & LSR, passing through some fine scenery. Worked in the last years almost entirely by diesel railcars. The Joint Committee was incorporated in 1906 by an Act which authorised the purchase of the existing Donegal system jointly by the GREAT NORTHERN RAILWAY OF IRELAND *and the* MIDLAND RAILWAY *of England.*

Constituents:

FINN VALLEY RAILWAY (originally built to 5ft 3in gauge)   Opened 1863.

WEST DONEGAL RAILWAY   Incorporated 1879. Opened 1882–9. Amalgamated 1892 with FINN VALLEY as DONEGAL RAILWAY. Subsequent extensions to Glenties, Killybegs, Ballyshannon and Londonderry.

STRABANE & LETTERKENNY   Incorporated 1903. Opened 1909.

The line between Strabane and Londonderry, opened 1900, became after 1906 exclusively owned by the MR (NCC), later LMS (NCC), and for a short time by BRITISH RAILWAYS, but worked by COUNTY DONEGAL JOINT COMMITTEE.

Route mileage: CDRJC jointly owned lines—91 miles.

STRABANE & LETTERKENNY—19 miles.

STRABANE & LONDONDERRY (owned by LMS but worked by CDRJC)—14½ miles.

Total worked by CDRJC—124½ miles.

Principal places served:

Londonderry, Strabane, Letterkenny, Stranorlar, Glenties, Donegal, Killybegs, Ballyshannon.

Railway entirely closed by 1960.

Apart from the Lough Swilly and a small penetration by the Great Northern at Bundoran in the south-west extremity, the only other railways to serve

Donegal were in the County Donegal group itself. This included the Strabane & Letterkenny, which was worked by the County Donegal and was the Lough Swilly's nearest neighbour, having a common meeting point with it at Letterkenny.

The two railways had a number of things in common: the nature of the country traversed, the 3ft gauge, and the fact that both had origins which were initially of 5ft 3in gauge. However, whereas the Lough Swilly was always independent and had to maintain itself by its own unaided efforts, the County

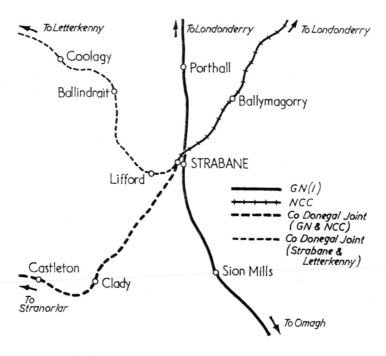

Donegal eventually became the joint property of two large railways, the very odd combination of the Great Northern of Ireland and the English Midland Railway, later the LMS.

Geographical conditions were largely the same in both the north-west and south-west parts of the county, served respectively by the two railways, the former with its Derryveagh range of mountains, having a highest summit of 2,466ft, which the Burtonport line had to circumnavigate, and the latter with the Blue Stack Mountains, the highest point of which is 2,211ft, intersected by the well-known Barnesmore Gap, through which the railway had to pass, with gradients of 1 in 60 on either side, to reach Donegal. Away from these wild and bleak areas both railways had comparatively flat agricultural land in their eastern halves and, in the case of the Donegal, also in its western extremities.

The origin of the Donegal system lay in the Finn Valley Railway, an independent 5ft 3in gauge line, which left the Irish North Western at Strabane, $14\frac{1}{2}$ miles out of Londonderry, and ran westwards to Stranorlar, along the valley of the River Finn, a distance of $13\frac{1}{2}$ miles. It was opened on 7 September 1863, and was worked by the INWR under a ten-year agreement.

At Strabane the Finn Valley at first used the INWR station, and to avoid the expense of a second bridge over the River Mourne, joined that company's tracks about half a mile to the south. Both of these facilities had of course to be paid for in the form of an annual rental of £375, which the Finn Valley considered excessive. In anticipation of the end of the ten years' agreement in 1872 the railway ordered its own rolling stock, although the Irish North Western continued to provide the motive power, and this arrangement continued after 1876 when the GNR was formed and absorbed the INWR.

The Finn Valley meanwhile had had thoughts of expanding westwards to the county town of Donegal, but this project was in fact brought about by the formation of a separate company, the West Donegal, incorporated on 21 July 1879, and opened through the Barnesmore Gap as far as Druiminin (later named Lough Eske), 14 miles from Stranorlar, on 25 April 1882, the remaining 4 miles to Donegal not being ready until 16 September 1889. The Finn Valley had a financial interest in the new line and was actually responsible for working it. As it had been constructed to the 3ft gauge however, new engines and rolling stock had to be obtained.

For the time being therefore Stranorlar station comprised two different rail gauges intermixed, but not, it is thought, any length of track common to both by means of a third rail. The curious situation during these years was that the GNR was working the Finn Vally Railway while that company was in turn working the West Donegal! In 1892 however the Finn Valley and the West Donegal were amalgamated into one company, the Donegal Railway. In the following year the decision was taken to alter the gauge of the old Finn Valley to conform with the 3ft of the West Donegal, and at the same time the opportunity was taken of diverting the trains at Strabane from the GNR station into a new one adjacent to it, which necessitated the construction of an independent bridge over the River Mourne, all this being achieved by July 1894.

Meanwhile two further extensions to the Donegal Railway had been authorised under the Light Railways (Ireland) Act of 1889. One of these was from Stranorlar, which now became the hub of the Donegal system, along the valley of the River Finn to Glenties, 24 miles distant, a small town of less than 1,000 inhabitants in very picturesque surroundings, and the other was from Donegal for 19 miles to Killybegs, a small fishing port of about 1,000 inhabitants, on an inlet of the north shore of Donegal Bay, with a good harbour and very fine coastal scenery. This line was opened on 18 April 1893, and the Glenties branch on 3 June 1895. Finally, in the western area was another 15½ mile extension from Donegal to Ballyshannon, third largest town in the county and 4 miles from the watering place of Bundoran. This was the last section of the Donegal Railway proper to be built, and was opened on 2 September 1905.

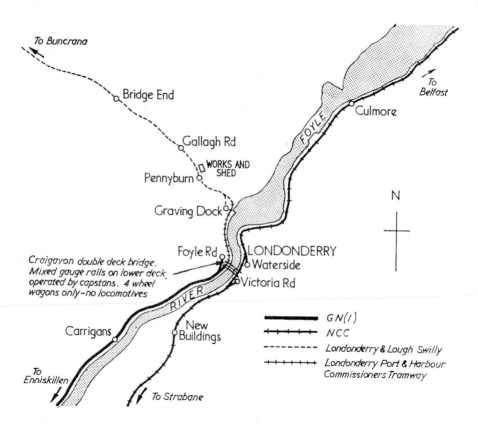

There had however been another line built by the Donegal Railway, so as to obtain its own access to Londonderry, independently of the GNR, which naturally opposed the scheme. The new line ran through a tract of country east of the River Foyle, whereas the GNR followed the west bank. This 14½ mile line was opened on 6 August 1900. Although essentially a very rural railway with small single platforms at intermediate stations serving but small villages, the terminus at Londonderry, Victoria Road, was a surprisingly commodious affair with overall roof, on the bank of the river which bisects the city.

Thus the railways in Londonderry were now four in number, two broad gauge and two narrow gauge, one of each gauge on either side of the river, and all using terminal stations. On the west side were the GNR and the L & LSR, and on the east side were the Belfast & Northern Counties and the Donegal. All these railways had intercommunication by means of mixed-gauge tracks on the lower level of Carlisle Bridge across the River Foyle; these lines were operated by the Londonderry Port & Harbour Commissioners, but could take only wagons and vans worked by capstans. The bridge was rebuilt in 1933 and is now named Craigavon Bridge.

The Midland, wishing to extend its operations in Ireland, offered to purchase the Donegal Railway outright. This however was opposed by the Great Northern, which saw the beginnings of an intrusion into what it naturally regarded as its own territory, and an agreement was reached by which the two railways became joint owners of the Donegal, with the exception of the Londonderry and Strabane section, of which the Midland secured sole ownership, though it was still worked by the County Donegal. By an Act of 1 May 1906 the Donegal Railway changed its name to County Donegal Railways Joint Committee, and was unique so far as Ireland was concerned in being the only joint railway of any size. There were however a number of small jointly owned sections of line, mainly around Dublin, Belfast and Waterford, and in its last years the Great Northern was operated by a joint board of the two Irish governments.

The last addition to what was now the County Donegal Joint system was the nominally independent Strabane & Letterkenny Railway. Originally known as the Strabane Raphoe & Convoy Railway, it was authorised in 1903–4 but not opened until 1 January 1909, which 19 miles brought the whole of the narrow-gauge network operated by the CDRJC up to 124½, although only 91 of the total was actually owned by them. The 14½ miles between Londonderry and Strabane was the property of the Midland and the Strabane & Letterkenny remained a separate entity, but all these lines were actually worked by the joint committee with its own locomotives. In fact in later years the rosters were so arranged that each engine visited Londonderry in turn, as by coaling there outside the boundaries of the Free State, some economies, possibly to do with customs duties, were obtained.

Even when physical contact with the Lough Swilly was at last achieved, at Letterkenny, very little through running ever materialised; in fact the two railways seemed to keep one another very much at arm's length, each with its own station at Letterkenny, side by side but with only siding connection. There was occasionally some small measure of co-operation; engines are known to have worked over each other's lines from time to time, and during the war visited each other's workshops for repair.

In 1902, just before being acquired by the GNR and MR, the Donegal Railway had made a profit of £10,854 and declared a dividend of 4½ per cent, a happy state of affairs unusual for a narrow-gauge railway. However, at the end of World War II, despite the economies of railcar operation, things were very different and closures were imminent. The Glenties branch was the least profitable part of the line, running through sparsely populated areas, and was the first to be closed to passengers on 3 December 1947, and completely on 12 March 1952. As a result the striking bridge across the River Finn at Stranorlar was demolished. Not surprisingly, this had been the first section to be turned over to railcars. The widespread use of such vehicles from the 1930s onwards, with the resultant economies in operation, undoubtedly enabled the railway to survive for many years longer than it could otherwise have done, and all of the rest of the system remained open until final closure on the last day of 1959. In fact some freight trains were operated between Stranorlar and Strabane until 6 February 1960. The company continued to operate road transport and its bus and lorry services passed to CIE on 1 January 1971.

The County Donegal became interested in alternatives to steam operation at a very early date, and was a pioneer in the use of diesel railcars. The first experiment occurred as early as 1907, when a small four-wheeled petrol-engined vehicle was obtained from Allday & Onions of Birmingham. It was intended really as nothing more than an inspection car, but with a capacity of ten it could sometimes be used in passenger service. It was later modified to some extent and has fortunately been preserved in Belfast Museum.

Further experimental cars were obtained during the following years but the really important breakthrough occurred in 1931, when the first two diesel railcars in the British Isles appeared in the shape of nos 7 and 8, built at the Great Northern Dundalk works with Gardner engines. They were of course primitive and by any standards uncomfortable things to travel in (a criticism which may still be levelled to some extent at many of their successors), but the County Donegal was quick to appreciate the annoyance caused to passengers by vibration, and in later examples, to try to overcome this drawback, the power unit was articulated to the passenger section, an improvement which regrettably has not been adopted as normal practice. These railcars were designed to haul trailers, and several interesting conversions were obtained from other sources.

Three classes of passenger accommodation were originally provided but the diesel railcars were one-class vehicles. The original eleven coaches built for the West Donegal were six-wheelers, but thereafter all were bogies, mainly of traditional compartment type, but with a few saloons, and in 1952 three corridor coaches, with the vestibules removed, formerly used on the Larne

Boat Train, were obtained from UTA. A few coaches provided lavatory accommodation for first- and second-class passengers, an amenity which third-class travellers had to do without. The livery changed over the years, the final turnout being a two-toned combination, red in the lower half (matching the engines) with cream upper panels, very similar in fact to the short-lived style first used on British Railways main-line stock. The considerable fleet of about 350 goods vehicles, open wagons, vans, cattle trucks, oil tank wagons and so on, were of usual design, but there were also some bogie flat wagons converted from passenger coaches.

Specimen tickets of CDRJC Constituents

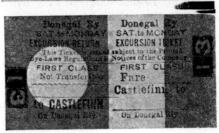

The County Donegal was not only a progressive and enterprising railway, it was also a very friendly line, the staff always being courteous and obliging, as indeed were most Irish railways, particularly the smaller ones. Its passing was very much regretted not only by the local inhabitants, but also by the many visitors from the outside world who had occasion to use it and enjoy some of the fine scenery through which it passed. The whole tract of country in the north-west of Ireland, north of Sligo and west of Londonderry, which includes the entire county of Donegal, is now entirely without railway communication.

LOCOMOTIVES AND ROLLING STOCK

The Finn Valley Railway was worked by engines from the INWR and the GNR and never had any of its own. The West Donegal originally had three 2–4–0Ts, built in 1882. These, together with all subsequent Donegal and County

Donegal engines, had both numbers and names, with the formation of the Donegal Railway in 1892, the gauge conversion of the Finn Valley in 1893, the Killybegs extension and other subsequent additions, more locomotives were progressively needed. First came six 4–6–0Ts in 1893, followed by two 4–4–4Ts in 1901 and four 4–6–4Ts in 1904; thereafter the remainder of the stock consisted of 2–6–4Ts, five in 1907 and the final three in 1912, in which year two of the 2–4–0Ts were scrapped, followed by the third in 1926. In 1930 four of the 4–6–0Ts, nos 4–7, were stored in the shed at Stranorlar and did not run again. Mr Forbes, the general manager, however, was always of an economical turn of mind and was loth to break them up, saying that they might come in useful some time, and there seemed no point in scrapping them when they were costing nothing for upkeep. How different from modern views on this subject! At that time no 9 was still in traffic, working the Glenties branch, and lasted a few years longer, together with no 8, which was lying derelict in Strabane shed as late as 1937. By then nos 4–7 had been broken up, but their side tanks, complete with nameplates, were still in the yard at Stranorlar. In 1930 no 10 was stationed at Ballyshannon, but no 11 was out of use; both were scrapped in 1933.

From the beginning of the 1930s the remaining engines, of which the 2–6–4Ts were undoubtedly the best, worked all the traffic until gradually displaced by railcars, which eventually took over nearly all of the passenger services. They were remarkably large engines for the 3ft gauge, matched only by the 4–8–4Ts and 4–8–0s of the Lough Swilly. Classes 4, 5 and 5A had cylinders of between 14 and 15½in by 21in, driving wheels 3ft 9in and 4ft, and boiler pressures of 160 and 175lb, giving tractive efforts between 12,755 and 14,295lb. All the 4–6–4Ts and some of the 2–6–4Ts later received superheaters, also unusual for a narrow-gauge design. The last three 2–6–4Ts nos 1–3 incidentally had Caledonian-type hooters.

The original livery was green, changed in 1906 to black with thin red lining out. From 1937 onwards a rather bright shade of red was adopted, described as 'geranium'. The nameplates were carried on the side tanks, with number-plates on the front cab panel.

Page 251 (*above*) Sligo Leitrim & Northern Counties Railway 0–6–4T *Lissadell* at Sligo in 1950. The railway (latterly almost entirely dieselised as far as passenger operation was concerned) was largely worked by engines of this wheel arrangement, five of this somewhat ancient appearance but another five considerably more modern, two of which were in fact the last new steam engines to be delivered to any Irish railway; (*below*) a reminder of the 'troubles' of the 1920s. Deliberate sabotage of the railway was widespread, and derailments such as this sometimes resulted in complete destruction of engines and rolling stock. Fortunately *Hazlewood*, sister engine to *Lissadell* above, survived, and was repaired to give many more years of service until the railway was obliged to close completely in 1957

Page 252 (above) Londonderry, showing the old Carlisle Bridge, rebuilt in 1933. The lower deck gave mixed-gauge rail intercommunication for goods vehicles between the four railways serving the city. The County Donegal Railway is depicted in the foreground, whilst the Great Northern station can be seen over the river. The bridge, now known as Craigavon, was rebuilt in 1933. It is no longer used for rail communication owing to the closure of three of the four railways, and road vehicles were first allowed on the lower deck in 1965, the approaches being reconstructed. The rails were finally removed in 1967; (below) Londonderry & Lough Swilly 4–8–0 12 taking water at Creeslough on the long run from Burtonport to Londonderry, 24 June 1937. The mountain peak in the background is that of Muckish, 2,197ft

CDRJC STEAM LOCOMOTIVES

Class	Original no and later no*		Name*	Type	Builder	Date	Works no	Scrapped
I	I		Alice	2–4–0T	Sharp Stewart	1881	3023	1926
	2		Blanche	2–4–0T	,,	1881	3021	1912
	3		Lydia	2–4–0T	,,	1881	3022	1912
2			Meenglas	4–6–0T	Neilson	1893	4573	1935
	5		Drumboe	4–6–0T	,,	1893	4574	1931
	6		Inver	4–6–0T	,,	1893	4575	1931
	7		Finn	4–6–0T	,,	1893	4576	1931
	8		Foyle	4–6–0T	,,	1893	4577	1937
	9		Columbkille	4–6–0T	,,	1893	4578	1937
3	10		Sir James	4–4–4T	,,	1901	6103	1933
	11		Hercules	4–4–4T	,,	1901	6104	1933
4	10	9	Eske	4–6–4T	Nasmyth Wilson	1904	697	1954
	13	10	Owenea	4–6–4T	,,	1904	698	1953
	14	11	Erne	4–6–4T	,,	1904	699	†
	15	(12)	Mourne	4–6–4T	,,	1904	700	1953
5	16	4	Donegal/ Meenglas	2–6–4T	,,	1907	828	†
	17	5	Glenties/ Drumboe	2–6–4T	,,	1907	829	†
	18	6	Killybegs/ Columbkille	2–6–4T	,,	1907	830	†
	19	(7)	Letterkenny/ (Finn)	2–6–4T	,,	1907	831	1940
	20	8	Raphoe/Foyle	2–6–4T	,,	1907	832	1955
5A	21	I	Ballyshannon/ Alice	2–6–4T	,,	1912	958	1961
	2A	2	Strabane/ Blanche	2–6–4T	,,	1912	956	Preserved in Belfast Museum
	3A	3	Stranorlar/ Lydia	2–6–4T	,,	1912	957	1961

* Class 5 engines were renumbered and renamed from 1937, but no 19 never received its new name. Class 5A engines were renumbered and renamed in 1928.

† On the closure of the line four engines, together with two railcars and a quantity of rolling stock, were purchased by a Dr Cox, of New Jersey, USA, for the purpose of setting up a small private railway in that country. Unfortunately the cost of shipping proved prohibitive, and at the time of writing, summer 1972, the three 2–6–4Ts were still in store in Ireland, nos 4 and 5 at Strabane, and no 6 at Stranorlar. There is a project to reopen a short length of the Londonderry line at Victoria Road as a preserved railway, utilising one or more of these engines.

P

CDJRC RAILCARS

Vehicle no	Description	Seating capacity	Builders	Source of acquisition	Disposal
1	Four-wheel petrol railcar	10	Allday & Onions 1906	Makers	Preserved in Belfast Museum
2 3	Four-wheel petrol railcars	17	Ford 1924	Derwent Valley Light Railway, re-gauged from 4' 8½" to 3'	Scrapped 1934
2	2–4–0 petrol rail-car, converted to trailer 1944	30	Cartledge 1925	Castlederg & Victoria Bridge Tramway	Scrapped 1960
3	2–2–2–2 petrol railcar, double ended, converted to trailer 1944	40	Drewry about 1926	1933, from Dublin & Blessington Tramway, re-gauged from 5' 3" to 3'	Preserved in Belfast Museum
4	Four-wheel petrol railcar	22	O'Doherty 1928 (assembled at Stranorlar)	New	Scrapped 1947
5	Four-wheeled trailer	28	O'Doherty 1929 Strabane & Dundalk	New	Scrapped 1960
6	2–4–0 petrol rail-car converted to four-wheel trailer 1945	30	O'Doherty 1930 Strabane & Dundalk	New	Scrapped 1958
7 8	2–4–0 diesel rail-cars, Gardner engines	32	Dundalk 1931	New	7 scrapped 1949, 8 pre-served in Belfast Museum
9 10	2–2–0 petrol railcars	20	Rebuilt Stranorlar 1933	Conversion from road omnibuses	9 scrapped 1949, 10 de-stroyed by fire, Bally-shannon, 1940
10	0–4–4 diesel railcar	28	Walker Bros 1932	1942 from Clogher Valley Railway	Preserved in Belfast Museum
11	*Phoenix* 0–4–0 diesel shunter	—	Atkinson Walker 1929, works no 114. Rebuilt Dundalk 1932	Conversion from steam tractor, Clogher Valley Railway	Preserved in Belfast Museum

Vehicle no	Description	Seating capacity	Builders	Source of acquisition	Disposal
12	0-4-4 diesel railcar	41	Dundalk 1934	New	Sold 1961 to Dr Cox, USA
13	Four-wheel trailer (conversion from petrol railcar)	16	Ford 1925	1933 from Dublin & Blessington Tramway (re-gauged from 5' 3" to 3')	Scrapped 1944
14	0-4-4 diesel rail-cars	41	Dundalk 1935	New	Scrapped 1961
15		41	1936	New	,,
16		41	1936	New	Sold 1961 to Dr Cox, USA
17		43	1938	New	Scrapped 1949 after accident
18		43	1940	New	Sold 1961 to Dr Cox, USA
19		41	1950 ⎫	New	Sold to Isle of Man Rail-way 1961
20		41	1951 ⎭		

With the exception of the Drewry no 3, all of the railcars were unidirectional and had to be turned after every journey.

CHAPTER 24

SLIGO LEITRIM & NORTHERN COUNTIES RAILWAY

In many respects a unique standard-gauge railway, consisting of a long main line, without branches, running through sparsely populated country, joining the GREAT NORTHERN RAILWAY *at its eastern end at Enniskillen and the* GREAT SOUTHERN RAILWAY *at Collooney, over which it had running powers into Sligo.*

Incorporated 1875. Opened in stages between 1879 and 1882.

Route mileage: 42¾ miles, plus 5½ miles of running powers into Sligo.

Principal places served:
Enniskillen, Sligo. The line ran through agricultural country, the headquarters of the railway being at Manorhamilton.

Closed completely in 1957 as a direct consequence of the severance of its main link with the rest of the Irish railway system at Enniskillen, a result of the enforced closure of the former GREAT NORTHERN RAILWAY *lines in the area by order of the Northern Ireland government.*

The Sligo Leitrim & Northern Counties Railway, which few people outside Ireland have ever heard of, was at the time of its regrettable demise in 1957 one of the two largest railway companies in the British Isles. By that time all the major systems in both Great Britain and Ireland were nationalised or under some form of state control, and none of them deigned to be described as companies. The other railway company was the Isle of Man Railway, which then operated 43 route miles of line. The operational length of the SLNCR was 48¼ miles, but only 42¾ miles was actually owned by the railway, the remaining 5½ being over the tracks of the CIE. It was however standard gauge as distinct from the 3ft gauge of the Isle of Man Railway. On the other hand the latter had sixteen engines against the Sligo Leitrim's modest total of seven at the end.

The 48¼ route miles of the SLNCR consisted of just one main line, unusually without any branches whatsoever, from Enniskillen, where it joined the Great Northern, westwards through the sparsely populated countryside of the counties of Fermanagh and Leitrim into Sligo, terminating at the county town of the latter. The first railway to reach Sligo had been the Midland Great Western in December 1862, and it was by virtue of running powers over the lines of that company that the SLNCR later ran its trains for the last few miles. Enniskillen, at the eastern end, had already had rail communication since 1854, by means of the Londonderry & Enniskillen Railway, later the Irish North Western, which became part of the Great Northern at the 1876 amalgamation. Thus the SLNCR became a link between the two largest railways in Ireland, the Great Northern and what eventually became the Great Southern. The railway was authorised by an Act of 11 August 1875, which provided for the construction of some 42 miles of line, with running powers over the MGWR into Sligo and at the other end for a short distance over the INWR into Enniskillen station. The actual point at which the SLNCR joined the MGWR at Collooney was at Carrignagat Junction.

In 1895 a third railway reached Sligo, also by virtue of running powers from Collooney over the MGWR, this being the Waterford Limerick & Western. This was the only instance in the whole country of three railways operating over the same length of main line track. Collooney, although only a small village with a population of about six hundred, was then served by three separate stations. There was also a separate loop, giving direct access to the SLNCR from the WLWR, put in by the latter (see map, page 81). At Sligo there was a separate branch to the quay, 1½ miles in length, over which the SLNCR also had running powers.

The first section of the line, from Enniskillen to Belcoo, 12½ miles, was opened in March 1879, but money was short, and a further Act had to be obtained on 29 June 1880, authorising the raising of further capital and an extension of time for completion. However another 5 miles on to Glenfarne was opened on 1 January 1880, and Manorhamilton, another 7½ miles, was reached by 1 December 1880. Here were established the headquarters and workshops of the railway. Westwards from Manorhamilton to Dromahair, another 8½ miles, and on to Collooney, in all 16¾ miles, were opened on 1 September 1881, but it was another year before the final link with the MGWR at Carrignagat Junction was at last completed and opened on 7 November 1882. The terms of agreement with the MGWR provided for the SLNCR to build a further parallel track as far as the next station, Ballysodare, to avoid single-line working over this section, the last 4½ miles into Sligo being already double.

So the railway was duly completed, not without difficulties mainly of a

SLNCR free pass

financial nature; it was never in any sense a prosperous line. Its most lucrative traffic was cattle, conveyed in large numbers over its two outlets at either end, but especially via Enniskillen, where its link with the Great Northern Railway, on which it was almost entirely dependent, gave it through access not only to Londonderry, but also to Belfast, Dublin and other parts of Ireland. As the country through which it passed was sparsely populated and became more so over the years, local traffic was never plentiful, and was subject to the usual encroachment by the bus and lorry from the 1920s onwards. Fortunately the Northern Ireland authorities in those earlier years refused permission for a competing bus service between Enniskillen and Sligo, an attitude which was reversed later. The SLNCR eventually operated a small road fleet of its own.

Three specimen SLNCR tickets

The 'troubles' associated with the partition of Ireland involved the SLNCR to a considerable extent and there were a number of acts of sabotage which resulted in derailments and damage. The railway was one of those unfortunate ones which crossed the border between Northern Ireland and the Free State, with all the nuisance of customs barriers, to say nothing of the more serious effects of the resulting change in traffic trends. However, along with the Great Northern and several smaller railways such as the Lough Swilly, it could not be absorbed into the Great Southern at the 1925 amalgamation, which may or may not have been an advantage, but it at least meant that it was able to retain its independence. Likewise the Ulster Transport Authority formed in 1948, could not acquire direct control over the Sligo Leitrim, but it effected its eventual closure indirectly by means of its hold on the Great Northern. The complete cessation of rail transport on the Great Northern at Enniskillen, the SLNCR's vital link with the outside world, rendered its closure on the same date inevitable. The last train ran on 30 September 1957.

Though usually in severe financial difficulties, the Sligo Leitrim & Northern Counties Railway battled on bravely, and in its later years was indebted to a very large extent to Mr G. F. Egan, who was not only locomotive and general civil engineer from 1925 until the end of the railway's existence, but who acted also in many other capacities, manager, secretary, solicitor and so on, officially or otherwise, and who in fact became the general 'Pooh Bah'. A charming man, whom I was privileged to meet on my several visits to the railway, always helpful and sympathetic to visitors interested in his line. On my last visit in 1955, the hospitality extended to myself and my son at his house overlooking the workshop in Manorhamilton was accompanied now and then by whistles from the engine of the evening goods into Sligo, by which we were to travel; it was already overdue but could not depart until Mr Egan was ready for it to do so, and it had to wait until we had finished our tea! This sort of thing could only happen in Ireland, and on a privately owned railway, but it was typical of the pleasant and easy-going ways of a past decade.

The Sligo Leitrim & Northern Counties Railway was a highly individual line; there was nothing quite like it even in Ireland, and unfortunately never can be again.

LOCOMOTIVES AND ROLLING STOCK

The first engines were a couple of 0-6-2Ts built by the Avonside Engine Company in 1877, works nos 1197-8. They were named *Pioneer* and *Sligo* and never bore numbers. This was a characteristic of the SLNCR: throughout its whole life it never numbered its engines. For a similar parallel one has to go back to the last years of the broad gauge of the Great Western Railway; right to the end in 1892 its famous 4-2-2s were known by names only. There were also the Isle of Wight Railway, with its small stud of 2-4-0Ts. *Pioneer* and *Sligo* worked until 1921, and after being laid aside for several years were sold for scrap in 1928.

Faugh a Ballagh was an 0-4-0ST used in the construction of the line, built by Hunslet in 1898, works no 178. It was later used on the building of the Claremorris and Collooney line of the WLWR, and then after a few years of miscellaneous duties on the SLNCR was disposed of in 1905 again for contractors' work, this time on the Castleblayney Keady & Armagh Railway. Its ultimate fate is unknown.

In 1882 there appeared the first of what was to become the railway's principal type, the 0-6-4T, of which there were eventually ten in all, of three classes.

The first five were of a distinctly archaic appearance, or at any rate gave this impression in their later years. N. W. Sprinks, in his book on the line, touches just the right note in describing them as 'having a curious spider-like grace'. They had some typically Beyer Peacock features, in particular the design of the copper-capped chimney (eventually replaced by one of Great Northern pattern) and the large brass bell-shaped dome with Salter safety valves; the latter were eventually superseded by the Ross pop-type, though the picturesque domes were retained to the end. They were very efficient engines, and together with their later successors formed the mainstay of the company's motive power.

Particulars of these first five are as follows:

Name	Date built	Beyer Peacock works no	Disposal		
Fermanagh	1882	2137	Withdrawn 1947, scrapped 1952		
Leitrim	1882	2138	Withdrawn and scrapped 1952		
Lurganboy	1895	3677	,,	,,	1953
Lissadell	1899	4073	,,	,,	1957
Hazlewood	1899	4074	Withdrawn 1957, scrapped 1959		

It was hoped on the closure of the line that *Hazlewood* would be sent to Belfast Museum, but unfortunately it was broken up by the scrap merchants.

In 1883 a 4–4–0T was obtained from Hudswell Clarke, works no 261, and was named *Erne*. It was very similar to the design built for the constituents of the Midland & Great Northern Joint Railway, one of which lasted in traffic until 1933, whilst another survived World War II on the Longmoor Military Railway, where it was used for rerailing exercises. The design however proved very unsuitable for the Sligo Leitrim even after rebuilding as a 4–4–2T. The engine was of very little use and was scrapped in 1912.

Waterford was an 0–6–0T built by Hunslet in 1893, works no 591, and was purchased secondhand in 1899. It worked on odd duties until about 1922 and was sold for scrap in 1928.

The first of three more 0–6–4Ts of an enlarged design and of much more modern appearance was built in 1904, followed by a second in 1905 and another in 1917. These were Beyer Peacock nos 4592, 4720 and 5943, and they were named *Sir Henry*, *Enniskillen* and *Lough Gill*. All lasted until the closure of the railway.

Two smallish 4–4–0s were purchased secondhand from the Great Northern in 1921, having been built by Beyer Peacock in 1885 and 1887. On the Great Northern they had been nos 118–19, *Rose* and *Thistle*, but they now became *Blacklion* and *Glencar*. They were somewhat underpowered for the requirements of the SLNCR, however; the two of them were rebuilt into one engine at Dundalk in 1928, this becoming *Blacklion*, which did only about three more years' work and after lying derelict at Manorhamilton for a further period was finally broken up in 1938.

During the next few years several o-6-os from the Great Northern worked on the SLNCR, mostly on hire, but three of these actually came into the stock of that company.

The first was *Glencar*, or *Glencar A* as it was at first known, to distinguish it from the 4-4-0 still in existence, the A being the former Great Northern class letter which it still carried on the cabside, but no doubt the same nameplate was used, being transferred from the 4-4-0. This had been Great Northern 31, originally named *Galway*. The second engine was *Sligo*, late Great Northern 149, formerly *Roscommon*. These two had been built by Beyer Peacock in 1890, works nos 3273-4. They were purchased by the SLNCR in 1928 and 1931 respectively. The last mentioned was scrapped in 1941 and replaced by a similar engine which assumed the same identity; this was Great Northern 79, originally named *Cavan*, Beyer Peacock 2116 of 1882. This second *Sligo*, together with *Glencar*, lasted until 1949.

Finally came two more o-6-4Ts, very similar to the three *Sir Henry* class, but with slight modifications. They were noteworthy in being not only the last engines obtained by the company, but the last conventional steam locomotives to be delivered to any railway in Ireland. They were built by Beyer Peacock in 1949, works nos 7138 and 7242. They had been ordered around 1946-7, despite the parlous financial position of the company at that time, being regarded as necessary in view of the poor condition of some of the existing locomotives. The company was however receiving some assistance from the Northern Ireland government at that time in the form of 'grant aid', but with increasing reluctance. The company had hoped to obtain a loan of £22,000 to purchase the new engines. Meanwhile the makers refused to effect delivery and it was not until a hire purchase agreement was concluded that the locomotives were shipped over in 1951. They carried plates on the backs of the bunkers, bearing the legend 'This locomotive makers No 7138 (7242) is the property of Beyer Peacock & Co Ltd, Gorton, Manchester, England'.

In accordance with tradition they received names only, *Lough Melvin* and *Lough Erne*. On closure of the line, they were sold by the makers, as owners, to the Ulster Transport Authority, being somewhat similar to four engines on the Great Northern, which were used for shunting in the Belfast area. They became UTA nos 26 and 27, and were employed for several years at York Road on the former NCC system.

Lough Melvin was withdrawn in 1965, but *Lough Erne* has fortunately been acquired for preservation and is now to be seen at the premises of the Railway Preservation Society of Ireland at Whitehead.

Whilst the principal locomotive shed was at Manorhamilton, the timetable required at least two engines to remain overnight at Sligo and one at Enniskillen, and there was usually in addition a spare engine at either end. At Enniskillen there were two small one-engine sheds and at Sligo they were accommodated in the Great Southern shed.

In 1932 trials were made with a light diesel railcar borrowed from the Great Northern. It was found that running costs were in the region of a quarter of that of a conventional steam train. This led the company to obtain in 1934 an even lighter vehicle, in fact an ordinary road bus adapted for rail operation, coupled with a small four-wheeled goods trailer. After a few years it was converted to diesel propulsion. Another similar vehicle was obtained in 1938. All of these were unidirectional, and had to be turned at Enniskillen and Sligo, but this was no different from steam practice, engines always being worked chimney first.

A very much larger and improved diesel car was built in 1947 by Messrs Walker of Wigan. This was an eight-wheeled vehicle with power unit and cab articulated from the coach body, providing a marked improvement in the riding qualities and comfort; it also had an increased passenger capacity. On the closure of the line it was sold to the CIE on which system it was still in use in 1972.

Until the introduction of diesel railcars the usual three classes of passenger accommodation were provided, but by 1950 nearly all passenger services were operated by railcars, which were one class only.

The general pattern of the timetable changed little over the years, consisting of three through trains daily from Sligo to Enniskillen and four in the opposite direction. The unbalanced working was an evening train from Enniskillen to Sligo which was mixed and was the only one regularly rostered for steam in later years. Towards the end even this could, if there was no worthwhile goods traffic, be worked by a railcar, much to the dismay and annoyance—to put it mildly—of many enthusiasts who had often travelled long distances to visit the railway.

Earlier passenger coaches were six-wheelers, but in 1924 there appeared three bogie vehicles, all tricomposites, one with a guard's brake compartment, and surprisingly they had clerestory roofs, an almost extinct feature for new construction at that time, which gave them a more ancient appearance than they merited. Two of them were electrically lit (the third being used only during daylight hours) and they were eventually fitted with steam heating, a luxury not hitherto enjoyed. They had only one first-class compartment, and the problem of providing accommodation for both smokers and non-smokers was solved by a central sliding partition. An oddity about the SLNCR coaching stock was that the door handles were on the left; the reason for this is obscure, but possibly the original designer was left-handed!

The goods stock consisted of the usual types of brake van, four-wheeled wagons and, by the nature of the railway's activities, a high proportion of cattle vans.

The livery of the steam coaching stock was unlined maroon, and of the railcars green for the lower body work and cream for the upper panels. The locomotives were at first in lined olive green but were later plain black. The handsome decorative nameplates were on the tank sides, or in the case of the few tender engines, on the splashers.

CHAPTER 25

CASTLEDERG & VICTORIA BRIDGE
TRAMWAY

Small roadside 3ft gauge steam tramway connecting the market township of Castlederg with the main GREAT NORTHERN *Londonderry line at Victoria Bridge.*

Incorporated 1883. Opened 1884.

Mileage: 7¼ miles.

Principal place served:
  Castlederg.

Closed 1933.

Incorporated by special Act of Parliament in 1883, the Castlederg & Victoria Bridge Tramway was a 3ft gauge roadside system 7¼ miles long, connecting the small town of Castlederg in County Tyrone, population about 850, with Victoria Bridge on the GNR main Londonderry line. The only hamlets en route in this sparsely populated district were Spamount, Crew and Fyfin, which were official stopping places, although the train would halt anywhere on request. The gradients were dependent on the undulating nature of the road, alongside which the tramway had its own reserved track, and were considerable, with many stretches of 1 in 30. The line was single and had no passing loops, only one engine being in service at a time. The journey took about forty minutes and the trains were timed to connect with the GNR main line at Victoria Bridge. Usually there were four or five trains a day, with a non-stop 'express' on Castlederg fair days. There was no Sunday service. The trains were mixed, being composed of one or more passenger coaches, as required, together with such vans and wagons as were to be conveyed. The coaches were of the single-deck tramcar type, at first four-wheelers, though bogie vehicles appeared later, and had first and second (later designated third) accommodation.

The railway was opened on 4 July 1884; although it served a need in the district and enjoyed a reasonable amount of traffic, until it met road competition in the 1920s, it was never in any sense a prosperous concern. The authorised capital was £20,000, which included a 5 per cent baronial guarantee, and until World War I it managed to pay a dividend of 3½ per cent. An extensive railway strike in 1933 finally sealed the company's fate; the trains never ran again, and the line was officially closed on 3 October of that year.

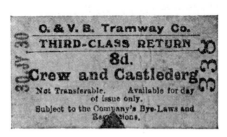

Specimen tickets of the CVBT

LOCOMOTIVES AND ROLLING STOCK

The headquarters and offices of the company were at Castlederg, where there was a sizeable yard, with engine shed and repair shop. The locomotive superintendent was C. S. Bracegirdle, who later went to the Donegal Railway. For the opening of the line there were two 0-4-0WT enclosed tram engines, built by Kitson in 1884, works nos T106 and T107. They were 1 *Mourne* and 2 *Derg*, after rivers in the vicinity, the names being later removed. They were originally fitted with a form of condensing apparatus, the resulting hot exhaust being used as feedwater, but this apparatus was dispensed with after some years. The original handbrakes were found to be unsatisfactory, and after an accident the company adopted Westinghouse brakes. These engines were scrapped on the arrival of new ones in 1904 and 1912.

No 3 also came from Kitson, in 1891, works no T257; it was a somewhat larger engine and was not totally enclosed. Like all the engines it had wheel guards on the left-hand side only. As the railway kept to one side of the road the whole way and the engines always faced Castlederg, there being no turning facilities, this was all that was necessary. It had a modified form of Walschaert valve gear, and remained as spare engine until 1928.

Mr Bracegirdle was succeeded in 1900 by R. Smith, who was followed by W. Holman in 1904. Two very much larger engines were then acquired from Hudswell Clark, no 4 in 1904, works no 698, and no 5 in 1912, works no 978. No 4 was of the very rare 2–6–0T type. Probably it had too rigid a wheelbase, as no 5 was very similar but an 0–4–4T and suffered in consequence from some lack of adhesion, as I found on my one and only visit to the line in 1930, when it was the engine at work. Nevertheless, despite some slipping it coped adequately with quite a long heavy train composed largely of cattle wagons. Between them these two engines handled most of the traffic until the railway closed, although another engine was obtained in 1928 by G. H. Pollard, the line's last locomotive superintendent, from 1918 until 1934.

This was a Beyer Peacock 2–4–0T of the type still to be found in the Isle of Man, which had been built for the Ballymena & Larne Railway in 1878, works no 1828. Originally numbered 4 on the BLR it became Belfast & Northern Counties no 66, later renumbered 105. On arrival at Castlederg it was fitted with a framework over the wheels, but not with totally enclosed sheeting as on the other engines. It was normally kept only as a spare engine, and it is doubtful whether it ever did a great deal of work. It was scrapped when the line closed, as was no 5, but no 4 was sold to the Clogher Valley Railway, which rebuilt it as a 2–6–2T. The engines were painted a rather dull shade of brick red, unlined, and were very little cleaned in their later years.

When the impact of road competition was severely felt in 1925, Mr Pollard built at the company's own workshops, with the assistance of a staff of two, a carpenter and a blacksmith, a paraffin railcar seating twenty-four passengers; it had a Fordson 20hp engine with four forward speeds. After some modification it was reasonably satisfactory, and ran about 30,000 miles till 1928. It certainly produced economies to tide the company over a particularly bad period, but by 1929 traffic was picking up again, and it was possible to revert to steam working. A diesel locomotive was also hired in that year, but proved unsatisfactory and was returned to the makers.

At the time of closure there were four of the tramway-type coaching vehicles, and thirty-one vans and wagons of various sorts, many of which were sold to the Clogher Valley Railway.

CHAPTER 26

CLOGHER VALLEY RAILWAY

Roadside 3ft gauge tramway, originally steam but operated largely by a diesel railcar in its final years, serving small townships in County Tyrone and Fermanagh, connecting at both ends with lines of the GREAT NORTHERN RAILWAY.

Incorporated 1884. Opened 1887.

Mileage: 37 miles.

Principal places served:
  Fivemiletown, Aughnacloy.

Closed 1941.

Similar in several respects to the Castlederg & Victoria Bridge Tramway was the Clogher Valley Railway, which lay some miles to the south of it, in the counties of Fermanagh and Tyrone. Another 3ft gauge line alongside a public road, it served a sparsely populated rural area and is famous for the fact that at its principal township of Fivemiletown it ran through the main street. Although it did not actually penetrate the Free State, it was at the eastern end close to the border, and after the partition in 1921 this lonely area gave good opportunities for smuggling both ways between the two countries. The railway benefitted for a considerable time from a remarkable and for a while unexplained increase in cattle and pig traffic, until the customs authorities became alive to the situation and vigilance tightened up!

The line was 37 miles long with no branches, and it made connection with the GNR at both ends, in the east at Tynan, on the Portadown–Clones section of the Londonderry line, and at Maguiresbridge, between Clones and Enniskillen. It was in fact the first tramway to be built in Ireland, under the Tramways and Public Companies Act of 1883, being incorporated by an Order in Council of 26 May 1884. The authorised capital was £150,000 with a baronial guarantee.

Page 269 (*above left*) County Donegal Railway 4–6–0T no 9 *Columbkille* at Stranorlar in 1930. Later engines were considerably larger machines of 4–4–4T, 2–6–4T and 4–6–4T wheel arrangements; (*above right*) in 1931 the CDRJC had the distinction of pioneering the use of the diesel railcar in the British Isles. This view, taken in 1937, shows no 8, one of the two original units, entering Stranorlar from Glenties over the fine girder bridge spanning the River Finn; (*below*) the Owencarrow viaduct of the Lough Swilly, in one of the wildest parts of Donegal. A train was blown over at this exposed spot in a high wind in January 1925

Page 270 (top) Castlederg & Victoria Bridge Tramway train at a roadside halt about 1929. The engine is a 2–4–oT obtained from the NCC and built in 1878 for the Ballymena & Larne Railway. It is of the well-known Beyer Peacock type still to be seen on the Isle of Man Railway; (centre) Clogher Valley Railway. No 6 Erne with a train at the roadside halt of Stoneparkcross, June 1937. The engines always worked bunker first and were fitted with a large headlight; (below) Bessbrook & Newry Tramway. Station and car sheds, Bessbrook, June 1932

It was promoted by the local landowners and constructed by Macrea & McFarland of Belfast; it was opened on 2 May 1887 under the title of Clogher Valley Tramway but this was changed to Clogher Valley Railway on 16 July 1894. It was proposed at one time that it should be extended in both directions, eastwards to Newry, near the coast in Armagh, and westwards to Bawnboy, where it would have joined up with the Cavan & Leitrim. Had this scheme come to fruition, the distance throughout between Dromod and Newry would have been well over 100 miles, much the longest continuous stretch of 3ft gauge in the country. There was an even more ambitious scheme for a 234 mile narrow-gauge line right across Ireland from Clifden in the west to Greenore in the east, and a bill was in fact promoted for it in 1902 under the title of Ulster & Connaught Light Railway but these lines were never built.

After 1928 the railway was managed by a joint committee appointed by the county councils of Tyrone and Fermanagh. It was to some extent worked as two end-on branches from the terminal junctions with the GNR, some trains terminating at Fivemiletown or Aughnacloy from either direction, although there was usually at least one train a day which made the through journey without a considerable wait at one of these places in an overall time of about two hours. The name Fivemiletown has no obvious origin, as it is not five miles from anywhere in particular, to the west being Brookeborough 6 miles away and to the east, Clogher, 8 miles distant, but perhaps this was considered near enough for Ireland!

Although much of the line was alongside the road there were some diversions where it acquired its own land to avoid severe gradients, particularly at the western end, where the first 3 miles out of Maguiresbridge was on the company's own right of way, and also other sections around Clogher and Aughnacloy. The line was single, with passing loops and sidings at the principal stations, Aughnacloy, Ballygawley, Augher and Fivemiletown, all of which had fully appointed stations built in red brick with waiting rooms and the usual offices, unusual for a light railway of this nature. In addition to this there were a number of other halts, sometimes indicated only by a nameboard, but some boasted shelters of a sort. As there was more than one train in operation and one engine in steam, a single-line train staff system was employed.

The headquarters of the railway were at Aughnacloy, where there was a well-equipped works and an engine shed where most of the locomotives would be found. There was a one-engine shed at Fivemiletown and covered accommodation for a couple of coaches. There was also a shed for one engine at Tynan.

By 1932 the fortunes of the railway, never a prosperous concern, were markedly on the decline through road competition, not the least of which was the operation by the Northern Ireland Transport Board of buses and lorries

Q

TIME TABLE.

30th MAY, 1937. and until further notice.

DOWN TRAINS.

			1. a.m.	2. a.m.	3. a.m.	4. noon.	5. p.m.	6. p.m.	Sundays a.m.	Sundays p.m.	SPECIAL MARKET TRAINS.	
G.N.R.	BELFAST ..	dep.	..	8–15	9–25	12– 0	3–10	7–10	9–30	7– 5		
	PORTADOWN ..	,,	..	9– 0	10–11	12–51	4– 2	7–55	10–20	8– 0		
	ARMAGH ..	..	..	9–21	10–30	1– 9	4–22	8–16	10–42	8–22	I.	
	TYNAN ..	arr.	..	9–34	10–42	1–26	4–36	8–30	10–56	8–36	a.m.	
			Rail- Coach.	Rail- Coach.		Rail- Coach.	Rail- Coach.	Rail- Coach.	Rail- Coach.	Rail- Coach.	Ballygawley Fair Days.	
TYNAN ..		dep.	6–15	9–40	10–45	1–40	4–40	8–35	11– 0	8–40	..	..
AUGHNACLOY ..		,,	6–45	10–11	11–30	2–10	5–25	9– 5	11–30	9–10	3–45	..
BALLYGAWLEY		,,	7– 1	10–27	11–50	2–25	5–45	9–19	11–45	9–25	4– 0	..
					p.m.					p.m.		
AUGHER ..		,,	7–18	10–42	12–10	2–40	6– 0	9–35	12– 5	9–45	4–15	..
CLOGHER ..		,,	7–24	10–48	12–20	2–50	6– 6	9–40	12–10	9–50	4–22	..
FIVEMILETOWN	arr.		7–45	11–10	12–48	3–10	6–25	10– 5	12–30	10–10	4–45	..
Do. ..		dep.	8– 5	11–35	..	3–15	..	..	..	..	..	..
BROOKEBORO' ..		,,	8–25	11–55	..	3–35	..	..	. ..	..	Second Friday	..
				p.m.							In Month.	
MAGUIRESBRIDGE	arr.		8–35	12– 5	..	3–45	..	..	..	..	..	..
G.N.R.	MAGUIRESBRIDGE	dep.	8–39	12–21	..	..	..	..	..	..	..	
	ENNISKILLEN ..	arr.	8–54	12–36	..	..	..	..	..	..	..	
	LONDONDERRY ..	,,	1–45	3– 5	..	..	..	..	. ..	..	..	

UP TRAINS.

			1. a.m.	2. a.m.	3. p.m.	4. a.m.	5 p.m.	6. p.m.	Sundays. a.m.	Sundays. p.m.	SPECIAL MARKET TRAINS.			
G.N.R.	LONDONDERRY	dep.	..	7–20	..	11–10	..	..	..	..	1. a.m.	2. p.m.	3. p.m.	4. p.m.
						p.m.								
	ENNISKILLEN ..	,,	..	9–30	..	1–35	3–10	..	..	..				
	MAGUIRESBRIDGE	arr.	..	9–46	..	1–51	3–35	..	..	..				
			Rail- Coach.	Rail- Coach.		Rail- Coach.	Rail- Coach.	Rail- Coach.	Rail- Coach	Rail- Coach	B'gawley Fair Days.	B'gawley Fair Days.	B'gawley Fair Days	B'gawley Fair Days.
MAGUIRESBRIDGE	dep.		..	9–50	..	1–55	3–55	x	..	..	..	..	2nd Friday	2nd Friday
BROOKEBORO'	..	,,	..	10– 0	..	2– 5	4– 5	..	..	..	..	..	in Month.	in Month
FIVEMILETOWN	..	arr.	..	10–25	..	2–25	4–25	..	..	..	..	..	..	..
Do.	..	dep.	7–45	..	1–15	2–30	5– 0	6–55	8– 5	6– 5	8–15	..	5–45	6–58
				p.m.								2nd Friday		
CLOGHER ..		,,	8– 5	12–21	1–45	2–51	5–20	7–19	8–26	6–25	8–55	in Month.	6– 8	7–25
AUGHER ..		,,	8–10	12–26	2– 0	2–56	5–25	7–24	8–32	6–30	9– 3	..	6–15	7–35
BALLYGAWLEY		,,	8–29	12–45	2–25	3–15	5–45	7–40	8–52	6–50	9–22	1–40	6–35	7–55
AUGHNACLOY ..		,,	8–46	1– 0	2–50	3x30	6– 2	7–55	9– 5	7– 5	2nd Friday	2–10	7–55	8–10
TYNAN ..		arr.	9–16	1–30	3–30	4x 0	6–32	8–25	9–35	7–35	in Month.	2–45	8–25	..
G.N.R.	TYNAN ..	dep.	9–20	1–32	3–35	..	6–44	..	9–41	7–41	..	..	..	..
	ARMAGH ..	arr.	9–37	1–46	3–48	..	6–57	..	9–52	7–54	..	..	..	..
	PORTADOWN ..	,,	9–58	2– 6	4–12	..	7–20	..	10–10	8–15	..	..	..	..
	BELFAST .	.. ,,	10–40	2–55	5– 0	..	8–15	..	11– 5	8–55	..	..	..	..

x Will not run on Ballygawley Fair Days.
All Trains will stop, if required, at all Halts to take up or set down Passengers. Tickets are issued subject to the
Bye-Laws, Regulations and Conditions shown in the Committee's Notices.

AUGHNACLOY, May, 1937.   D. N. M'CLURE. General Manager

Clogher Valley Railway 1937 timetable showing GNR connections to Belfast and
Londonderry

conveying livestock, one of the railway's principal sources of revenue. Even at that time the Northern Ireland government was bent on closing as many of the railways as possible and replacing them with road transport.

In an endeavour to reduce costs two diesel units were obtained in 1932, one for passenger service and the other for goods. The railcar consisted of a coach body seating twenty-eight passengers, which was articulated from the driving cab and engine, a 74hp six-cylinder Gardner diesel. The other was similar except for the substitution of a lorry body for the passenger coach. It was however sometimes employed on passenger service by attaching an ordinary coach. The passenger unit could also attach a van when necessary. This new method of working reduced locomotive costs in the first eleven months from £3,531 to £2,248, notwithstanding that passenger mileage increased from 61,940 to 66,628. Steam mileage was reduced from 69,945 to 37,887 during the same period, the two diesel units running 33,818 miles. The general manager and locomotive superintendent at this time was D. N. M. McClure.

Specimen CVR ticket

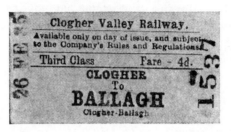

Under these conditions the railway managed to survive into World War II, but it was finally forced to close on 31 December 1941. The locomotives and rolling stock were scrapped or sold, and the remaining property, including the station buildings, was disposed of by auction in 1944.

LOCOMOTIVES AND ROLLING STOCK

For many years the locomotive stock comprised six 0-4-2Ts, the wheels and motion being enclosed by hinged flaps for running alongside the public roads, a Board of Trade requirement. A peculiarity was that the engines were always run backwards, with the cab leading, thus giving the driver a better lookout, and they were fitted with protective 'cow-catcher' buffer beams—although in fact the only actual buffing gear was incorporated in the single central coupling fitted to all of the stock, a normal practice on the narrow-gauge lines. They carried a large headlamp to illuminate the road ahead.

These engines were built by Sharp Stewart in 1886-7, works nos 3369-74, no 1 *Caledon*, 2 *Errigal*, 3 *Blackwater*, 4 *Fury*, 5 *Colebrooke* and 6 *Erne*. In 1907 an 0–4–4T was obtained, no 7 *Blessingbourne*, built by Hudswell Clarke, works no 914, but it does not appear to have been much liked and was not often used. The last steam locomotive was obtained from the Castlederg & Victoria Bridge, when it closed in 1934. This was a 2–6–0T, which the CVR rebuilt in its own works at Aughnacloy as a 2–6–2T, a brass plate 'Rebuilt CVR 1936 Augna-cloy works' proudly proclaiming the fact. It was numbered 4 but had no name. It was also painted in a pleasing dark red livery, which was subsequently applied to the other remaining engines, whereas previously they had been green. The original no 4 *Fury* had been withdrawn in 1929, but its side tanks and other remains were still to be found in the works yard in 1937. No 1 was scrapped in 1935 and no 5 in 1936, the others lasting until the closure of the line.

In 1928 experiments had been made with a light Atkinson Walker steam tractor with an upright high-pressure boiler of 280lb psi, but in spite of later receiving a larger boiler it was never a success and was returned to the makers, Walker Brothers of Wigan. Subsequently it was acquired by the County Donegal, fitted with a diesel engine and proved a very useful shunter; it is now in Belfast Museum.

The passenger coaches were handsome clerestory bogie saloon vehicles with end verandahs and steps to the ground, somewhat American in style. They were electrically lit. Originally they had two classes, first and third, but the former was abolished in 1928.

CHAPTER 27

BESSBROOK & NEWRY TRAMWAY

A 3ft gauge small electric tramway built mainly for conveyance of mill workers, together with raw materials and finished products, between Newry and the mill at Bessbrook in County Armagh.

Incorporated 1884. Opened 1885.

Mileage: 3 miles.

Places served:
  Newry, Bessbrook.

Closed 1948.

This small 3ft gauge line had something in common with the Giant's Causeway Portrush & Bush Valley, in that both were electrically operated from the start and were amongst the first electric railways in the British Isles. Bessbrook is a small manufacturing town in Armagh, with some 3,000 inhabitants, and owes its existence to J. G. Richardson, a Quaker, who in 1846 developed the old-established Bessbrook Flax Spinning Mills into a large linen manufacturing concern, with good housing for the workers. It must be unique in the whole of Ireland in being the only township of any size without a public house, this being forbidden under a local bylaw no doubt originated by Mr Richardson himself. Although within three miles of Newry the line was a little off the beaten tourist track, although the observant railway traveller could get a fleeting glimpse of it where its track passed under the large viaduct at Craigmore on the Great Northern main line.

To facilitate the carriage of coal and flax from Newry to Bessbrook, and finished products in the other direction, the Bessbrook & Newry Tramway was incorporated on 26 May 1884 under the Tramways (Ireland) Act of 1883. Construction of the line proceeded rapidly and it was opened to the public in October 1885. The total cost was £15,000.

It was worked electrically from the start, although a steam line was originally proposed. Like the Giant's Causeway line, already in operation, the power was provided by hydro-electric generators, current pick-up being from a third rail placed between the two running rails. The power house was at Millvale, about a mile from Bessbrook; here the line crossed a public road, where for a distance of 50 yards the current was obtained by means of an overhead wire, for which the cars were provided with bow collectors. There was a small platform provided here, and also at Craigmore, where there was a secondary smaller mill. At Newry there was a small sheltered platform adjacent to the Great Northern station at Edward Street, but the headquarters of the line, shed and workshops were at Bessbrook.

The rolling stock comprised four power cars and five trailers, of various designs obtained over the years, together with twenty-seven miscellaneous goods vehicles, four-wheeled, and with both open and closed bodies. These were flangeless, and could be adapted to run on both road and rail to avoid transhipment. The track, of 3ft gauge for train operation, also embodied outer rails ⅞in lower, on which the wagons ran, kept in position by the main running lines which acted as check rails.

The power cars were unusual in tramway operation in that they had driving cabs at one end only, and because of this a run-round loop was provided at each terminus.

The passenger stock, all single deckers and mostly with clerestory roofs, may briefly be summarised as follows:

No in stock	Description	Seating capacity	Builders	Notes
1	Bogie power car	24	Ashburys 1885	Withdrawn 1921
2	,, ,, ,,	34	,, ,,	Preserved at Bessbrook by Bessbrook Spinning Co
3	Bogie trailer	44	,, ,,	—
1	Bogie power car	40	Hurst Nelson 1921	Preserved in Belfast Museum
4	,, ,, ,,	32	,, ,, ,,	—
5	Four-wheeler trailer open top	20	,, ,, ,,	
6	Four-wheeler trailer covered top	12	Built about 1922, maker not known	
7	Bogie trailer	26	⎧Purchased 1928 from ⎨Dublin & United Tram-	
8	,, ,,	24	⎩ways, formerly used on Dublin & Lucan Tramway	

There were originally two classes, but first was later abandoned. The journey time for the 3 miles was about 20 minutes, with an hourly service, augmented morning and evening for the benefit of the mill workers, many of whom lived in Newry and who formed the mainstay of the passenger traffic. In its most prosperous days the line carried some 100,000 passengers and 16,000 tons of goods annually, but it gradually declined in favour of road transport and was closed on 10 January 1948. All the rolling stock was sold for scrap to G. Cohen & Sons of Sydenham, Belfast, apart from the two cars which have been preserved.

Specimen ticket of Bessbrook & Newry Tramway

CHAPTER 28

DUBLIN & BLESSINGTON and DUBLIN & LUCAN TRAMWAYS

Roadside tramways, both at first steam-worked, the first being of standard 5ft 3in gauge, and the second 3ft gauge, later widened to 3ft 6in and ultimately to 5ft 3in.

DUBLIN & BLESSINGTON   Incorporated 1887. Opened 1888.
POULAPHOUCA EXTENSION   Incorporated 1889. Opened 1895.
DUBLIN & LUCAN   Incorporated 1880. Opened throughout 1883.

Route mileage: DUBLIN & BLESSINGTON (including POULAPHOUCA EXTENSION)—
    19½ miles.
        DUBLIN & LUCAN—7 miles.

Principal places served:
  Blessington, Lucan.

Date of DUBLIN & BLESSINGTON *closure, 1932.*
Date of DUBLIN & LUCAN *closure, 1925.*

Both these were roadside systems serving villages some distance out of Dublin. Blessington was 15½ miles from the terminus at Terenure, on the outskirts of the city, and Lucan a picturesque village 7 miles from Phoenix Park, both lines being reached by the Dublin United Tramways from the city centre. At Terenure there was actual physical connection, as both systems were of 5ft 3in gauge, but there was no through passenger running, as the Dublin & Blessington was steam operated, and the tramway system, previously horse worked, was electrified in 1898. Goods traffic for the Dublin & Blessington was taken through the streets at night, electrically hauled. The Dublin & Lucan, on the other hand, was built to 3ft gauge, and consequently no through running was possible. The Dublin & Blessington, incorporated in 1887, was opened on 1 August 1888.

An extension from Blessington to Poulaphouca, another 4 miles on, was incorporated in 1889 by a separate company of that name, opened on 1 May 1895, and worked at first with rolling stock borrowed from the Dublin & Blessington, which eventually took over the working and ran through trains from Terenure to Poulaphouca. Plans for a lengthy extension to Rathdrum, which would have included a 1,600ft climb over Wicklow Gap, never materialised.

The Dublin & Lucan, authorised in 1880, was opened as far as Chapelizod, $1\frac{3}{4}$ miles, in June 1881, and reached Lucan on 2 July 1883. Here again an extension westwards was promoted by a separate company, the Lucan Leixlip & Celbridge Steam Tramway, but only the Leixlip section of $1\frac{7}{8}$ miles was completed. What would have been a $3\frac{3}{4}$ mile branch to Celbridge, together with another 7 miles to Clane, never got beyond the planning stage.

Both systems followed the contours of the roads and consequently were of an undulating nature with severe, if short, gradients of as much as 1 in 20 in places.

The $15\frac{1}{2}$ mile journey to Blessington occupied about 1hr 25min. There were many intermediate stopping places, the principal one being at Templeogue, $\frac{1}{2}$ mile out of Terenure terminus, but only about four of these possessed anything that could in any way be described as a station, perhaps just a seat. At Templeogue were situated the company's workshops and sheds; at Embankment, about half way, there were watering facilities for the engines. Blessington itself is a typical Irish village, population less than 500, with the usual generous proportion of establishments selling the well-known national beverage. The tramway had a yard with a shed for its coaching stock and the usual engine facilities.

Lucan, situated amid the charming scenery of the Liffey valley, was a larger township, population about 1,600, and at Leixlip, which is near the border of the county of Dublin and boasts a twelfth-century castle, there is now a large hydro-electric station.

Such slow and inconvenient roadside tramways as these were quite incapable of meeting the bus competition which grew up after World War I. Plans for electrification of the Dublin & Blessington never came to anything, but the Dublin & Lucan was so converted under an Act obtained in 1896 and at the same time the gauge was widened to 3ft 6in, but why this was not done to 5ft 3in, which would have enabled through running over the Dublin United Tramways, is something of a mystery. The name of the company was changed to Dublin & Lucan Electric Railway. Bus competition however finally caused the closure of the tramway on 1 January 1925. The Leixlip extension had already shut down as early as 1896, but $\frac{1}{2}$ mile of the route was restored in 1909

DUBLIN AND BLESSINGTON TRAMWAY.

TIME TABLE FROM AND AFTER 1st JUNE, 1929.

☛ This Time Table is liable to alteration on all Bank Holidays. Particulars of running on those days can be obtained at Booking Office.

Weekdays.

FROM DUBLIN.

Station	a m	a m	a m	a m	p m	p m	p m	p m	p m	p m	p m	p m	p m	p m	p m	p m
TERENURE	7 7	9 0	10 4	11 0	12 7	1 7	2 0	2 35	3 0	3 14	4 0	4 7	5 0	5 4	6 0	6 7
TEMPLEOGUE	7 14	9 7	10 14	11 7	12 14	1 14	2 7	2 42	3 7	3 14	4 7	…	5 7	5 14	6 7	6 14
BALROTHERY	7 5	9 14	10 14	11 14	12 24	1 24	2 7	2 49	3 14	3 20	4 14	…	5 14	5 20	6 14	6 20
TALLAGHT	7 20	9 20	10 20	11 30	12 28	1 30	2 20	2 55	3 20	3 30	4 20	4 28	5 20	…	6 20	6 30
JOBSTOWN	7 30	7 40	…	…	…	…	2 55	…	…	…	…	…	…	…	6 45	6 55
EMBANKMENT (For Saggart & Rathcoole)	7 55	…	…	…	…	…	3 11	…	…	…	…	…	…	…	6 50	7 7
CROOKSLING	8 2	…	…	…	…	…	3 30	…	…	…	…	…	…	…	6 55	7 10
BRITTAS	8 12	…	…	…	…	…	3 37	…	…	…	…	…	…	…	7 17	7 25
LAMB	…	…	…	…	…	…	3 42	…	…	…	…	…	…	…	7 20	7 35
BLESSINGTON	8 30	…	…	…	…	…	3 58	…	…	…	…	…	…	…	7 30	7 40

Runs to Jobstown on Weds. & Sats. — 9 30, 9 37, 9 47, 9 50, 10 50 / 10 30, 10 37, 10 42, 10 50

TO DUBLIN.

Station	a m	a m	a m	a m	a m	p m	p m	p m	p m	p m	p m	p m	p m	p m	p m	p m
BLESSINGTON	8 55	9 35	10 20	…	12 33	…	2 30	…	4 10	…	5 15	…	6 30	…	7 30	…
LAMB	…	9 18	…	…	…	…	2 30	…	4 28	…	…	…	6 36	…	7 35	…
BRITTAS	9 18	9 25	…	…	…	…	2 36	…	4 37	…	5 22	…	6 43	…	7 43	…
CROOKSLING	9 35	9 45	…	…	…	…	2 43	…	4 45	…	5 28	…	6 50	…	8 0	…
EMBANKMENT (For Saggart & Rathcoole)	8 20	9 55	…	12 40	…	1 25	2 40	…	5 0	…	5 35	…	…	…	8 45	…
JOBSTOWN	8 30	9 36	11 30	12 46	1 30	2 46	3 40	4 40	5 12	…	6 39	7 30	…	…	8 55	…
TALLAGHT	8 36	9 36	11 36	12 46	1 36	2 46	3 46	4 46	5 22	…	6 43	7 36	8 8	…	9 0	…
BALROTHERY	8 43	10 7	11 43	12 53	1 43	2 53	3 53	4 53	5 28	…	6 50	7 43	10 16	…	9 8	…
TEMPLEOGUE	…	10 10	…	1 0	…	3 0	4 0	5 0	5 35	…	…	7 50	10 23	…	9 15	…
TERENURE	8 50	10 15	11 50	1 0	1 50	3 0	4 0	5 0	5 35	…	…	7 50	10 30	…	9 20	…

From Jobst'n at 10 o'clock on Weds. & Sats.

Sundays.

FROM DUBLIN.

Station	a m	a m	a m	a m	p m	p m	p m	p m	p m	p m	p m	p m	p m	p m	p m	p m
TERENURE	9 7	10 4	11 0	12 7	1 30	2 15	3 0	3 25	4 0	5 0	6 0	6 45	7 30	8 30	9 30	10 30
TEMPLEOGUE	9 7	10 7	11 7	12 7	1 37	2 22	3 7	3 30	4 7	5 5	6 7	6 52	7 37	8 36	9 37	10 37
BALROTHERY	9 14	10 14	11 14	12 14	1 44	2 30	3 14	3 35	4 14	5 10	6 14	7 5	7 44	8 44	9 47	10 42
TALLAGHT	9 20	10 20	11 30	12 28	1 50	2 35	3 20	3 40	4 20	5 15	6 20	7 5	7 50	8 50	9 50	10 50
JOBSTOWN	9 30	…	…	…	2 10	…	3 50	…	…	…	6 40	…	…	…	…	…
EMBANKMENT (For Saggart & Rathcoole)	9 40	…	…	…	2 25	…	…	…	…	…	6 55	…	…	…	…	…
CROOKSLING	9 55	…	…	…	2 30	…	…	…	…	…	7 2	…	…	…	…	…
BRITTAS	10 2	…	…	…	2 37	…	…	…	…	…	7 10	…	…	…	…	…
LAMB	10 10	…	…	…	…	…	…	…	…	…	…	…	…	…	…	…
BLESSINGTON	10 25	…	…	…	2 55	…	…	…	…	…	7 30	…	…	…	…	…

TO DUBLIN.

Station	a m	a m	p m	p m	p m	p m	p m	p m	p m	p m	p m	p m	p m	p m	p m
BLESSINGTON	10 40	…	12 40	…	3 32	…	4 10	…	5 5	…	6 0	…	…	9 30	…
LAMB	10 55	…	1 0	…	3 40	…	4 26	…	5 10	…	6 6	…	8 52	…	…
BRITTAS	11 0	…	1 15	…	3 46	…	4 37	…	5 22	…	6 13	…	9 0	…	…
CROOKSLING	11 10	…	1 25	…	3 53	…	4 45	…	5 28	…	6 20	…	9 10	…	…
EMBANKMENT (For Saggart & Rathcoole)	11 40	12 33	1 35	2 40	4 0	5 5	5 35	…	…	…	9 20	…	…	…	…
JOBSTOWN	11 45	12 40	1 50	2 46	…	5 12	…	6 39	7 30	8 40	9 30	…	…	…	…
TALLAGHT	11 50	12 46	1 53	2 53	4 33	5 22	…	6 43	7 36	8 46	9 36	…	…	…	…
BALROTHERY	11 55	12 53	2 0	3 0	4 40	5 28	…	6 50	7 43	8 53	9 43	…	…	…	…
TEMPLEOGUE	…	1 0	…	…	…	5 35	…	7 0	7 50	9 0	9 50	…	…	…	…
TERENURE	…	1 0	2 0	3 0	4 40	5 35	…	7 0	7 50	9 0	9 50	…	…	…	…

Time Bills.—The published Train Bills of this Company are only intended to fix the time at which Passengers may be certain to obtain their Tickets for any Journey from the various Stations; it being understood that the Trains shall not start before the appointed time. The Company do not undertake that the Trains shall start or arrive at the time specified in the Bills. The right to stop the Trains at any Station on the Line, although not marked as a Stopping Station, is reserved.

Timetable for the Dublin & Blessington Tramway

as far as the Spa Hotel by a new company, the Lucan & Leixlip Electric Railway, worked by the Dublin & Lucan.

In 1915 the Dublin & Blessington obtained two petrol electric railcars, but they were very unreliable. Parts of the bodies were used in the construction at Templeogue of two small Ford railcars, and in 1926 a larger eight-wheeled Drewry railcar was obtained, which could be driven from either end. This was eventually sold to the County Donegal, was regauged to 3ft and survives in Belfast Museum. One of the Ford cars also went to the County Donegal, where the body was converted to a railcar trailer and was used in this capacity for some years.

Specimen Dublin & Blessington ticket

Otherwise the Dublin & Blessington remained steam worked to the end, which came on 31 December 1932, one of the last steam roadside tramways in the British Isles.

LOCOMOTIVES AND ROLLING STOCK

The Dublin & Lucan's first vehicle was a 2–4–2 Perrett coke-fired steam-car, a double-decker built at Nottingham in 1881, but it was very soon superseded by standard Kitson 0–4–0 enclosed tram engines hauling bogie tramcars, sometimes made up into trains of several vehicles.

Nos 1–3 were built in 1882–3, works nos T57, T74 and T81, 4 and 5 in 1884, T104 and T108, and no 6, an enlarged version, in 1887, T224. The last engine no 7, came from T. Green in 1892, works no 169. It was a two-cylinder Worsdell von Borries compound and was built for the Leixlip line. It was sold in 1896. Nos 1–3 were scrapped in 1899 and 4–6 in 1912.

The tramcars which replaced steam working were of the conventional bogie type, with two decks, built by Dick Kerr from 1899 onwards, and there were also a few single-deckers, and an electric locomotive for goods traffic.

The Dublin & Blessington's first engines were also of the 0–4–0 enclosed tramway type; nos 1–6 were built by the Falcon works, Loughborough, in 1887, works nos 125–30 but not in the same order. Nos 7–10 were much larger 2–4–2T engines, not enclosed, and unique in being double-ended, with cabs at both ends and duplicate controls. No 7 was built by T. Green of Leeds in 1892, works no 179, and no 8, an 0–4–2T, in 1896, works no 218; no 9 came from Brush of Loughborough in 1899, works no 284, and no 10 (at first no 2) again from T. Green in 1915, works no 267.

In addition to these locomotives, in 1916 the company obtained an 0–4–0WT from the Dublin & South Eastern, but it was unsatisfactory. It was a conversion of the engine part of what had originally been a steam railmotor built by Kerr Stuart in 1905. It went to the GSWR in 1918, which replaced it with an engine named *Cambria*. This was an 0–4–0ST which had been built by Hunslet in 1894 for the Wexford & Rosslare Railway. It became Dublin & Blessington no 5 and lasted until 1928. Of the others, no 1 was scrapped in 1912, 2 in 1906, 3 in 1927, 4 in 1898, 5 in 1911 and 7 and 8 in 1915. The remainder, nos 6, 9 and 10, lasted until the closing of the line and were broken up in 1933. The engines were painted in a middle green, with two thin bands of yellow lining.

The passenger vehicles were of the double-decked bogie tramcar type, roofed over but with open sides, at first right down to floor level. The resultant view from the road below was however objected to on decency grounds by the ladies of the period, and the sides were partly boarded up. Whether the present generation would be so particular is open to question. Two classes were provided on both decks, and in spite of the very long chimneys on the engines, the passengers were exposed in windy conditions to a very smoky journey, such as could be appreciated only by the dedicated steam lover. The delights of a ride in such an outmoded form of transport, even for that time, was a experience I should have been sorry to have missed. It was in fact the last steam tramway of its type in the British Isles, with double-decked tramcar vehicles, once much used in city and urban areas. Similar concerns were the Swansea & Mumbles and the Wolverton & Stony Stratford. One or two roadside steam tramways still existed for some time afterwards; the Glyn Valley Tramway operated a passenger service a year after the end of the Dublin & Blessington but finally closed in 1935, leaving only the Wantage and the Wisbech & Upwell, both of which had run only goods trains for many years.

CHAPTER 29

LISTOWEL & BALLYBUNION
RAILWAY

The famous so-called mono-railway, although in effect more accurately a three-rail system, with unique twin-boilered engines.

Incorporated 1886. Opened 1888.

Length: 9¼ miles.

Principal place served:
  Ballybunion.

Closed 1924.

There can be very few, if any, railway enthusiasts alive today who actually had the experience of travelling over that wonderful and unique freak of railway engineering, the Lartigue mono-rail system which once enjoyed a life of thirty-six years in the south-west of Ireland. To my lasting regret, I am not one of them. Although I explored the Irish railways extensively from 1929, I was already five years too late to include it in my first programme of visits. All that was to be seen when I passed through Listowel in 1934, was the carriage shed, the concrete base of one of the turntables and a small overbridge near the terminus. Being in a remote area, it must have been seen by very few of the railway explorers of those days—there were not many of us in any case—and there cannot be very many local inhabitants or visitors still around who have anything but faded recollections of travelling over it, other than perhaps some of the men who actually worked on it.

  Ballybunion is a seaside resort in south-west Ireland, in County Kerry, on the mouth of the Shannon overlooking the Atlantic, with a present population of some 1,200. Once the railway between Tralee and Limerick had been built, it naturally sought more direct communication with the outside world by means of a branch from its nearest point, Listowel, eight or nine miles away.

First proposals in 1883 included a 5ft 3in branch off the Waterford & Limerick and tramways of 3ft gauge. These were promoted by the Munster Steam Tramways Company and the Limerick & Kerry Light Railways, but they did not materialise.

It was in 1885 that a Frenchman, Charles Lartigue, appeared on the scene. He had patented an entirely new principle in light railway building, termed a mono-rail but more accurately a three-rail system, and one such short experimental railway was already in operation in France. Wishing to extend its operations the Lartigue Railway Construction Company rather surprisingly chose this remote part of the British Isles for a further trial. The main advantage claimed was cheapness in construction, the necessity for a really sound road-bed such as could take a conventional track being eliminated. There were however severe operational disadvantages, the most obvious of which was the clumsiness of any arrangement for switching from one line to another, not to mention the necessarily awkward design of the rolling stock, all of which, engines, passenger coaches and goods vehicles, had to be designed in two halves so as to straddle the centre-running rail. Anything in the nature of a level crossing obviously presented problems.

It was a true mono-rail system only in that there was a single running rail which took the whole weight of the engine and train; this was supported by A-shaped angle-iron trestles, 3ft 6in high, near the base of which on either side were horizontal rails facing outwards; along these ran guide wheels fitted to the engine and stock. The only means of transfer from one track to another was by a turntable, large enough to accommodate one engine or two small wagons at a time, an awkward and time-consuming process but perhaps not of great importance in the leisurely Irish south-west.

An Act of 16 April 1886 authorised construction of the railway, which proceeded rapidly, and it was opened on 29 February 1888, Leap Year Day, and quite appropriate indeed, as crossing the new line would inevitably necessitate some manner of 'leap'! With a length of 9¼ miles, the total cost, including the track, various bridges, three engines and a good number of items of coaching stock, was £30,000, which sounds modest, even allowing for the much higher value of money at that time, though labour costs must have been much lower than would apply today.

There was an intermediate station, at Liselton, which had a passing loop, and also a halt at Francis Road. The problem of level crossings for access to farms and the like was provided for by a small section of the line being hinged, so that it could be turned at right angles. For use at stations a pair of small ladders was fitted to the ends of the coaches, and to allow a public road to cross the line there was a sort of crude model of London's Tower Bridge; the two halves of the drawbridge normally rested on the elevated mono-rail girders but could be raised for the passage of a train.

The journey took 40–45min, with speeds of between 15 and 20mph, and there were for most of the railway's existence three trains each way daily, with an extra one on Saturdays, together with two (sometimes three) return trips on Sundays. The headquarters were at Ballybunion, but there was an engine shed at Listowel to accommodate one locomotive, which worked in on the last train at night and took out the first one in the morning.

Specimen ticket of Listowel
& Ballybunion Railway

Traffic never came up to expectations, and by 1897 the line was already in the hands of a receiver; it managed to continue a precarious existence, although it was latterly incurring a loss of £30 a week. Unfortunately the Great Southern Railways, formed in 1924, refused to have anything to do with it, making its demise inevitable, and the last train ran on 14 October 1924, after which the line was entirely dismantled by T. W. Ward of Sheffield. Apart from one or two buildings nothing now survives, except for a maker's plate from the original vertical boiler engine. What a tourist attraction it would have been had it survived, and an unrivalled subject for preservation. One cannot help wishing that perhaps one day some wealthy railway enthusiast might have a full-sized replica made of this unique railway, which would undoubtedly be an enormous attraction. The engines would of course be the major expense, but an advantageous factor might be that the makers of the original locomotives, Hunslet of Leeds, are practically the only firm still in business as such in this country.

LOCOMOTIVES AND ROLLING STOCK

There were in all four locomotives, but not a great deal is known about the first one, which was used in the construction of the line. Like the later ones, it was necessarily a twin engine, but with upright 'coffee-pot-type' boilers. Such records as exist show that it was built at Tubize in Belgium. Unfortunately the only known photograph of it is a general view of the yard at Listowel during construction, which must have been taken about 1887 and which included this interesting engine by chance. It seems to have been withdrawn about 1900.

The three engines which worked the line were built by Hunslet in 1887, numbered 1–3, works nos 431–3, and had a wheel classification on the Whyte system of 0–3–0. The tenders, which had two coupled axles, were at first fitted with cylinders to supply additional power, but as the boilers were unable to provide sufficient steam, these cylinders were later removed. As originally built, however, the engines could quite accurately be described as 0–3–2–0s. They were painted green and had 2ft diameter driving wheels, cylinders 7in by 12in, and a boiler pressure of 150lb, with a combined heating surface of 140sq ft and grate area of 5sq ft in the two boilers; their total weight was 9½ tons in working order. The driver occupied the side of the cab where the controls were, and had to fire the boiler on that side too, while the fireman on the other side seems to have had an easier time of it, as he had only to look after his one boiler.

The passenger stock, like the engines, was in two halves, straddling the elevated rail and facing outwards; the goods vehicles were similar, and care had to be taken to equate the loads on either side as far as possible. An old story well illustrates this. A farmer wished to transport a cow over the line, but there was no suitable balancing weight available for the other side. He solved the difficulty by balancing the cow on the outward journey with two calves which duly returned by themselves, one on each side of the wagon. There were twenty-one freight vehicles of various sorts, and thirteen passenger coaches, providing both first- and third-class accommodation, the former enjoying the luxury of cushioned seats. Those unwilling to pay the extra fare had to make do with wooden slats. By all accounts travel was very noisy, since the passengers sat almost on top of the wheels.

Page 287 (above) Dublin & Blessington Tramway. Train taking water at Embankment, a roadside stopping place, June 1932, with double-ended 2–4–2T no 10; (below) the unique Listowel & Ballybunion Railway, with twin boiler Lartigue engine and rolling stock. Note the steps provided to enable people to cross the line. View taken in 1914

Page 288 (above) O. V. S. Bulleid's last effort to keep steam as a viable proposition for railway operation. The Irish version of his abortive 'Leader' class, built for British Railways in 1949, was in effect an adaptation to burn that country's natural fuel, turf, although it was designed with a view to conversion to oil burning. It never got beyond the experimental stage; (below) the diesel age arrives. A view typical of the Irish train of today is this one taken at Campile on 6 June 1964, on the occasion of the last all-embracing steam railtour organised by the Irish Railway Record Society

CHAPTER 30

INDUSTRIAL RAILWAYS

As Ireland is in the main an agricultural country with little heavy industry, private railway systems built purely for industrial needs have been few and far between, and even then usually on a very small scale. By far the largest undertaking was that in connection with the hydro-electric scheme on the River Shannon. The size of the project can well be gauged by the fact that there were 106 steam locomotives in use at one time or another and 3,000 wagons. The contract, which occupied five years between 1925 and 1929, was awarded by the Irish Free State government to the German firms of Siemens, Schuckert-werke, and Siemens Bauunion.

The powerhouse itself is situated at Ardnacrusha, a few miles north of Limerick, and to serve it a mile long branch was constructed from Longpavement Halt (now closed), 4 miles out of Limerick on the line to Sligo. Ardnachrusha harnesses the water power of the River Shannon, the level of which falls 100ft in the course of the 18 miles between Lough Derg and Limerick. This flow is directed through a canal, or head race, 7½ miles long, and is capable of producing 38,000 horsepower through the turbines. The construction of the barrage, with its associated earthworks and reservoirs, the largest of its kind ever undertaken in Ireland, necessitated the building of an intricate railway network, mostly to a gauge of 90cm (about 2ft 11½in) but some of a more portable kind to a gauge of 60cm (1ft 11⅝in). All this disappeared on completion of the work in 1929 and few traces are now to be seen, although the standard-gauge branch to the power station still remains. All the machinery and equipment came from Germany and was shipped back on completion of the contract. The 106 locomotives, for both gauges, were all 0-4-0Ts, and were built by various makers, Henschel, Borsig, Hanomag and others. There were also four electric engines.

At Portarlington the Bord Na Mona, Irish Turf Board, constructed an extensive 3ft gauge system to transport peat recovered from the bog. It is now entirely worked by diesel engines, but there were also three steam locomotives one of which is now used on a pleasure railway at Shane's Castle, Antrim, whilst another is preserved at Stradbally Museum, Laois, and the third has been brought to Wales for eventual use on the Talyllyn Railway.

Sugar beet is another important rural industry, and there are large factories at Carlow, Mallow, Thurles and Tuam, all of which have internal standard-gauge systems. Some steam locomotives are kept in reserve, mainly of German origin, 0–4–0Ts, built by Orenstein & Koppel of Berlin, but Carlow had three Belgian engines with vertical boilers. These systems are owned by the Comhlucht Siuicre Eireann Teo (Irish Sugar Beet Limited).

The largest internal industrial system, and by far the best known, was that operated at Dublin by the old-established firm of Arthur Guinness Son & Company Limited, whose famous brew hardly needs any description (or recommendation!). An extensive 1ft 10in gauge network around the works was constructed from 1874 onwards. Initially this was confined within the brewery premises, but in 1878 an Act of Parliament allowed Arthur Cecil Guinness to extend the system into the adjoining streets, which were of course public property and required such sanction. The extensive internal railway included a spiral tunnel, a miniature edition of those found in mountainous countries such as Switzerland, between different levels, previously served by a hydraulic lift. The layout had a number of triangular junctions to avoid reversing trains, and there was a good deal of constant cyclic working by an engine hauling nine bogie flat wagons. Three such trains could be successively moved by a single engine with one driver and conductor, working a twelve-hour shift, during which 8,000 casks would be conveyed. This could be regarded as an early equivalent of the modern 'merry-go-round' principle. The first engine was an 0–4–0T built by Sharp Stewart in 1875, works no 2477, followed by two strange-looking machines from the firm of T. Lewin of Poole, Dorset, which also built some similar engines for the Laxey lead mines in the Isle of Man. They had single cylinders driving a shaft fitted with a flywheel; the shaft had a pinion which engaged a large gear wheel meshed with a gear on the rear running axle. These fascinating little engines were appropriately named *Hops* and *Malt*. The later engines comprised a fleet of 0–4–0Ts, again of unusual design. A particular feature of them was that they could be mounted on a 5ft 3in gauge transporting conveyor of special design, so that the locomotive wheels came into contact through suitable gearing with the carrying wheels, thus enabling it to take transfer traffic over the broad-gauge lines to the Great Southern; this traffic was also provided for by two Hudswell Clarke 0–4–0STs. Latterly there were also some diesel locomotives. Regrettably the whole system has now been abandoned. The broad-gauge link line between the works and Kingsbridge yard which was opened in 1874, was finally closed in May 1965, all traffic thereafter being conveyed by a road tractor.

One of the broad-gauge steam engines has been acquired by the Railway Preservation Society of Ireland, and several of the narrow-gauge engines, which ultimately numbered nineteen, all except the first built by Spense's Foundry of Dublin between 1882 and 1920, have been preserved, some by various bodies in England and Wales.

The Londonderry Port & Harbour Commission had 1½ miles of track on the wharves, opened in 1867, and eventually owned two broad-gauge locomotives. No 1, an 0–6–0ST built by Robert Stephenson in 1891, is preserved in Belfast Museum and no 3 *R. H. Smyth*, an 0–6–0ST by Avonside in 1928, is privately preserved. Few details exist of no 2; it was built in 1902 but was probably scrapped in 1928, when no 3 arrived.

At Larne Harbour the British Aluminium Company had some 3ft gauge track worked by three Peckett 0–4–0Ts, one of which is now in Belfast Museum, and another on Shane's Castle Pleasure Railway. The large works of Courtaulds, Carrickfergus, also had a couple of Peckett 0–4–0STs.

Another Peckett 0–4–0ST, of that firm's standard Beaufort class, works no 1556 built in 1920, had an interesting history in that it was sold by its industrial owner, Allman's Distillery, Bandon, Cork, to the Great Southern in 1930. It was numbered 495 and was used for shunting at Cork until 1949. In Great Britain engines were often sold by main-line companies to collieries and the like, though such cases were rare in Ireland, but it was virtually unknown for an industrial locomotive to be sold to a main-line company.

A similar fate occurred to an 0–6–0ST built in 1892 by Hunslet, works no 557, for T. H. Falkiner of Kerry, and acquired by the Fenit Harbour Commission for use on the pier. It was then named *Shamrock*. It passed into the hands of the Great Southern & Western, which numbered it 299 and removed the name, and saw many years further service, its last duties being on the Timoleague & Courtmacsherry; it was scrapped in 1955.

BIBLIOGRAPHY

The following is a list of the main sources consulted, with apologies for any inadvertent omissions.

Baker *Irish Railways Since 1916*

Barrie, D. S. M. *The Dundalk Newry & Greenore Railway*

Creeder *The Cork & Macroom Railway*

Currie *The Portstewart Tramway*

Fayle, H. *Narrow Gauge Railways of Ireland*

Fayle and Newham *The Dublin & Blessington Tramway*

Flanaghan, Patrick J. *The Cavan & Leitrim Railway*
Transport in Ireland 1880–1910

Flewitt *The Hill of Howth Tramway*

McGrath *Industrial Railways of Ireland*

McGuigan *Giant's Causeway Tramway*

McNeill *Ulster Tramways and Light Railways*

Murray *The Great Northern Railway, Past present and future*

NCC official *NCC Centenary* booklet

Newham *The Cork Blackrock & Passage Railway*
The Cork & Muskerry Railway
The Listowel & Ballybunion Railway
The Schull & Skibereen Railway
The Waterford & Tramore Railway

O'Cuimin *Baronial Lines of the MGWR*

Patterson, Edward M. *The Belfast & County Down Railway*
The Clogher Valley Railway
The County Donegal Railway
The Great Northern Railway
The Londonderry & Lough Swilly Railway

Pender and Richards *Irish Railways Today*

Whitehouse, P. B. *The Tralee & Dingle Railway*

Bradshaw's Railway Manual and Directory 1869

Bradshaw and other railway timetables

Journals of the Irish Railway Record Society

The Railway Magazine, particularly articles by E. L. Ahrons and H. Fayle

The Railway Year Book

ACKNOWLEDGEMENTS

I must express my deep appreciation for the help of my friend for many years, Mr R. N. Clements, who can rightly be regarded as the foremost expert today on Irish railway history, and who has made very many useful suggestions and provided me with much material which I would otherwise have found difficult if not impossible to unearth.

Most of the older illustrations are from photographs of unknown authorship, but credit should be acknowledged to the following:

W. A. Camwell, pages 69 (top) and 105 (bottom).

Coras Iompair Eireann, page 33 (bottom).

Locomotive Publishing Company, page 87 (bottom).

D. Morris (Courtesy Irish Railway Record Society), page 179 (bottom).

National Library of Ireland, page 34.

K. A. C. R. Nunn (by courtesy of the Locomotive Club of Great Britain), pages 52 (bottom) and 233 (top).

The remainder are largely the work of the author and of his son, R. M. Casserley, who is responsible for pages 88 (top), 136 (bottom) and 179 (top).

INDEX